ANDOVER
MASSACHUSETTS
HISTORICAL SELECTIONS
FROM FOUR CENTURIES

JULIET HAINES MOFFORD

Introduction by James Batchelder

Merrimack Valley Preservation Press

First Printing 2004
ISBN: 0-9758993-9-2

The Merrimack Valley Preservation Press was established by the Merrimack Valley
Preservation Group, Incorporated. The MVPG, Inc. is a non-profit organization dedicated
to preserving the historical, cultural, and architectural heritage of the seventeen Massachusetts
communities situated along the banks of the Merrimack River.

Merrimack Valley Preservation Group, Incorporated
P.O. Box 813
Andover, MA 01810

www.mvpginc.org | Tel. 978.749.0634

COVER ILLUSTRATION:
Woodblock engraving, *View of Andover,*
from John Warner Barber's *Massachusetts Historical Collections,*
published in 1839, by Dorr, Howland and Co., Worcester, Massachusetts.
Courtesy of Daniel Gagnon.

BOOK DESIGN: John Hadley
COPY EDITOR: Martha Ough Briggs

PUBLISHER'S NOTE

A SPECIAL THANK YOU
to the members of the
MERRIMACK VALLEY
PRESERVATION GROUP
INCORPORATED
and to the many volunteers
whose support has made this
publication possible.

AUTHOR
ACKNOWLEDGEMENTS

ೲ

EACH STORY HERE HAS ITS OWN STORY. Some are new discoveries but others have been with me in many different places through decades. This book really began in 1967 when I informed my step-father that our family had just moved here.

"Andover!" John Marshall exclaimed. "That's where my ancestors attended theological school. My great-grandfather, Samuel Francis Smith wrote *My Country 'Tis of Thee* when he was a student there." I immediately made my way to the Andover Historical Society where the author of *America* became my first local history project.

Early town records on microfilm were culled for my first book *And Firm Thine Ancient Vow: The History of the North Parish Church of North Andover, 1645-1974.* This was completed on a hilltop overlooking the Mediterranean in Spain. Soon, I was at the American Cultural Institute in Madrid, researching a dozen biographies for the *Eagle Tribune's Bicentennial Editions.*

The annotated bibliography of Andover, North Andover, Methuen, and Lawrence that I was contracted to produce upon my return, required reading every book and pamphlet on these towns, some located in the dusty archives, cellars, and closets of area libraries and historical societies. Jobs at the Merrimack Valley Textile Museum and Stevens Memorial Library in North Andover generated further research. One summer was spent hiking Andover streets and in historical society files, working on an architectural survey for the Massachusetts and Andover Historical Commissions.

This town's exemplary environmental history was uncovered when I was commissioned to write *AVIS: A History in Conservation. Alice Buck and Indian Ridge* was first a play produced for Andover Village Improvement Society's Centennial and still presented by Susan Lenoe in local schools.

Although I worked in Maine for eight years, then at the Lowell Historic Preservation Commission, I returned to Andover periodically to lecture and teach. In 1992, Dr. Paul Hudon, Dee Liffman, and I presented Andover's story at the Salem Witch Trials Tercentenary Conference. Andover's accused went with me when I taught courses on the 1692 witch hunt for Elderhostel and several community colleges.

Andover's 350th Anniversary Celebrations presented the opportunity to create new programs, requiring research trips to the Stowe Center at Hartford, Franklin Pierce's New Hampshire homes, and directing my daughter as nineteenth-century author Elizabeth Stuart Phelps, in an original one-woman show. The community play, *Cry Witch!*, sponsored by the Andover & North Andover Historical Societies under grants from the Massachusetts Cultural Council, was presented in 1998 and 1999.

Space prevents naming all who contributed their unique and valuable knowledge over these many years. Andover and North Andover are indeed, fortunate in having Sarah Loring Bailey's book published in 1880, which is every local historian's first source. Forbes Rockwell's work with early town and land records is also indispensible. Bessie Goldsmith and Frederick Allis were also first-rate Andover historians on their special topics. Eleanor Richardson's *Andover: A Century of Change, 1896-1996* proved immensely helpful on the twentieth century. I am grateful to my colleagues, particularly former Andover Historical Society Director, Barbara Thibault and former Curator Tom Edmonds; Phillips Academy Archivist Ruth Quattlebaum; and historian Joan Patrakis, whose Andover Historical Society newsletter articles never fail to inspire and teach. My gifted editor, Liz Nelson, offered expertise and valuable insight both as a reader and fellow author. I also wish to thank the many teachers and students whose questions about Andover history over the years have challenged me to search out more stories to share.

Finally, enduring love and appreciation must go to my husband and best friend, Tad, whose support, patience, and enthusiasm, continue to make all creative projects possible. And to Eric, Lindsay, and Lauren, who grew up hearing my Andover stories and were ever willing to join their parents in exploring old burial grounds, touring historic houses, locating books in many different libraries, and assisting with interviews. Now they are picking the best stories to pass down to our grandchildren: Sarah, Emily, and Juno, as I hope you will do. Enjoy! ∾

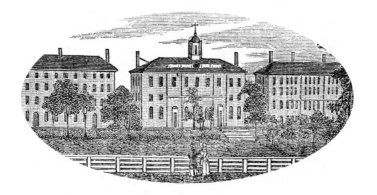

ANDOVER, WHERE THE OLD RELIGION FLOURISHED AS NOWHERE ELSE—the last great wave of the Puritan faith, its final crusade to redeem the world...and little boys played preacher as their chief amusement.

VAN WYCK BROOKS
New England Indian Summer
1865-1915

TABLE OF CONTENTS

ILLUSTRATIONS

INTRODUCTION

◍

ANDOVER, MASSACHUSETTS: HISTORICAL SELECTIONS FROM FOUR CENTURIES is a chronicle of the people and events that have shaped the history of Andover. Prior to the incorporation of Andover in 1646 and into the mid nineteenth century the towns of Andover, North Andover and the city of Lawrence south of the Merrimack River shared a common history as all were within the same border of the original inland plantation once known as Cochichawicke.

Juliet Haines Mofford, the author of this history presents the issues of the times. A list of topics include; politics, witchcraft, domestic violence, anti-slavery, religious influence, woman's rights, immigration, education, war, conservation, industrialization and tales of pastimes that have become unique to Andover alone. The stories presented in a chronological order and grouped by century provide the reader with a unique insight as to issues of our past that can often run parallel to our present day lives. Although names and boundaries have been redefined over the last three hundred and fifty years, our history continues to be the common thread that binds all our communities together.

As a teacher in the Andover Public School system I quickly realized what a valuable resource this book would be to colleagues, students and researchers of local history. The book highlights some of the major events of our times, but in a local setting. Many of the stories create thought provoking questions about the mores of the time and force the reader to re-examine truth from fiction. What could be better than to be challenged by a story and then wanting to know more?

Juliet has published many books on history; *Cry Witch! The Salem Trials of 1692, Talkin' Union: History of American Labor, Child Labor, A History of Conservation 1894-1980: Andover Village Improvement Society*. Juliet has also researched and scripted several *Living History* interpretive plays that have brought local issues to life for children and adults alike. Juliet Haines Mofford holds degrees from Tufts University and Boston University.

She has taught both elementary and secondary levels in Japan, Spain, and the West Indies. Juliet has worked professionally to develop museum-to-schools curricula as Cultural Director for the Lowell Historic Preservation Commission at the Museum of American Textile History, Old York Historical Society, in York, Maine, Greater Lawrence Underground Railroad Committee and the Northeast Regional Council for Social Studies and the New Hampshire Social Studies Council.

We are indebted to Juliet who made this idea a reality and hope that these pages will not only answer some questions, but also stimulate more dialogue throughout our communities and among the people that read them.

JAMES BATCHELDER

Andover Preservation Commission
and West Parish Garden Cemetery, Board of Directors.

THE SEVENTEENTH CENTURY

As the coastal towns established by the Puritans grew more crowded, men followed the rivers inland to establish new settlements. Their belief in a sacred covenant bound them to create new Cities of God in the American wilderness. The majority of the earliest English settlers at Cochichawicke previously resided at Newbury or Ipswich in Massachusetts Bay Colony.

Following negotiations between the Native Americans and the General Court, Cochichawicke was renamed Andover in 1646. The original settlement was concentrated in the area now known as the Old Center of North Andover, where the first meeting house was built. Home lots were assigned according to status and measured four to ten acres, with each man also receiving a meadow, wood lot and land for planting. Before long, men began to build houses closer to their allotted lands near the Shawsheen River, where they could harness the power to run saw mills, fulling and grist mills.

Andover was considered remote, situated at the edge of a vast, unexplored frontier. In 1654, Captain Edward Johnson wrote that "the land was well-fitted for the husbandman's hand," but "distance from market force the planters to carry their corn far." From the time of King Philip's War in 1675 through the first decades of the 18th century, inhabitants lived in fear of Indian raids and actually considered abandoning the settlement altogether.

The Puritan dream of building a New Zion, based on the Bible, was fading. Insecurity and strife within the community and dissension in the church were among the factors that led to the witch hunt. In 1692 more men, women, and children from Andover were accused, arrested, and confessed than from any other Massachusetts Bay town.

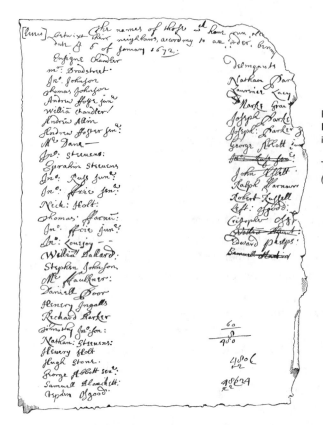

I. **List of the first twenty-three Freeholders.** Individuals are listed in the order they came to Andover.

Town Meeting Records, 1656–1709. *(Courtesy of Memorial Hall Library)*

2. **The Old Red House.** Ancient Homestead of the Abbots, Central Street. Built 1704; razed 1858. Example of a typical First Period House in Andover. *(Courtesy of Andover Historical Society)*

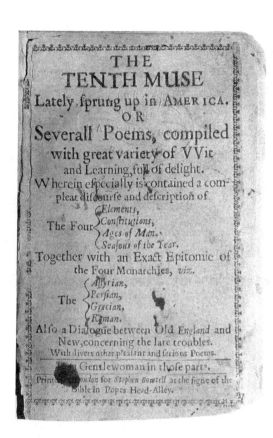

3. **Title page of Anne Bradstreet's book.** The Reverend John Woodbridge, Andover's first minister and Bradstreet's brother-in-law, took her manuscript along with him to England, apparently without the author's permission.
The Tenth Muse Lately Sprung up in America… was published in London in 1650. Original edition is owned by the Stevens Memorial Library, North Andover

Claude M. Fuess, *Andover: Symbol of New England.* *(Courtesy of the author.)*

4. **Gravestone of the Reverend Thomas Barnard.** Old Burying Ground, Academy Road, North Andover.

Born in Hartford, Connecticut, Thomas Barnard graduated from Harvard College in 1679 and served the North Parish Meeting House for thirty-seven years. The Reverend Samuel Phillips of South Parish eulogized Parson Barnard as "An able minister of the New Testament and a faithful Steward in the House of God; naturally caring for the flock…Truly of a meek and quiet spirit and clothed with Humility…"

His son, John, who followed him in the North Parish pulpit wrote that his father was "a good Pastor, one after God's own Heart, a pleasant, carefull Husband, a very Tender prudent father, and an accessable neighbour…"

Photo by Gayton Osgood for *And Firm Thine Ancient Vow: The History of North Parish Church of North Andover* by Juliet Haines Mofford, 1975, p. 59. *(Courtesy of the author)*

5. **Map of Andover, 1692.** The map indicates house locations and families involved in the witch hunt; created from early land records by historians from Andover and North Andover Historical Societies in 1992.

(Courtesy of Andover and North Andover Historical Societies)

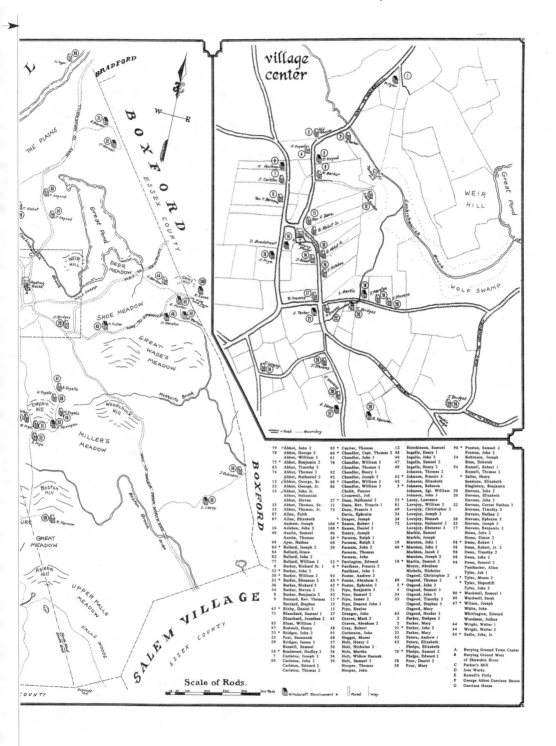

*This town
is called Andover
and hath good store of land
improved for the
bigness of it.*

CAPTAIN EDWARD JOHNSON
1654

SIX POUNDS AND A COAT

In 1646, English Puritans bought the land known as Cochichawicke ("Place of Great Cascade") that now includes Andover, North Andover and part of South Lawrence, from a Massachusetts Sagamore called Cutshamache. The English settlers were represented by the Reverend John Woodbridge and Mister Edmond Faulkner.

> *Cutshamache, Sagamore of ye Massachusetts came into ye Corte, May 6, 1646 and acknowledged Ye for the sum of 6 pounds and a Coate which he had already received, that he sold to Mr. John Woodbridge, in behalfe of ye inhabitants of Cochichawicke now called Andover, all his rights, interests and privilege in ye land Southward from ye towne two miles eastward to Rowley bounds, be ye same more or lesse, Northward to the Merrimac River…*

This agreement also insured the rights of a handful of Native Americans who already made their home here. The "Indian called Roger and his company" could fish for alewives in the Cochichawicke River "for their own eating, but if they either spoyle or steale any corne or other fruite to any considerable value of ye inhabitants there, this liberty of taking fish shall forever cease, and ye said Roger is still to enjoy four acres of ground where he now plants."

Although a few squatters, including Job Tyler, were already living here, it was "those Rowley men" who prompted legal permission for this new settlement. In 1641, John Woodbridge wrote Governor John Winthrop that "Some men from Rowley were scheming to take 100 acres of meadow from the Cochichawicke plantation." He urged something be done quickly as "some of our company have sold themselves out of house & home & so desire to be settled as soone as may bee…and I think I must resolve to labour to better myselfe."

As the first coastal settlements became crowded with much of the land already claimed, the Puritans followed the rivers inland to start new towns which they called plantations. Their Sacred Covenant decreed that they establish Cities of God in the American wilderness. With the establishment of new towns and the acquisition of land, a man could also increase his financial holdings and social status. For each new settlement, one was required to make application to General Court, then find ten freemen to sign on. These proprietors had to be church members and thus, eligible to become land-holders. An "able and orthodox minister" was also required for each new settlement. By law, a meeting house for worship and all town business had to be erected within three years. and no house could be built more than half a mile from that meeting house. John Woodbridge, a son-in-law of Deputy Governor Thomas Dudley, was ordained to serve the new church at Andover. He was the first minister in Essex County and the second to be ordained in New England.

After Bradstreet and Woodbridge, John Osgood is the third name on the list of the ten freeholders who established the new town in the area around what is presently the Old Center of North Andover. Cochichawicke was soon renamed Andover, presumeably after the market town near Osgood's home in Old England. The other original proprietors were Robert Barnard, John Frye, Nicholas Holt, Richard Barker, Joseph Parker, Nathan Parker, Richard Blake and Edmond Faulkner. They did not come directly from England but had been living in Newbury or like the town's chief magistrate and largest landholder, Simon Bradstreet, at Ipswich, before moving to Andover. Home lots were assigned, measuring four to ten acres each, depending on a man's wealth and social status. Each settler also received a meadow, wood lot and land for planting. John Osgood was elected Andover's first representative to the General Court in 1651.

The first written description of the new town appeared in *The Wonder Working Providence of Zion's Saviour in New England* by Captain Edward Johnson, published in London in 1654:

> *About this time there was a Town founded about one or two miles distant from the place where the goodly river of Merrimack receives her branches into her own body, hard upon the river of Shawshin…the honored Mr. Simon Bradstreet taking up his last sitting there hath been a great means to further the work, it being a place well-fitted for the husbandman's hand, were it not that remoteness of the place from the towns of trade bringeth forth some inconveniences upon the planters who are enforced to carry their corn far to market. This town is called Andover, and hath good store of land improved for the bigness of it.* ∞

THE FIRST POET

❧

Anne Dudley Bradstreet was to the manor born about 1612, in Northampton, England, yet she would spend most of her life facing difficult challenges on the primitive frontier. Her father, Thomas Dudley, a future governor of Massachusetts Bay Colony, was a steward in the employ of the Earl of Lincoln. Anne and her brother were educated by tutors, along with the Earl's children. Anne was permitted access to the library where she devoured His Lordship's books on history, literature and the classics. At the age of sixteen, having barely survived smallpox, Anne Dudley married her father's protege Simon Bradstreet, who had a master's degree from Emmanuel College, Cambridge. In 1630, the couple sailed with the Dudley family on Governor Winthrop's flagship, the *Arbella*, to help establish Massachusetts Bay Colony for the Puritans.

New England must have been a shock to the young wife who had been raised in the English castles and gardens of Tattershall and Sempringham in Lincolnshire. Many years later, Anne Bradstreet recalled her reaction in a journal she left her children and grandchildren:

> *I changed my condition and came into this country, where I found a new World and new manner, at which my heart rose. But after I was convinced it was the way of God, I submitted to it and joined the church at Boston.*

After brief stays at Salem and Charlestown, the Bradstreets joined family and friends in establishing several new Cities of God, first at Newtown (later Cambridge), then Agawam (Ipswich), and by 1645, Andover. Anne's husband, who remained her dearest friend throughout her life, was chief magistrate of the new Andover settlement. Simon Bradstreet, who became governor of Massachusetts Bay Colony after Anne's death, then served as secretary to the Court of Assistants. His political duties required frequent absences from home and Anne's poems show how much she missed him. Anne Bradsteet's love poems are timeless and explode the persistent myth that Puritans are cold-hearted and repressed.

To My Dear and Loving Husband

If ever two were one, then surely we.
If ever man were lov'd by wife, then thee;
If ever wife was happy in a man,
Compare with me ye women if you can.
I prize thy love more than whole Mines of gold,
Or all the riches that the East doth hold.
My love is such that Rivers cannot quench,
Nor ought but love from thee, give recompense.
Thy love is such I can no way repay,
The heavens reward thee manifold I pray.
Then while we live, in love lets so persevere,
That when we live no more, we may live ever.

Simon and Anne eventually had eight children, all of whom grew up to marry and have children of their own. In spite of her duties as wife of the local magistrate and daughter of the deputy governor and sometime governor of Massachusetts Bay Colony, Anne Bradstreet found time to write poetry. She wrote to stretch her mind, filled as it was with the literature and history that she had read and lived in Old England. Writing poetry was her manner of soul-searching, something Puritans were expected to do on a regular basis on their personal path to salvation. Anne also penned meditations of home and hearth as well as concerned poems about family members and the births and deaths of her grandchildren, although these were not published during her lifetime.

Andover's first minister, the Reverend John Woodbridge, was married to Anne's sister, Mercy, and had established Andover with Simon Bradstreet and the other free holders. Several years later, when Oliver Cromwell came to power and Puritans could safely practice their faith, Woodbridge returned to England. Unknown to Anne (though probably not to her husband and father) Woodbridge took her poems along with him. Anne was mortified when she saw the small book with the big name: *The Tenth Muse Lately Sprung up in America. Or Severall Poems, compiled with great variety of Wit and Learning, full of delight By a Gentlewoman in those parts*…that had been published in London in 1650. Anne Bradstreet had become the New World's first published author in the English language. Since neither her brother-in-law nor the printer dared put a woman's name on the title page *A Gentlewoman in Those Parts* remained the by-line for what the London publisher called "one of the most vendible books."

Anne never got the opportunity to revise her poems and now, here they were in print! In a subsequent poem, she compared her embarrassment to sending one's child out in public with a dirty face. Nor did her Andover neighbors think much of a woman who wasted time writing poetry instead of tending to her needlework. Woodbridge and others felt compelled to defend the author's reputation: "These poems are but the fruit of some few hours, curtailed from sleep and other refreshments." Poetry had not kept the author from domestic duties, Anne's brother-in-law assured readers, for this "*Gentlewoman in Those Parts* is honored and esteemed where she lives, for her gracious demeanor, her eminent parts, her pious conversation…" Even Harvard College's president confessed "her lines left him weltering in delight." Andover neighbors remained unimpressed causing Anne to write:

> *I am obnoxious to each carping tongue*
> *Who says my hand a needle better fits*
> *A Poet's pen all scorn I should thus wrong*
> *For such despite they cast female wits;*
> *If what I prove well it won't advance*
> *They'll say it's stol'n, Or else it was by chance.*

One summer night in Andover, a careless maid neglected to extinguish some live coals from the fireplace and the Great House belonging to Andover's first family burned to the ground. Some 800 books were lost, most of which had been brought from England, along with any furniture and personal possessions that linked the Bradstreets to their former life at Lincolnshire. In a long poem, *Verses Upon the Burning of Our House in Andover, July 10th, 1666,* Anne Bradstreet expressed her despair and attempted to reconcile the family's loss with her religious beliefs.

> *In silent night, when rest I took,*
> *For sorrow near I did not look.*
> *I wakened was with thundering noise*
> *And piteous shrieks of dreadful voice.*
> *That fearful sound of "Fire!" and "Fire!"*
> *Let no man know, is my desire.*
> *I, starting up, the light did spy,*
> *And to my God my heart did cry…*
>
> *When by the ruins oft I passed*
> *My sorrowing eyes aside did cast,*
> *And here and there the places spy*
> *Where oft I sat, and long did lie…*
> *Here stood that trunk, and there that chest;*
> *There lay that store I counted best;*
> *My pleasant things in ashes lie,*
> *And them behold no more shall I…*
>
> *In silence ever shall thou lie.*
> *Adieu, adieu; all's vanity…*
> *There's wealth enough; I need no more.*
> *Farewell, my pelf; farewell, my store;*
> *The world no longer let me love.*
> *My hope and treasure lie above.*

Andover Massachusetts: Historical Selections from Four Centuries

Anne Bradstreet's life was a dramatic contrast between genteel breeding and upper-class amenities and deprivation and uncertainty in new settlements. She drew strength from her creative, inner life to cope with cultural shock. Writing poetry must have been a necessary comfort as she struggled to reconcile the many challenges and physical difficulties that she was forced by faith and circumstance to meet. She also wrote to remember Old England, forever left behind. Much of her poetry reflects from her knowledge of ancient history, interest in English politics, and her admiration of other poets, particularly the French Huguenot, Du Bartas.

Anne Bradstreet's most enduring poems were penned in Andover, where she spent the final twenty-seven years of her life and died in 1672. Although no gravestone remains, she was likely buried in the town's earliest cemetery on Academy Road in North Andover. In September, 2000, a memorial plaque was erected here to commemorate the 350th anniversary of the publication of *The Tenth Muse.* ∞

An "Outside Town"

Andover was a frontier town on the edge of a vast wilderness. Packs of wolves attacked livestock so regularly that in 1686, town fathers voted that "those that catch wolves in the Town of Andover shall have 10 shillings for each wolfe paid by the town." The head of a wolf nailed on the meeting house door often greeted worshippers.

The Native American threat was nearly constant beginning with King Philip's War in 1675, followed by the French and Indian Wars, that series of conflicts between France and England in their struggle to dominate North America. There was virtually no peace in New England until 1713, when the European powers signed the Treaty of Utrecht. Andover citizens lived in a state of fear, never knowing when they might be ambushed in their fields or attacked in their beds. In the winter, the enemy came silently on snow-shoes and in summer, glided down rivers in canoes.

English settlers, having had little or no previous experience with diverse cultures, considered the Indians, with their shamanistic rituals, strange clothing and painted faces, "agents of the Devil." Some ministers back in England actually preached that Indians represented a lost tribe of Israel selected by Satan to settle as far as possible from the Christian gospel. Clergy also told their congregations that decades before the Great Migration of the 1630s, God had cleared the way for Puritans by sending epidemics upon the Northeastern Indian population.

The General Court officially designated Andover a "frontier town" on May 3, 1676 and ordered soldiers from Andover in service elsewhere to return and defend their homes. However, this did little to quell citizens' fears and the settlement was nearly abandoned, "as we being an outside town and in great danger..." In October of 1676, Lieutenant John Osgood dispatched a desperate letter to the Boston Council of Massachusetts General Court:

> We find we are not able to go to work improving our own lands, but
> are liable to be cutt off. Nor are we able to raise man at our charge to defend
> ourselves. We fear greatly that we shall not be able to live in this town to
> improve our lands to raise a subsistence...our men are liable to be shot when-
> ever we stir from our houses and our children taken by the cruel enemy; it does

so distress us that we know not what to do; if some defense not be made by ye forces we must remove off we cannot tell where, before we have lost all lives and cattle and horses by the enemy; we are completely able to fend ourselves in our garrison if we have warning but otherwise out of our house we are in continual danger."

The Court responded with an order for the building of twelve garrisons, "which we hope through God's blessing may be sufficient to secure them from any sudden surprisal of the enemy…Let God arise and our enemies be scattered."

On June 1, 1677, Dudley Bradstreet was appointed captain of the foot company at Andover. He immediately ordered soldiers to guard farmers at work in their fields. There was relative peace until 1689, when brothers John and Andrew Peters were ambushed and killed by a raiding party. Seven years later, a third Peters brother was killed outside a garrison.

By the summer of 1690, 200 soldiers "well appointed with arms and ammunition," and 80 mounted troops, making up four companies had been put on border guard for the protection of Andover and similar frontier settlements. The last direct raid on Andover occurred in 1698 with the deaths of five, the capture of three, the burning of houses and barns and torture of cattle. Some early land and town records were also lost during this raid. In 1704, four blockhouses were built including one in Shawshin Fields "as no garrison or dwelling house was nearby and corn and rye were grown by many here." A fifth was erected in 1722 and three repaired at the town's expense.

John Barnard, the minister's son grew up in Andover and returned here to teach school following graduation from Harvard. When he resigned in 1710 to accept another teaching position in Boston, Andover selectmen despaired: "We cannot compell gentlemen to come to us and we doe suppose they are something afraid by the Rason we doe lye so exposed to our Indian enemies." ∞

TIMOTHY ABBOT'S CAPTURE

❧

Legend has it that for his entire adult life, Timothy Abbot never allowed his children nor anyone else, to complain about being hungry nor to gripe about any food served, for they could not possibly know the meaning of hunger. Abbot was also known to provide a sumptuous meal to any person who appeared at his door.

On April 8, 1676, as King Philip's War raged, Ephraim Stevens spotted an Indian party in war paint, mounted his horse and galloped off to sound the alarm to Andover citizens, who immediately made for the nearest garrison.

The Indians pursued Stevens but according to town records, "did no mischief" until they arrived in the south end of town where Joseph Abbot was cutting elder bushes by the swamp with his younger brother, Timothy. Both were sons of original settler George Abbot. Twenty-four-year-old Joseph, had seen military action the previous winter in the Narragansett War swamp fight and on his way back from battle had burned Namesit wigwams. The written records tell us that Joseph put up a brave fight, killing several before being slain in sight of his father's garrison house.

The Indians captured thirteen year old Timothy. He was forced to walk to Canada, where he was to be sold to the French. However, after enduring months of cold, an Indian woman returned him to his family "much pined with hunger." Apparently, the boy did not much care for the Native American fare of snakes, boiled bark, and ground acorn patties fried in bear grease. ∞

TYLER'S TROUBLES

Job Tyler's name appears frequently in the Essex County Court Records. He obviously had trouble keeping out of trouble. In 1658, Job apprenticed his teenage son, Hopestill, to Andover blacksmith Thomas Chandler. After the legal agreement had been drawn up, the boy broke his bargain and hid his indenture paper. This legal document stated that apprentice Hope Tyler should serve Thomas Chandler "faithfully for nine years and a half…" and that Master Chandler "should teach him the trade of blacksmith." Chandler was also bound to teach Hopestill "to read the Bible and to write so as to be able to keep a book, so as to serve his turn for his trade and to allow unto said apprentice convenient meat and drink, washing, lodging, and clothes." Apparently, Chandler was an unkind master who worked his apprentice relentlessly.

Controversy in the courts over this matter raged back and forth between Job Tyler and Chandler for nearly a decade and in the end, Tyler paid dearly for suing a man of Chandler's position. Thomas Chandler was Andover's deputy to the General Court and one of the town's wealthiest citizens.

In 1665, another case between these two men was brought before the court, this time for defamation. The court decreed that Job Tyler, "being poor, should not be fined above six pounds," then ordered that

> *Job Tyler shall nail up or fasten upon the posts of the Andover and Roxbury Meeting Houses, in a plain legible hand, this acknowledgement: 'I Job Tyler have shamefully reproached Thomas Chandler by saying he is a base lying, cozening, cheating knave and that he hath got his estate by cozening in a base reviling manner and that he was recorded for a liar and that he was a cheating, lying, whoring knave fit for all manner of bawdery, wishing the devil had him…Therefore, I Job Tyler do acknowledge that I in these expressions most wickedly slandered the said Thomas Chandler…that without any just ground can do no less but express myself to be sorry for my cursing of him.* ∞

TWO MINISTERS FOR ONE CHURCH: ONE TOO MANY

In 1681, in the 32nd year of his Andover ministry, the Reverend Francis Dane "ceased preaching on a regular basis" and asked the town to provide for another minister. At this time, there was only one meeting house where all Andover residents gathered for town business, worship services and weekly lectures. Preaching was very important to Puritans and sermons, the highlight of the week. A minister called to a parish was expected to "settle" for life. This parson (from "person") or Elder, generally the most educated person in town, served as the congregation's resident guide on the path to salvation. By his sacred calling, training and knowledge of Scripture, the minister was expected to protect public morality and keep members of the community from the Devil's snares. Now, whether due to illness, mid-life crisis, or some change in personal theology, the Reverend Mr. Dane suddenly proposed to leave his flock without religious leadership.

The town fathers asked Parson Dane to forfeit his salary "considering the large accommodation of land and meadows given him by the town." Dane refused a pay cut so the selectmen wrote the General Court at Boston concerning their "sad and solemn condition…the wont of a preaching minister among us makes us in a sorrowful and very uncomfortable condition."

The court appointed a committee to meet at Andover which included clergy from four neighboring communities as well as magistrates. A month later the court returned a recommendation that the Town pay Mr. Dane thirty pounds a year in consideration of his many years of service and urged him "to endeavor to improve his utmost diligence and ability to carry on the publick worship of God and to carry it to his people with that tender love and respect, forgetting all former disgusts, as becomes a minister of the Gospel, and as duty doth oblige him, so the townspeople would more freely and cheerfully contribute his salary which they feared would not come easily from the town unless Mr. Dane resumed some of his duties with the help of the Reverend Thomas Barnard."

Thomas Barnard, who came to Andover in 1682 to assist Parson Dane, represented the new breed of Harvard educated Puritan clergy. He was thirty-four and had been teaching school in Roxbury when offered this position in Andover. To support two ministers for one meeting house must have seemed an unnecessary expense to Andover citizens, whose taxes salaried the minister. After 1683, the Reverend Mr. Dane, previously paid half his salary in wheat and the other half in Indian corn, began receiving five pounds of his thirty-pound salary in silver "during his abode in the ministry." Parishioners were also still required to provide his fuel, along with Parson Barnard's.

Andover's dispute with the Reverend Francis Dane had been legally settled, yet it appears likely that some members of the congregation, displeased with the committee's recommendation and the court's ruling, may have led the opposition against Dane's family a decade later. Ten of the senior minister's family members would be accused during the witch hunt, more than from any other single family. ∞

"EXCESS & DISORDER" AT HORSESHOE TAVERN

⅋

Hoping to control the consumption of liquor in Massachusetts Bay towns, the Colonial government granted annual licenses to sell liquor and keep public houses to men considered responsible citizens. At a town meeting in 1678, Andover Selectmen attempted to control this growing problem by setting a curfew and ordering the church sexton to toll the bell every night at nine. Tythingmen were instructed to report any breaches and to fine offenders.

In 1687, four of William Chandler's neighbors and his brother petitioned court requesting a Publick House or tavern be opened at Chandler's house, conveniently located in Andover on the road from Ipswich to Billerica.

Being *disguised with drink* is the most common crime in early records. Men frequented taverns to meet friends, to catch up on the latest political news, and to barter. Bulletins of auctions, land sales and runaway servants were posted on tavern walls. Names of "Common Tipplers" were also posted and a vintor could lose his license if he sold drinks to reputed drunkards, repeat offenders, or to blacks and Indians.

Gaming (billiards, dice, horse races, cock fights, wrestling matches and bull and bear baiting (a popular sport that pit dogs against these much larger, chained adversaries) were all betting matches. Both gaming and gambling were illegal in 17th-century New England, yet these laws were seldom enforced. Local ministers regularly cleared taverns on Saturday evenings and sent local citizens home to prepare for the Sabbath.

In March of 1690, William Chandler was called into court for permitting "all manner of Excess and Disorder in his tavern at the Sign of the Horseshoe" (symbol of the Chandler family's blacksmith trade). Some thirty-five Andover citizens submitted a petition requesting Chandler's tavern be shut down. Their formal complaint was that of "an epidemicall evill that overspreads and is like to corrupt the greater part of our town if not speedily prevented." They told the General Court that Chandler, in his

> *desire for money hath proved an evil root…for through his over forward-*
> *ness to promote his own gaine he hath been apt to animate and to entice*
> *persons to spend their money and time to ye great wrong of themselves and*

family they belong to; and to that end will encourage all sorts of persons both old and young to spend upon trust, if they have not money, & to some he will offer to lend them money to spend rather than that they should be discouraged...Servants & children are allowed by him in his house at all times unseasonable by night and day, sometimes till midnight and past & till break of day, till they know not their way to their habitations. And gaming is freely allowed in his house by which means the looser must call for drink.

The petitioners further requested that Chandler "be restrained from the selling of drink, else our town will be for the greatest part of our young generation so corrupted thereby that we can expect little else but a cours of drunkenness of them..." Because Chandler was "unable to undertake hard labor," the court renewed Chandler's license "to keep a common house of entertainment and common selling of ale, beer, syder in his Dwelling House known by the sign of the horseshoe," rather than remove his livelihood, but only on condition he

not permit, suffer nor have any playing at Dice, Cards, Tables, Quoits, Loggets, Bowles, Ninepins, Billiards or any other unlawful Games in his house, yard, garden, or backside; nor shall suffer to be or remain in his House any persons not being of his own family upon Saturday nights after it is Dark, nor at any time on the Sabbath Day or Evening after the Sabbath...nor shall he sell any Wine or Liquors to any Indians or Negroes nor suffer any servants or apprentices to remain in his house tippling or drinking after nine of the clock in the night; nor buy or take to Pawn any stolen goods, nor willingly harbor in his said House, Barn, Stable or otherwhere any Rogues, Vagabonds, Thieves, nor other notorious offenders whatsoever...∞

"PEMAQUID" CHUBB

When the Algonquins raided the North Parish of Andover during the Winter of 1698 that was, according to the Reverend Cotton Mather, "the severest that ever was in the memory of Man," they were seeking revenge against a former soldier by the name of Pasco Chubb.

In February, 1696, Chubb became commander of Fort William Henry, the newly rebuilt British fort at Pemaquid on the Maine Coast, to defend the New England Colonists against its French enemies. With fifteen cannon and nearly one hundred British soldiers, this stone fortress replaced an earlier one that burned, and was now considered impenetrable. Unfortunately, the only well had been located outside those thick walls.

That Spring, a dozen Indians, including the Chiefs of the Machias and the Penobscots, approached Fort William Henry by water, bearing a flag of truce in order to negotiate a prisoner exchange. Commander Chubb welcomed them with plenty of West Indies rum. While discussions were in progress, Chubb and his soldiers attacked their guests and killed four, including the two chiefs, and took the others hostage.

On July 14, the French leader Frontenac sent three ships of war under Iberville, to rendezvous with nearly three hundred Abenakis led by Baron St. Castin, to take Fort William Henry. When they ordered the English soldiers to surrender, Chubb refused, announcing boldly that he would not give up the fort, "Not even if the sea were covered with French vessels and the entire land with Indians!"

The mortar shells that the French sent exploding over the fortress walls represented the latest in modern warfare and terrified the King's Army. The rifle fire from the French's Native American allies was ceaseless. Most critically, the British soldiers inside Fort William Henry were cut off from their water supply. French Commander Castin dispatched a note to Major Chubb warning that if the French took the fort, the British soldiers would be handed over to the Indians who were eager to avenge the murder of their chiefs. Then the walls of the bastion that Massachusetts Bay's Royal Governor, Sir William Phips' had boasted strong enough to resist all the Indians in America, started to crack under the vibration of the cannons. Major Chubb surrendered, pleading for safe passage back to Boston for himself and all the soldiers under his charge.

The loss of this bastion to French forces in 1696 was a terrible blow to New Englanders. Chubb was immediately arrested for "gross misconduct" in deserting his post and for his "horrible piece of villainy committed against the Colony's Indian enemies." On November 18, Pasco Chubb petitioned the Court from the Boston jail, requesting that either he be quickly brought to trial or released to Andover "on payment of bail in order to take some care of his poor family for their subsistence in this hard winter season."

On February 22, 1698, a sizable war party, led by Chief Assacumbuit attacked Andover. They broke into the house in the North End where "Pemaquid" Chubb had been living since his release from prison. Chubb's wife, Hannah, daughter of one of Andover's original proprietors, Edmond Faulkner, died with her husband at the hands of the Indian avengers.

Eighteen-year-old Penelope Johnson and Major Wade, a relative visiting the Bradstreets, were also killed. Twenty head of cattle perished when barns were torched. Several other houses were raided, including those belonging to Parson Thomas Barnard and Colonel Dudley Bradstreet, who had filled his father's former position as Andover's chief magistrate.

The Bradstreets were taken captive, then quickly released. According to Abiel Abbot, the town's first historian, "This was a singular instance of mercy in a people who had always shown themselves to be cruel and to have no mercy." He claims that an Indian who lived at Newbury supposedly had high regard for Colonel Bradstreet. He agreed to lead the war party to Andover and show them Pasco Chubb's house, on the condition that they "neither kill nor captivate any of the Bradstreet family." ∞

The Seventeenth Century

ANDOVER'S FIRST MURDER

Hugh Stone, a carpenter, moved to Andover in 1667 and married Hannah Foster, the daughter of Andrew, a Scotsman who had been one of the town's first settlers. After twenty-two years of marriage and seven children, Hannah was expecting her eighth child, when on April 20, 1689, her husband slit her throat in a drunken rage. The Reverend Cotton Mather published an account of the murder in *Magnalia Christi Americana*, explaining to his readers that the particulars of the case were told him by a minister who attended the prisoner…

> *One Hugh Stone upon a quarrel between himself and his wife about selling a piece of land, having some words, as they were walking together on a certain evening, very barbarously reached a stroke at her throat with a sharp knife, and by that one stroke fetched away the soul of her who had made him a father of several children, and would have brought yet another to him if she lived a few weeks longer in the world. The wretched man was too soon surprised by his neighbors to be capable of denying that fact and so he pleaded guilty upon his trial…*

Mather reported that a minister, (most likely the Reverend Thomas Barnard), accompanied Stone to the scaffold where he made a final address to the spectators gathered there. According to Puritan belief, no one should be launched into eternity without an opportunity to prepare to meet his or her Maker. Confession was basic to Puritan theology, signifying God's forgiveness and a chance for regeneration. Thus, until the moment appointed for execution, ministers met with convicted prisoners to urge remorse and bring about religious conversion.

Hangings provided important lessons in morality for the early New England community and served as a means of social control. Advertised as Publick Spectacles, executions typically took place in natural amphitheaters that allowed as many people as possible to witness the event. Crowds thronged to hear the much-anticipated gallows speech since those close to death were supposed to impart special lessons for the living. Vendors hawked refreshments and mothers brought their children for this important learning experience.

The Reverend Cotton Mather reports that Hugh Stone did not believe he had broken *all* of the Ten Commandments. Yet Stone's attending minister insisted that the condemned man had "broken them all in your mind a thousand times."

"Indeed, Sir. I confess it: I see my sinfulness greater than I thought it was!" Stone admitted. When the cleric asked him what led him to commit murder, Hugh Stone replied, "It was contention in my family." He said he had once been careful about religion, "but upon contention between me and my wife, I left off the ways of God and you see what I am come to."

From the gallows Hugh Stone urged the crowd to follow God and honor the commitment to marriage vows. "Young men and maids, observe the rule of obedience to your parents and servants to your masters, according to the will of God...If you take up wicked ways, you set open a gate to sins to lead in bigger one..." Hugh also claimed that his wife had disobeyed him and warned other wives to keep their place. Stone admitted that it "was under the effect of strong drink that he gave way to passion. When thou hast thy head full of drink, remembrance of God is out of thy heart. I have cause to cry out and be ashamed of it, that I am guilty of it because I gave way to that sin more than any other and then God did leave me to practice wickedness and to murder that dear woman whom I should have taken a great deal of contentment in."

Prior to execution, Hugh Stone also delivered a "slanderous account" against his mother-in-law, Ann Foster. This would be remembered when Goody Foster was accused of witchcraft in 1692. At the age of seventy-two, Ann Foster became a confessed and convicted witch and died in prison, awaiting her own execution.∾

PARSON DANE
DIDN'T BELIEVE IN WITCHES

Like most up and coming clerics of his day, Andover's assistant minister Thomas Barnard, a Harvard graduate, believed that to fulfill his aim of destroying the Christian religion, the Devil routinely attempted to recruit witches as agents.

The Reverend Francis Dane, on the other hand, seems to have been among relatively few people then living in Old or New England, who did not believe in witches. In 1665, Dane testified in defense of one John Godfrey, "herdsman and laborer" and "resident at Andover or elsewhere at his pleasure," whom folks blamed for "losses suffered in their persons and estates that came not from any natural causes." John Godfrey was also accused of "injuring by Satanic acts," the wife of Job Tyler.

In depositions made with his wife and teenage son and daughter, Tyler explained they "saw a thing like a black bird, to wit as big as a pigeon, come down at the door of their house which did fly about." He and John Godfrey, then working as Tyler's hired man, tried to catch it but the bird vanished through a jointed board. Job Tyler told the court that Godfrey said "the bird came to suck your wife." Indeed, Goody Tyler "had afterwards fallen into strange fits and sickness." In his testimony, the Reverend Francis Dane agreed itinerate laborer, John Godfrey was an "ill-disposed person…" Yet the minister publicly rejected any supernatural manifestations in the Godfrey case. John Godfrey was acquitted, then sued his accusers for libel.∞

CARRIER OF SMALLPOX

✌

In late May of 1692, Martha Allen Carrier was the first from Andover charged and imprisoned for witchcraft. Some years before Martha had married a Welshman twenty years her senior "after naming him the father of her first child." Thomas Carrier was said to stand over seven foot tall and was known for his incredible strength and "fleetness of foot." In seventeenth-century New England, anyone outside the norm was viewed with suspicion. The big man from Wales was a man without roots who drifted from town to town, hiring himself out as a field hand.

The Carriers had been living in Billerica with Martha's sister, Mary Toothaker (who herself would be arrested and later confess to witchcraft). Mary's husband, a doctor with malpractice suits hanging over his head and an accused witch, would die in prison. Poverty was another significant issue in witchcraft accusations, for Puritans believed the poor to be out of God's favor.

Thomas Carrier was unable to support his wife and four children. The Billerica selectmen, fearing they would become public charges, warned the family out of town. The Carriers moved back to Andover, where Martha had grown up, a daughter of one of the earliest settlers, Scotsman Andrew Allen. The family, ironically named *Carrier*, apparently brought smallpox with them.

Andover had never suffered a smallpox epidemic, although the disease was all too common in Boston and other port towns, where it came in on ships. Puritans, who believed everything was part of God's plan, considered epidemics to be divine judgment upon an entire community.

On October 24, 1690, Martha's three year old nephew, Andrew Allen, Jr. was the first to die. Within a matter of months, her father, both brothers, her sister-in-law and several more nephews were dead of smallpox. As the first victims lay ill, the Andover Selectmen warned Martha Carrier out of town "for spreading the distemper with wicked carelessness." They implored her brothers to take responsibility for "your sister Carrier and some of her children (who) are smitten with that contagious disease the small pox and have been so inconsiderate as to think that their care belongs to the Selectmen of Andover which it does not…"

Not only did Martha refuse to leave, she demanded the town assume financial responsibility for her family until every one regained health. This feisty woman entered into a battle of wills with the town fathers, who understood quarantine was their only defense against spread of smallpox. The Carriers were banned from "public meeting till they may come with safety to others…"

Following the deaths of her father and both brothers, Martha broke the gender rules of her day by taking charge of the family property. Carrier was typical of many women accused of witchcraft in Old and New England. A woman who refused to stay in her place and had the reputation of being a "scold," might easily be suspected of witchcraft. At a time when being a "good neighbor" meant spying and tattling on others, Martha Carrier was "a quarrelsome neighbor." In one petition dispatched to Court in his attempt to put a stop to the 1692 witch hunt, the Reverend Francis Dane, Andover's senior minister, who was Martha's uncle, said "that there was suspicion of Goodwife Carrier before she was apprehended, I knew." Parson Dane claimed his niece was merely "the victim of malicious gossip."

Thirty-one-year-old, Benjamin Abbot believed Martha Carrier "had a great hand in my sickness and misery." After Goody Carrier threatened him during an argument over boundary lines, he started to suffer unbearable pains in his side. Then his foot swelled to such a size that he could not walk, and his body broke out in gruesome boils. Although Andover's Doctor Prescott lanced his sores, Abbot "hovered near death" until Martha was arrested, after which he made "a remarkable recovery."

"You lie! I am wronged!" Carrier shouted during her examination May 31, when five "afflicted girls fell into the most intolerable cries and agonies." As the Salem maids writhed under Goody Carrier's alleged pricking of them with pins, she told the judges, "It is false! I have not done it!"

"I see the souls of thirteen persons murdered by Goody Carrier!" exclaimed one girl, referring to the victims of the smallpox epidemic Martha Carrier supposedly brought to Andover.

"The devil is a liar and it is a shame for you to mind what these girls say that are out of their wits!" Martha spoke boldly in her own defense. "It's no matter though these girls' necks be twisted off! For if I speak, you will not believe me!"

The court scribe noted that "the tortures of the afflicted were so great that there was no enduring of it." So Goody Carrier was ordered away to be bound hand and foot. The scribe wrote that "when the accused was well bound, all had strange and sudden ease."

There was no lack of evidence when Martha Carrier went on trial for her life. Tavernkeeper William Chandler's daughter, eleven-year-old Phebe, claimed to have been struck deaf by Martha's voice and temporarily crippled by her glance. Martha's nephew, Allen Toothacker told the court he'd been knocked down by Cousin Richard Carrier and was unable to get up until he saw Goody Carrier's specter rise off his chest. Toothacker had also lost a heifer, a yearling, then a cow, "and knew not of any natural causes, yet feared it hath been ye affect of my Aunt Carrier, her malice." Mary Lacey, Jr., an Andover teenager convicted of witchcraft, told the court that she "heard the Devil promise Goody Carrier that she might rule as "Queen of Hell." Mary's grand-mother, Ann Foster, gave the magistrates details of her ride through the air to attend witches' meetings with Martha Carrier.

Seventy-two-year-old Ann Foster (mother of the murdered Hannah Stone) also reinforced Martha's role in Andover's smallpox epidemic. "Goody Carrier came to me and would have me bewitch two children of Andrew Allen's. I had two poppets made, and stuck pins in them to bewitch the children. One of the children died, and the other became very sick…"

Martha's four children were arrested, apparently to coerce their mother's confession. John Proctor who was executed with Carrier on August 19, 1692, wrote from his prison cell that Martha's teenage sons were, like his own son "tied neck to heels," prior to confessing to witchcraft and accusing their mother. Seven-and-a-half-year-old Sarah Carrier, coaxed by zealous magistrates determined to rout Satan from Massachusetts Bay Colony, said her mother's specter had come to her in the shape of a cat and made her a witch too.

Martha Carrier remained unrepentant all the way to the gallows. Had she confessed to being a witch, as so many did, her life might have been spared. Nor did Martha Carrier ever accept responsibility for Andover's smallpox epidemic.

In his *Diary*, Judge Samuel Sewall recorded his "particular surprise at Carrier's protestations of innocence, since she had enjoyed so long and so thoroughly a reputa-tion for witchcraft." To add insult to injury, Thomas Carrier was billed fifty-six shillings in prison fees to cover room and board, as well as costs incurred for the manacles and chains locked on his wife and children. ∞

THE TOWN WITH THE MOST WITCHES

❧

New Englanders were generally convinced that the Colony's troubles were caused by what Cotton Mather called "a dreadful knot of witches." Many believed that God and Satan were involved in a struggle for the very soul of New England and by the summer of 1692, it seemed to townspeople that Andover was their final battle-ground. The Devil's goal was to rout the Christianity from the country, destroy their Cities of God and set up Satan's Kingdom. If many of the Massachusetts Bay Colony leaders had not been convinced of this "Conspiracy of Satan," the Salem Trials would never have become such a tragedy

William Barker Sr., a farmer who lived in what is now North Andover, admitted he "wickedly, mallitiously, and felloniously a Covenant with the Devil did Make, and did Signe the Devill's Booke with Blood, and gave himself Soule and Body to the Devill." Accused by afflicted Andover girls, Abigail Martin, Rose Foster, and Martha Sprague, this "detestable witch" admitted getting into the "Snare of the Devil" three years before because he had a large family and the "world went hard with him." The Devil had promised to pay all Barker's debts and "he could live comfortably." In several confessions, Barker gave the magistrates and clergy just the sort of information they were longing to hear. He provided details of a meeting of one hundred witches held at Salem Village. Barker had been haying all day, so his spectre went. "There are already 307 witches in the colony who are much disturbed with the Afflicted Persons because they are discovered by them…Satan's design is to abolish all the churches in the land and set up his own worship." Barker beat the judges at their own game and then, escaped from prison.

Between July 15 and September 17 of 1692, more than fifty persons were accused in Andover, a town with a total population of about six hundred. Some forty warrants were signed by local magistrate Dudley Bradstreet. Finally, refusing to sign any more, he threw down his quill, and was himself accused, along with his family. They managed to escape to New Hampshire until the witch hunt was over. However, the dog belonging to his brother, John Bradstreet, was hanged in Andover, presumed guilty of being that witch's "familiar."

Of the forty-eight arrested, forty-two were related through extended families. Thirty-seven were females; while the ages of females and males ranged from seven to seventy-two, nearly half of the accused were under the age of twenty. Sixty percent of all those who confessed to witchcraft in 1692 came from Andover. During their Examinations before the magistrates, many implicated members of their own families.

"Hence we so easily parted with our neighbors of honest and good report," the Reverend Francis Dane wrote. "Hence we so easily parted with our children when we knew nothing in their lives nor any of our neighbors' to suspect them, and thus things were hurried on; hence such strange breeches in families." According to Elder Dane, "Had charity been put on, the Devil would not have had such advantage against us…"

Three from Andover were hanged on Gallows Hill in Salem: Martha Carrier on August 19; Samuel Wardwell and Mary Ayer Parker (widow of original Andover settler, Nathan Parker) on September 22nd. Ann Foster had been condemned but died in prison, awaiting execution. ∾

THE ANDOVER TOUCH TEST

❧

Poor Andover does now rue the day that ever the afflicted went among them;
they lament their folly, and are an object of great pity and commiseration.

—Thomas Brattle, *Letter*
Boston, Massachusetts, October 8, 1692

The afflicted girls of Salem Village were considered gifted persons by most magistrates and ministers because God permitted them to see inside the spiritual world and experience things that ordinary folks could not. Many colonists were convinced that the ability of afflicted persons to spot witches might save Massachusetts Bay Colony. During examinations and trials, accused persons were ordered to place their hands upon the afflicted who were in the throes of seizures and undergoing an imaginative variety of tortures. If, when an afflicted person was touched their torments ceased, it meant that the evil force had flowed back into the accused, thus proving guilt. Known as spectral evidence, this also meant that the alleged witch's spirit could leave the witch's body in order to inflict pain on others far away. Although controversial throughout the trials, this was the grounds for conviction of all nineteen hanged as witches in 1692.

Although Martha Carrier had been locked in Salem Prison since the end of May, no one else in Andover had been accused of witchcraft. Then, in mid-July, when herbal remedies and bloodletting failed to cure Elizabeth Ballard's lingering illness, her husband suspected she might be a victim of witchcraft. Joseph Ballard rode to Salem Village and brought back two of the afflicted girls. After Parson Barnard had offered prayers, they were taken to Goodwife Ballard's bedside, as well as to other houses around Andover where someone lay ill. When the girls proclaimed Goody Ballard bewitched and blamed the widow, Ann Foster, mother of the murdered Hannah Stone, Goodman Ballard quickly filed a warrant for Foster's arrest

Only in Andover did a community-wide touch-test take place. Intent upon routing out all possible "devil's agents" in their midst, this horrific event seems to have been orchestrated by Andover's assistant minister, the Reverend Thomas Barnard who sanctioned it with a prayer. The Reverend Francis Dane, Andover's seventy-six-year-old senior minister, was noticeably absent. Staged at the meeting house September 7, it resulted in the arrests of seventeen citizens, causing Cotton Mather to comment that "in this town was discovered the most horrid crew of witches that ever disgraced a New England town."

Mary Osgood, wife of the church deacon, was among the accused that day and from her prison cell, she described what happened.

> *After Mr. Barnard had been at prayer, we were blindfolded and our hands were laid upon the afflicted persons, they being in their fits and falling into their fits at our coming into their presence...some led us and laid our hands upon them, and then they said that we were guilty of afflicting them. Whereupon, we were all seized as prisoners, by a warrant from the Justice of the Peace and forthwith carried to Salem...knowing ourselves altogether innocent of the crime, we were all exceedingly astonished and amazed, and consternated and affrighted even out of our reason. And our nearest and dearest relations, seeing us in that dreadful condition and knowing our great danger, apprehended there was no other way to save our lives but by confessing ourselves witches...*

Confessions were considered the most desirable means of conviction for a confessed witch promised community regeneration and would bring the blessing and protection of God over the entire town. Hence, Abigail Dane Faulkner was urged to "Confess, for the credit of the town." Andover confessions tended to focus more on religion, typically describing Baptism by the Devil and mock celebrations of the Christian Sacrament. Some are filled with ancient English folklore, as when William Barker, Sr. described "Satan's cloven foot."

Andover had more confessed witches than any other town. By mid-summer, it was likely clear to most people that those who confessed to witchcraft remained in prison while those who had denied any dealings with the Devil, had gone to the gallows. Convicted witches were often brought into court to testify against others, but they had not yet been executed. Word had also gotten around that those who confessed to witchcraft were not locked into manacles and chains. ❧

THE TOWN FORTUNE-TELLER

Although Puritan clergy abhorred all such practices as "tools of the Devil," magic prevailed in early New England, particularly among the poor who saw little evidence of being among God's Elect. Folk practices like astrology and predicting the future were simply part of the cultural heritage that many New England settlers brought along with them from Europe. Andover citizens had a reputation for dabbling in the occult, what Cotton Mather and other ministers called "wicked little sorceries."

In a letter dated October 8, 1692, Thomas Brattle, a prominent Boston lawyer, wrote, "Now I am writing concerning Andover, whereas there is a report spread abroad the country, how they were much addicted to Sorcery and there there were 40 men in it that could raise the Devil as well as an astrologer…"

The Reverend Francis Dane refused to accept such slurs against his town. In one letter to the court, he rejected the "diverse reports" of magical practices in his parish as "scandalous and unjust."

The carpenter, Samuel Wardwell was Andover's favorite fortune-teller. Following his arrest on August 22, Thomas Chandler told the court he'd heard Wardwell predict the future and when the carpenter did so, "cast his eyes down, as if consulting the Devil." Furthermore, the clairvoyant carpenter had correctly predicted the genders of Ephraim Foster's children before they were born, telling Foster he would father five daughters before a son joined the household.

Wardwell admitted to the Court that he had been "foolishly led along with the telling of fortunes which sometimes came to pass." Furthermore, when he was angry, he would curse, "The Devil take it!" Perhaps the Devil had "taken advantage of that." And indeed, it was true: he *did* have the power to make animals come to him whenever he called them.

Wardwell confessed making a bargain with the devil some years before when he had "fallen into a discontented state of mind over a maid named Barker who had not returned his love." About that time, he had seen some cats gathered in front of Captain Bradstreet's house. One cat suddenly assumed the shape of the Devil and promised Wardwell he could "live comfortably and be a captain" if he signed the book. The carpenter told the magistrates that he was then "dipt all over in the Shawsheen

River" and "renounced his former baptism." Wardwell was convicted of witchcraft and sent to Salem Prison. Then, less than two weeks later, Wardwell recanted his confession and was quickly brought to trial again. He went to the gallows on September 22, 1692. ∞

"Our Sin of Ignorance"

❧

Throughout the witch hunt, which he referred to as "Our Sin of Ignorance," Andover's senior minister, Francis Dane prevailed as the voice of reason. Even while some ten members of his family were incarcerated, including several eight-year-old grandchildren, Dane maintained his courageous and unpopular point of view, standing firm against most fellow clergy and magistrates. He questioned the integrity of accusers and disapproved of methods employed by the judges at examinations and trials, particularly the use of spectral evidence.

"The conceit of spectre evidence as an infallible mark did too far prevail with us…We know not who can think himself safe, if the accusations of children and others who are under a Diabolical influence shall be received against persons of good fame…I believe many innocent persons have been accused and imprisoned." Dane's petitions and appeals to the Governor and court eventually helped turn public opinion against the Trials and bring an end to the witch hunt.

On September 17, 1692, Abigail Dane Faulkner, one of Dane's daughters was cried out against. Married to the son of Edmond Faulkner, the original settler credited with purchasing the Cochichewicke plantation from Native Americans, Abigail was about forty years of age when she became one of Andover's ten citizens sentenced to death for witchcraft. Goodwife Faulkner refused to confess and denied all the charges against her. "God would not require me to confess that which I was not guilty of," she said.

She did admit being angry at what folks said about members of her family. "My spirit being raised, I pinched my hands together. Perhaps the Devil took advantage of that…although if the devil was working through me, I was not aware of it and did not consent to it." Abigail's eight and ten-year-old daughters also confessed and told the judges that their mother had made them witches. The minister's daughter was sentenced to death but since she was then expecting her seventh child, her date of execution was postponed.

Faulkner's plea for mercy penned from prison, show that she was educated and articulate at a time when many women could neither read nor sign their names. She wrote the Governor of the Colony, begging release to return to her family. She feared her husband and children would perish during her incarceration and wrote that the charges against her were based only on the testimony of afflicted persons. After four months in prison, the Governor granted her release.

Abigail soon gave birth to a son, calling him "Ammi Ruhammah" from the Old Testament, meaning "my people have obtained mercy." Abigail Faulkner's life was spared by the "General Gaol Delivery," signed by Governor Phips the following January, yet the names of those convicted had not been legally cleared. They had no legal rights and could not reclaim their property. She remained under sentence and unable to regain her "former rights and reputation." Her father, who died in 1697, could not help. Goody Faulkner and her family worked at menial tasks in Parson Barnard's household: spinning, sewing garments for his sons, and weaving with her daughters who had also served prison time. Her husband labored in the minister's fields and tended his livestock.

Because her sentence had not been lifted, Abigail Dane Faulkner was terrified of being accused of witchcraft again. In 1703, she addressed the Massachusetts General Court with a courageous letter which helped bring closure to the Salem Trials.

> I am as yet suffered to live but this only as a Malefactor convicted upon record of ye most heinous crimes that mankind can be supposed to be guilty of, which besides its utter ruining and defaming my reputation...will certainly expose myself to Imminent Danger by new accusations which will thereby be the more readily believed and will remain a perpetual brand of infamy upon my family. I do humbly pray that the High and Honorable Court will...order the Defacing of ye record.

The minister's daughter led the way for survivors and families of those who had been executed to petition legislature for reparations suffered in lives and property. In 1709, twenty-one individuals and families petitioned for a redress of the loss of their civil rights and property and two years later, the Massachusetts Court passed the Act to Reverse the Attainders. Five hundred and ninety-eight pounds was paid in various amounts to the petitioners, the General Court declaring "all charges and convictions brought against those accused and found guilty of witchcraft be declared null and void...judgments and attainers were to be repealed and reversed...and no corruption of blood or forfeitures of goods and chattels be incurred and they be reinstated in their just Credit and reputation." ∞

ENDNOTES: THE SEVENTEENTH CENTURY

SEVENTEENTH CENTURY
Page 3: Captain Edward Johnson. "Wonder-Working Providence of Sion's Saviour in New England". London, 1654.

CHAPTER 1-SIX POUNDS AND A COAT
Page 9: (Cutshamache, Sagamore) Massachusetts Bay Records, Vol. II, p. 159.
(Letter of Woodbridge to Governor Winthrop, 1641) Reverend Cotton Mather, Magnalia Christi Americana, "Woodbridge."
Page 10: Captain Edward Johnson, Op. Cit.

CHAPTER 2- THE FIRST POET
Page 11-13: Jeannine Hensley, Editor. *The Works of Anne Bradstreet*. Cambridge, Mass.: Harvard University: Belknap Press.

CHAPTER 3- "AN OUTSIDE TOWN"
Page 15: Town Meeting Records , 1656-1709. March, 1686.
Page 15-16: (Osgood to Massachusetts General Court, October, 1676) Massachusetts Archives , Vol. l xviii, p. 202; cited by Sarah Loring Bailey. *Historical Sketches of Andover, comprising the present towns of North Andover & Andover, Massachusetts.* Boston: Houghton Mifflin & Co., 1880, p. 175

CHAPTER 4 - TIMOTHY ABBOT'S CAPTURE
Page 17: Joseph Abbot, see Andover Vital Records, Deaths;
Abiel Abbot. *History of Andover From Its Settlement to 1829.* Andover: Flagg & Gould, 1829

CHAPTER 5 - TYLER'S TROUBLES
Page 18: Op. Cit ., Sarah Loring Bailey, pp. 47-48

CHAPTER 6 - TWO MINISTERS FOR ONE CHURCH: ONE TOO MANY
Page 19: Town Meeting Records, 1656-1709, October 10, 1681. *Records of the Massachusetts General Court*, October 12, 1681. Op. Cit., March 6, 1681/2

CHAPTER 7 - "EXCESS AND DISORDER" AT HORSESHOE TAVERN
Pages 21-22: Ibid ., Sarah Loring Bailey, 68-69 cites Essex County Court Papers,

Vol. I, 74.
Page 22: Bailey, Op. Cit., p. 71

CHAPTER 8 – "PEMAQUID" CHUBB
Pages 23-24: Op. Cit., Bailey, pp. 181-183.

CHAPTER 9 – ANDOVER'S FIRST MURDER
Page 25: Reverend Cotton Mather. Magnalia Christi Americana; also Sarah Loring
Bailey, pp. 79-81.

CHAPTER 10 – PARSON DANE DIDN'T BELIEVE IN WITCHES
Page 27: Job Tyler vs. John Godfrey, Essex County Court Records, March 7; March
13, 1665. Records of the Court of Assistants, 2, pp. 158-159. See also Sarah Loring
Bailey, p. 54.

CHAPTER 11 – CARRIER OF SMALLPOX
Page 28-29: Town Records , October 14, 1690; November 4, 1690; April 9, 1690.
See also Sarah Loring Bailey, pp. 201-203; 231-232. Andover Vital Records, Deaths.

Reverend Francis Dane. "Letter to the Court of Oyer et Terminer," Essex County
Court Papers , vol. I, p. 142.

Page 29-30: Examination of Martha Carrier, May 31 & August 3, 1692. Paul Boyer &
Stephen Nissenbaum, Editors. *Salem Witchcraft Papers*. NY: Da Capo Press, 1977, pp.
183-203 (also Electronic Text Center, University of Virginia).

Page 29-30: *Queen of Hell, Testimony of Mary Lacey*, Jr., Ibid., p. 523

Examination & Confession of Ann Foster. Op. Cit. 341-344.

Page 30: Judge Samuel Sewall, Diary, 1692. Fifth Series, Vol. V. Massachusetts
Historical Society.

CHAPTER 12 – THE TOWN WITH THE MOST WITCHES
Page 31: Examination & Confessions of William Barker, Sr. Op. Cit., pp. 63-69.
Page 32: Reverend Francis Dane, "Letter to Court, January 2, 1692/3." Essex County
Court Papers , vol. 1, p. 142; see also Sarah Loring Bailey, pp. 231-232.

CHAPTER 13 – THE ANDOVER TOUCH TEST
Page 33: Thomas Brattle, "Full & Candid Account of the Delusion Called Witchcraft,"
October 8, 1692. Massachusetts Historical Society Collections; see also Sarah Loring

Bailey, pp. 228-229.

Page 34: Description of Touch Test: Reverend Increase Mather's Interview with Mary Osgood in Salem Prison. Juliet H. Mofford. *Cry Witch! The Salem Witchcraft Trials, 1692.* Carlisle, Mass.: Discovery Enterprises, Ltd., 1995, p. 44.

CHAPTER 14 – THE TOWN FORTUNE-TELLER
Page 35: Op. Cit., Thomas Brattle.
Pages 35-36: Examination of Samuel Wardwell, September 1, 1692. Paul Boyer & Stephen Nissenbaum, Editors. *Salem Witchcraft Papers.* NY: Da Capo Press, 1977, pp. 783-789 (also Electronic Text Center, University of Virginia).

CHAPTER 15 – "OUR SIN OF IGNORANCE"
Page 37: Reverend Francis Dane, "Letter to Court, January 2, 1692/3." Essex County Court Papers , vol. 1, p. 142; see also Sarah Loring Bailey, pp. 227-228.
Examination of Abigail Faulkner, August 11, 1692. Salem Witchcraft Papers, Op. Cit., pp. 327-333
Page 38: Abigail Faulkner, "Petition to Massachusetts General Court, March 2, 1703;" and "Act to Reverse the Attainders," October 17, 1711. Province of Massachusetts Bay. Juliet H. Mofford. *Cry Witch: The Salem Witchcraft Trials, 1692.* Carlisle, Mass.: Discovery Enterprises Ltd. 1995, pp. 55-57.

THE EIGHTEENTH CENTURY

❧

By order of the General Court, the town of Andover was divided into two separate parishes in 1709, each with its own meeting house and minister. Second and third generations of the first families relocated South and West of the original town center near Lake Cochichewicke.

Throat distemper, smallpox, and other infectious diseases in the 1720s and '30s resulted in a religious revival known as the Great Awakening in Andover, as well as throughout New England.

As England and France continued to wage war for the control of North America until 1764, Andover militia men served on battle fronts as far away as Nova Scotia. For their service in the King's forces, many moved out of Andover, starting new lives in new places. Acadian families brought down from conquered Canada, were quartered in town, exposing citizens to a new culture and religion.

As Mother England imposed punishing taxes on the Colonists, Andover citizens became increasingly self-sufficient in producing their own cloth rather than to continue their dependence on British imports. When war came, Andover was enthusiastically committed to independence. More blacks from Andover fought at the Battle of Bunker Hill than from any other town.

In the midst of the Revolutionary War, Phillips Academy was founded by two old friends, who were also busy manufacturing gun powder for the Continental troops. A local visit from the first President of the new United States seemed a fitting and happier end to this century of conflict. ∞

6. **Portrait of the Reverend Samuel Phillips.**
Graduated from Harvard 1708; ordained October 7, 1711 as the first minister at South Parish, where he for served fifty-nine years. He died June 5, 1771.

Historical Manual of the South Church in Andover, Massachusetts, 1859, by the Reverend George Mooar.

(Courtesy of Memorial Hall Library)

7. **The Second Meeting House in South Parish.** Dedicated March 19, 1734 and in use until 1787. The present church is the fourth and was erected in 1864 on approximately the same spot.
(Courtesy of Andover Historical Society)

8. **Portrait of Samuel Phillips, Jr.**
   (1752-1802), grandson of the first
   minister of South Church; founder
   of Phillips Academy, manufacturer
   of gunpowder and paper, Lieutenant
   Governor and State Senator.
   Unsigned portrait owned by Phillips
   Academy and reproduced in "*An
   Illustrious Town – Andover*," Reverend
   F. B. Makepeace, *The New England
   Magazine and Bay State Monthly*,
   April, 1886, p. 305.

   (Courtesy of the author)

9. **Portrait of James Otis, Jr.**,
   Frontispiece: Reverend F. B. Makepeace,
   "An Illustrious Town–Andover,"
   *The New England Magazine and
   Bay State Monthly*, April, 1886.

   (Courtesy of the author)

10. **Page from South Parish Church Manuscript Records.**
This page has notation of deaths in the 1778 Powderhouse explosion.

(Courtesy of Andover Historical Society)

11. **Phillips Academy in 1778.** *(Courtesy of Phillips Academy)*

12. **Sketch of Andover Hill.** Rendered by Ralph Robin Naizot. View of Phillips Academy, 1778.
(Courtesy of Phillips Academy)

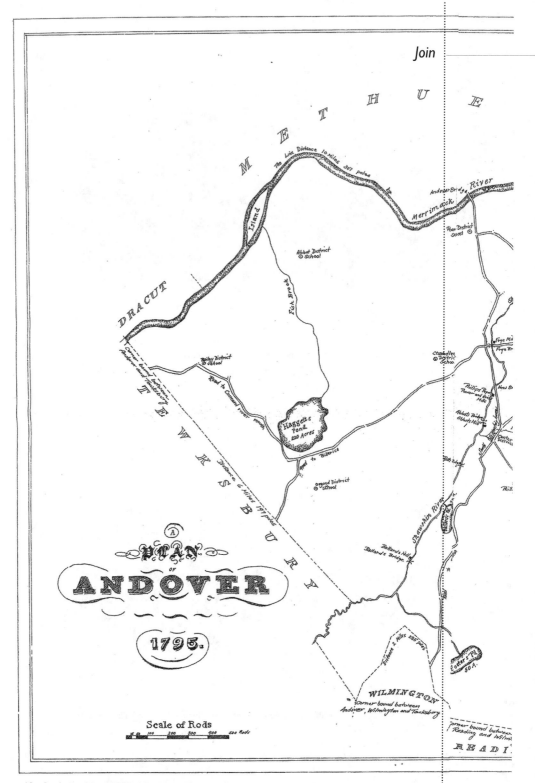

13. **Andover Map, 1795.** (*Courtesy of Andover Historical Society*)

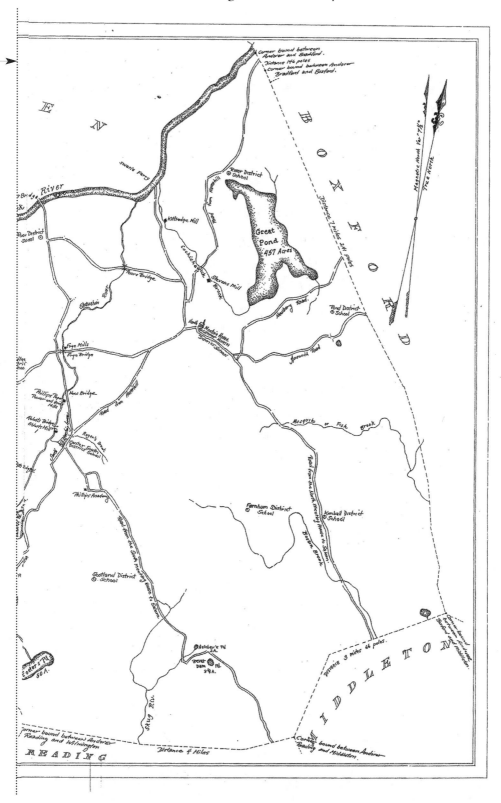

*But since the
Glorious Lord of the Sabbath
has given you such a shaking of late,
I hope to see no more sleepers
in the Meeting House!*

REVEREND SAMUEL PHILLIPS

SERMON AT SOUTH PARISH
AFTER THE EARTHQUAKE OF 1775

THE PARSON WHO RULED

In 1705, the citizens of Andover voted to build a new meeting house "as sufficient and convenient for the whole town as may be." Their only church, located near what is now the Old Center of North Andover, was too distant, particularly during inclement weather, for many parishioners to travel to Sabbathday services, town meetings, and mid-week public religious lectures. By this time, the southern end of Andover had become more heavily populated than the original settlement area. Controversy raged over where to locate the new meeting house. Forty-five freeholders then filed a petition with Massachusetts General Court to build the new church in the south end of town. The court sent a committee to Andover to study the situation and instructed the Reverend Thomas Barnard to decide where his pulpit should be. The minister, who lived in the North Parish, could not or would not decide. The controversy dragged until it became clear that no compromise was possible. On November 2, 1708 the General Court decreed that the town could support two churches and would "be divided into two separate precincts, each with its own meet-ing house for the Worship of God and as a convenient place to conduct town affairs: South's to be set at ye Rock on the West side of Indian Roger's Brook."

Twenty-two-year-old Samuel Phillips was called as South Parish's first minister three years after graduation from Harvard College. He was the great-grandson of the Reverend George Phillips, who had sailed with the Winthrop Fleet in 1630 to help establish Mass Bay Colony. Samuel Phillips was ordained October 17, 1711, and the parish "voted to pay the minister 60 pounds annual while he is in an unmarried state and 10 pounds more when he shall see reason to marry." Firewood and corn would be provided by parishioners. Young Phillips promptly wed Hannah White of Haverhill.

For the next sixty one years, the Reverend Mr. Phillips, a zealous Calvinist, preached the orthodox doctrine of predestination and original sin at South Parish Meeting House. Local historians claim that he "demanded justice from his flock in their dealings with him, even instructing them when they proved delinquent in the payment of his salary."

Andover residents were accustomed to seeing Sabbathday processions of this minister and his wife arm in arm, with his African slave, Salem, by his right side and her maid "servant" Ramah, also from Africa, at her left, followed by the five Phillips children in descending age order. After the minister's death, these household slaves became the property of his successor in the pulpit, while their children were inherited by Phillip's eldest son, a North Parish resident.

The congregation would stand as this entourage entered the Meeting House and sit only after Parson Phillips ascended the steps to the pulpit and took his place beneath the sounding-board. Men sat on the right side and women on the left. Seating was assigned according to social rank and parishioners bought or rented their pews. A Tything Man, appointed at town meeting, occupied the front seat in the gallery or paced up and down the aisle. He carried a long rod which he brought down hard on anyone caught whispering or dozing. Restless and giggling youngsters were removed from the meeting house and their parents subsequently fined. Blacks and Indians were designated the upstairs gallery. There was no bell until 1792, some time after South Parish's second meeting house was built in 1734.

Mr. Phillips showed little sympathy when his flock complained of the cold when required to sit through his sermons that ordinarily lasted until the sands of the hour glass had been turned three or four times.

"Although the communion bread is frozen hard and rattling on the silver plates, the Lord sends forth His Word to thaw you. Stoke the hot coals of your foot-warmers for I can pray down any man, heathen, or devil!"

"Remember, Children study your catechism. Practice self-examination for the sake of your souls. How far are you governed in regard to the opinions, customs, and fashions of this world? Would you rather be regarded as fashionable or as meek and holy? Do not frolic, nor even go fishing, on the Sabbath. And you women, never cook on the Sabbath for the smell of food is an abomination to the nostrils of the Lord!"

After the earthquake of 1755, Parson Phillips admonished his flock upon the duty of watchfulness and of being ready to meet the sudden summons of the Lord; rebuking them for "sleeping away a great part of sermon time…But since the Glorious Lord of the Sabbath has given you such a shaking of late, I hope to see no more sleep-ers in the Meeting House!"

In 1769, the Reverend Samuel Phillips actually put out a warrant for the arrest of one particular youth, Peter Fry, who "in the time of divine service sported and played and by indecent Gestures and Wry faces, caused laughter and misbehavior among Beholders and thereby greatly disturbed the Congregation."

Another story still told is how the minister was stopped by a stranger on the road.who asked, "Are you the Parson who serves here?" Phillips' immediate reply: "Why, Sir, I am the Parson who *rules* here!" ∽

ANDOVER'S FIRST ALIENS

❧

Although the French had ceded Nova Scotia or Acadia to Great Britain in 1713 as part of the Treaty of Utrecht, Cape Breton Island and the islands of the Saint Lawrence River still belonged to France and that nation's ships continually threatened New England's trade routes and fishing rights. Acadians stubbornly refused to sign any Oaths of Allegiance to the British Crown unless exempted from bearing arms in the ongoing struggle of France and Great Britain for the domination of North America.

In 1745, Governor Shirley ordered Massachusetts militiamen under Sir William Pepperrell to storm Fort Louisbourg, that formidable French bastion with thirty-foot-high stone walls on the Coast of Cape Breton. During the sea and land battles that ensued, when the weather suddenly turned in favor of the British troops, Massachusetts militiamen were convinced that God had raised His Hand to defeat the "popery" they so detested. Sixteen Andover men died "in the King's Service" at the Siege of Cape Breton and during the occupation that followed from "putrid fevers, dysentery and hunger."

In 1754, 2000 English troops were dispatched to finally oust the Acadians from Nova Scotia and replace then with British settlers. Between 1755 and 1764 more than 6000 French Acadians were forcibly removed from their homes and deported back to France or dispersed throughout the English colonies.

In 1756, five of these displaced refugee families, numbering twenty-two individuals, were quartered with Andover families. Their older children were bound out as servants and laborers in other homes, shops, and farms around town. Selectman's records show reimbursements to various local citizens for assisting these refugees: Asa Carleton for "Necessaries for Keeping House to the French Neutrals at the House of Ebenezer Abbot" and Dr. Joseph Osgood "for doctoring the French & Poor of the town" are but several examples. One Acadian family, that of elderly Germaine Landry ("Laundry" was how Andoverites wrote it) had seven sons and thirteen daughters and "one more born since," according to the town records. Several newcomers were placed "on the estate of Jonathan Abbot—to his annoyance." Jacques Ebert was housed at Widow Abigail Frye's and since spelling was phonetic, this Frenchman's name has been preserved in Andover records as "Jockey Bear."

Mr. Bear (as he was locally known) was among those Acadians who sent a petition from Andover to Massachusetts General Court, begging for a redress of grievances on behalf of their children:

> *The loss which we have suffered at your hands, of our houses,*
> *and being brought here and our separation from one another is*
> *nothing to compare with what we experience at present, that of*
> *losing our children by force before our eyes. Nature herself cannot*
> *endure that. If it were in our power to have our choice we should*
> *choose rather to lose our body and our soul than to be separated*
> *from them. Wherefore we pray your honors that you would*
> *have the goodness to mitigate this cruelty...*

This petition achieved the intended result. No more Acadian children were to be bound out in Andover and housing would be provided each family "that they might keep together." Local historians say they planted flax fields and tended gardens around their lodgings until 1760, when many removed to Springfield. Sarah Loring Bailey, writing in 1880, assures readers that most of Andover's Acadians were "industrious and frugal...conquered the prejudices of the community and practiced the rites of their religion in an inoffensive manner." ∞

"The Patriot's" Sudden Death

❦

The Revolutionary leader whom John Adams, second President of the United States, nicknamed "Flame of Fire," died a strange death in Andover. John Adams said that it was James Otis who "set the Revolution on its feet and made it respectable in the eyes of the world," .

Fourteen years before "the shot heard 'round the world," James Otis resigned his post as customs agent in protest against the Writs of Assistance, those warrants imposed by the Crown that allowed British agents to storm any citizen's shop or private home in search of smuggled goods. The five hour, landmark speech that Otis delivered in Boston's Old South Meeting House denouncing those Writs, is considered the first formal statement articulating the causes of the American Revolution. According to John Adams "American Independence was then and there born"

Otis' speech included the familiar phrase, "Taxation without representation is tyranny!" Whenever you hear the cliché "A man's house is his castle," it is a tribute to James Otis. The small minority who then supported a break with Great Britain lost Otis' leadership after September 5, 1769. Detested by Royalists and Loyalists alike who wished to see him put on trial for treason before British Parliament, Otis got into a political argument with an Crown customs agent named John Robinson in a Boston coffee-house. A brawl ensued during which Otis was knocked to the ground and bludgeoned. He suffered severe head wounds which caused intermittent insanity for the rest of his life. It marked the end of a brilliant legal career and robbed the Founding Fathers of their leading voice.

In January of 1770, John Adams sadly remarked, "Otis rambles and wanders like a ship without a helm." The following year, James Otis was legally declared *non compos mentis*. On June 17, 1775, he borrowed a gun and rushed through flying bullets at the Battle of Bunker Hill. He occasionally fired guns out the windows of his Boston home throughout the Revolutionary War. In a subsequent civil action, Otis received two thousand pounds in damages for his injuries but returned the money after receiving a personal apology from Robinson.

James Otis was eventually brought to the farm of his old friend, Jacob Osgood in West Andover. Here "The Patriot," as he was known, lived a quiet life where he tutored Osgood's children in Latin and Greek and taught school when able. According to contemporary reports, Otis slept a great deal and was partial to bread and milk. The high-fashion woolly, white wig that he always wore barely hid the terrible deep scar across his skull.

"My dear sister," he confided in a letter to Mercy Otis Warren, herself a playwright and recorder of contemporary political history, "I hope when God Almighty, in his righteous providence, shall take me out of time into eternity, that it will be by a flash of lightning." On May 23, 1783, Andover experienced a sudden and severe spring storm. James Otis was standing at the front door, leaning on his cane against the doorway and telling a story to the Osgood family who had gathered in the front room. Eyewitnesses described a deafening explosion of thunder "which seemed to shake the solid earth, followed by a flash and Otis fell forward, instantly dead." No one else was injured nor did the house catch fire.

The funeral of James Otis was said to have been the biggest ever before seen in Boston. Yet, fifty years later, few could recall where "The Patriot" had been buried. Numerous books and pamphlets mistakenly had James Otis buried in Andover. A marker was finally placed in Boston's Old Granary Burial Ground in 1897, where his remains lay near his old friend and fellow Revolutionary radical, Samuel Adams. ∞

WAR CLOUDS

❧

Andover stood united against the Stamp Act, and all tax increases imposed by Great Britain. The town's representative to General Court was instructed "not to give assent to any active assembly that shall signify any willingness to submit to any internal taxes."

Samuel Phillips, Esquire, the minister's son and prominent North end merchant, was chairman of the local committee to draft resolutions on Andover's reaction to British policies. In 1768, townspeople went on record "to secure to ourselves and transmitting to posterity those invaluable rights and privileges both civil and religious, which have been dearly purchased by our predecessors, the first settlers of this country." The committee decreed it "absolutely necessary that the inhabitants use their utmost endeavors…for the suppressing of extravagance, idleness and vice, and for the promoting of industry, economy and good morals; and endeavor to discountenance the importation and use of foreign superfluities…Also, "anyone using tea of foreign importation should incur the Town's displeasure."

War fever was running high. Hangings in effigy and destruction of property belonging to British sympathizers became increasingly common in New England. Andover, as other towns, sought to prevent the "Sons of Liberty" from becoming over zealous, "voting utter detestation and abhorrence of all such violent proceedings." Andover, like some other communities, formed a Committee of Safety to maintain "peace and harmony and to suppress all unwarrantable mobs and riots and to promote good will and affection toward one another."

The local militia increased training and drilling through 1774 and 1775. In 1775, the town voted a watch be kept, whereby "sentinels were required to question every person walking the streets after nine o'clock in the evening, concerning their business. If any person being called on, neglects or refuses to reply, the sentinel shall immediately fire. If then not given a satisfactory account, the sentinel shall by force, detain and confine him…" That same year, Andover's enlisted men were furnished with bayonets at the town's expense and formed the Fourth Regiment of Militia of Essex County.

Andover unanimously declared its support for independence on June 12, 1776: "The question being put—whether, should the Honorable Congress, for the safety of the Colonies, declare them independent of the kingdom of Great Britain? If so you will solemnly agree to engage your lives and fortunes to support them in the measure." ∞

LATE FOR LEXINGTON

⁌

When the alarm was sounded on the morning of April 19, 1775 by church bell, drum beats and messengers on horseback, Andover militia men assembled at the North Parish Meeting House with muskets and bayonets, ready to march to Lexington and Concord. There were four companies: fifty four minutemen under the command of Captain Benjamin Farnum. Captain Benjamin Ames led fifty more who were attached to the previously formed regiment of Colonel James Frye. Captain Charles Furbush and Captain Thomas Poor led the other divisions, making a total of some 329 Andover Minute Men. Many were veterans of the French and Indian Wars. Old men followed the troops, carrying provisions; boys accompanied their fathers and slaves marched alongside their masters, including fifty-two-year-old Pompey Lovejoy.

By the time Andover soldiers arrived at Lexington the battle was over. They pursued the retreating British forces until dark, as far as Arlington and there they camped, bone-weary after marching some thirty-five miles. ⁌

ON THE HOMEFRONT

The town's two ministers urged their congregations to unite in the common cause of freedom and did their best to prepare parishioners for what lay ahead. The Reverend William Symnes of North Parish preached austerity, declaring "It is not God's ordinary method to rain down bread for the food of man!" He encouraged home industry so Colonists would no longer depend on imported goods and even sponsored spinning bees at his parsonage. "Let us show ourselves and Britain that we are able to feed and clothe ourselves," Doctor Symnes preached. "Citizens, give preference to clothing produced from our own flocks and our own fields."

Farmers were urged to improve their numbers and breed of sheep in order to produce more local wool. A Committee of Inspection was formed to "encourage frugal economy and industry, and promote agriculture and manufactures of this Province." The town provided hay for the army in 1776 and furnished Andover soldiers with "one pair of shirts, two pair of stocking, one pair of shoes and a blanket" at town expense.

SALEM POOR,
"A BRAVE AND GALLANT SOLDIER"

He was purchased as an infant at the Salem slave market by Lydia Abbot, who supposedly brought him home to Andover by horseback on the bow of her saddle. She called him Salem Pony and had him baptized at North Parish Church in 1747.

Salem Poor purchased his freedom July 10, 1769 for twenty-seven pounds from John Poor, the third, who did "freely give and grant full liberty to depart and go out from under my command and control and to acquire to himself and to his own rise and benefit all such gains and profits as he can by any lawful business or employment during his natural life…" The ex-slave was issued an official manumission.

The *Andover Vital Records* lists the former slave's marriage to Nancy Parker, "former servant of Captain James Parker," in 1771 and the birth of a son, Jonas, in 1776. One of the issues considered at town meeting in 1774 was "Whether the town will be at whole or any part of the charge of supporting the wife and children of Salem, the servant of John Poor 3rd: passed in the negative."

Salem Poor was twenty-eight when he marched off to war in Captain Ames' Company. Six months after the Battle of Bunker Hill, fourteen officers who fought beside Poor, petitioned Provincial Congress to award him a citation, the only man known to have been singularly honored in this manner. The petitioners stated that "we do in justice to the character of so Brave a Man), that under Our Own observation, Wee declare that a Negro Man, called Salem Poor…in the late Battle at Charlestown, behaved like an Experienced officer, as well as an Excellent Soldier, to set forth Particulars of his conduct would be tedious, Wee Would Only begg leave to say in the Person of this said Negro Centers a brave and gallant soldier…"

His name is listed on a company return October 6, 1775. He rejoined the militia in Captain Samuel Johnson's First Andover Company of the Continental Army. Then, as General Burgoyne was mustering his advance against upstate New York, the Americans issued a call for more recruits. Poor enlisted May 14, 1776 in Captain Abram Tyler's company, Colonel Edmund Phinney's regiment of the Maine militia and served at Fort George, then at Saratoga, Valley Forge and Monmouth.

Salem Poor was discharged March 20, 1780. If he did return to Andover, he was not living here ten years later since his name does not appear on the 1790 Census among the ninety-four blacks listed living in Andover's North and South Parishes. Salem Poor's wife, Nancy, seems to have been part Native American, part African-American, and part folklore. Legend has it that she was the last Native American to live in Andover, in a wigwam in the Carmel Woods, near the village center. Another source says her home was on Pine Island in the Merrimack River, not far from an early 17th-century Native American site later verified by archaeologists. Contemporaries described her as tall, "wild-looking" and said that she was fond of "calling out cuss-words." She was considered a hard worker who supported herself as a spinster, going door to door with her spinning wheel strapped on her back.

Although the date and place of Salem Poor's death remains unknown, the "brave and gallant soldier" has not been altogether forgotten. In 1975, a ten-cent Bicentennial stamp was issued in his honor. ∞

CAPTAIN BENJAMIN FARNUM

When two companies of Minute Men were raised in Andover before the "shot heard 'round the world," Benjamin Farnum was appointed First Lieutenant of one. When the Massachusetts Provincial Army was organized, he was promoted captain of the regiment commanded by Colonel James Frye.

Farnum was wounded June 17, 1775 at the Battle of Bunker Hill. John Barker, a private in his company saw Captain Farnum lying in the path of the retreating Minute Men. Private Barker lifted the officer on his shoulders crying, "Now hold on, Ben. The Regulars shan't have you!" Farnum's children carried their father back to Andover on a litter.

Two years after Bunker Hill, Farnum was commissioned in the Continental Army as a company commander in the 11th Massachusetts Regiment and fought in the battle against General Burgoyne at Ticonderoga which resulted in this Redcoat leader's surrender. His regiment then joined General Washington's army and Farnum wintered at Valley Forge. He was discharged with smallpox in 1778 and returned to his Andover farm. The old soldier served as town constable and was the North Parish Church deacon for over forty years.

When Benjamin Farnum limped down the aisle each Sunday, it must have been a poignant reminder of the terrible cost colonists had paid for independence. Although one British musket ball had been surgically removed from his leg, he carried the other in his thigh until his death in 1833 at the age of eighty-seven. One descendent claims that under the linoleum of the floors at the old family homestead, the marks from Captain Farnum's dragging leg can still be seen. ❧

THE REVEREND JONATHAN FRENCH: WITH MUSKET AND MEDICAL KIT

Born in Braintree in 1740, a direct descendant of John and Priscilla Alden, South Church's second minister started out a soldier. Jonathan French enlisted in the Colonial Army at the age of seventeen and served in the French and Indian Wars. Promoted to sergeant, he served as the surgeon's assistant at Castle William in Boston Harbor, where he studied medicine and practiced surgery. Colleagues urged him to become a physician, but by this time, French had decided on the ministry, hoping to become a missionary to the Indians. Local historian Sarah Loring Bailey writes that he "delivered up his sword only on the day he entered a Freshman at Harvard," at the age of twenty-seven.

It was French's Harvard classmate, Samuel Phillips, Jr. who invited him to consider filling the South church pulpit, when it was vacated by the death of Phillips' grandfather. The Reverend Jonathan French served this church from 1772 until his death in 1809, regularly attending to the medical, as well as spiritual needs, of his flock.

On June 17, 1775, when Parson French heard that Charlestown was under attack, he immediately left his pulpit for battle. The fighting parson grabbed his musket, Bible and surgeon's box and rode to Breed's Hill. "Our houses of public worship were generally shut up," the minister later wrote; "When the news of the battle reached us, the anxiety and distress of wives and children, of parents, of brothers, sisters, and friends was great. It was not known who were among the slain or living, the wounded or the well. It was thought justifiable for us who could to repair to the camp to know the circumstances, to join in the defense of the country and prevent the enemy from pushing the advantages they had gained, and to afford comfort and relief to our suffering brethren and friends."

According to Bailey, Jonathan French was "An active participant in town affairs, a zealous patriot, and a promoter of every proper measure of Revolutionary tendency…" The minister instructed divinity students in his home and regularly visited local schools to make certain that the duty of learning catechism was not being neglected. French helped establish Phillips Academy, where he became an original trustee and a teacher of religion. He is also credited as the first person to express the idea of opening a theological seminary at Andover.

During his ministry, Parson French was "often subjected to no small inconvenience by the neglect of the people to meet his salary." Unlike his predecessor, he had no means of his own and sometimes, was forced to plead with his congregation and remind them of their delinquency. Part of his salary, according to contract, was to be provided in firewood. One Sunday after he had read the Massachusetts Thanksgiving Proclamation, he addressed the entire congregation: "My brethren, you perceive that our Governor has appointed next Thursday as the day of Thanksgiving. According to custom, I am to prepare two discourses for that occasion, *provided I can write them without a fire!*"

A romantic tale of Mr. French's courtship passed down through the family. He was already engaged to Abigail Richards of Weymouth when he began studies for the ministry. Realizing how long his training would take, the couple released each other from their promise for seven years, agreeing that if, at the end of that time, either wished to renew the engagement, he or she should write the other. After seven years, Jonathan had not changed his mind and told Abigail this in a letter which he entrusted to the captain of a coasting vessel sailing to Weymouth. According to family lore, the captain happened to be a rejected suitor of Miss Richards. Jealousy and curiosity led him to break the seal on the letter, read it and throw it into the sea. Swimming nearby, Abigail's brother noticed a paper floating on the water and fetched it, amazed to find it addressed to his sister. Thus, Jonathan's love letter reached its intended destination and the couple soon wed.

"Do what you can and leave the rest," Parson Jonathan French later advised his son who also became a minister. "Never be discouraged." ∽

ANDOVER'S GUNPOWDER MILL
HELPED WIN THE WAR

෨

Perhaps the town's most important contribution to the Revolutionary War effort was the manufacture of gunpowder undertaken at Samuel Phillips, Jr.'s personal expense. This powder mill, located on the Shawsheen River near the present Stevens and North Main Streets, is said to have been the first operational munitions plant in the country.

Lack of gunpowder for the defense of Boston was an embarrassment to General Washington, Commander of the Continental Army stationed at Cambridge in 1775. The General was unable to attack for want of gunpowder. To make a public appeal for ammunition or to reply to the criticism he was then receiving for not ordering his troops to fire their muskets when the enemy was in range, would have meant revealing their desperate situation to the British.

Samuel Phillips, Jr., grandson of South Parish's first minister, understood his country's immediate and desperate need and saw an opportunity to combine patriotism with profit. He asked his old friend and former Dummer Academy and Harvard College classmate, Eliphalet Pearson to develop the chemical components for manufacturing gunpowder. Pearson, trained in chemistry, tore up floors of old barns all over Andover in his search for the nitrous earth required to make salt petre. He borrowed a stove from South Parish Church and dismissed school in order to cover the students' desks with formula pans and work twenty-four hours non-stop on his experiments. Pearson even feared blindness, having worked over poisonous fumes so long, but their gunpowder mill was in operation within several months.

According to George Washington, "Congress agreed to furnish Samuel Phillips with saltpeter and sulphur at cost for a year and pay eight pence a pound for what he could produce. Phillips agreed to sell only to the government and keep a guard on duty at the mill to prevent any wicked and designing person from destruction." The new mill ran day and night, seven days a week and was soon producing 1200 pounds of ammunition for the Continental Army per week. Phillips obtained permission for men employed at the mill to be excused from military duty, so necessary was their work to the war effort.

Washington was not at all impressed with the quality of the Andover gunpowder in the beginning. "There must certainly be either roguery or gross ignorance in your powder makers," the General complained in a letter dated April 8, 1777, "because the powder made in the other states is esteemed better than that imported from Europe…It is a matter of so much importance that it should be strictly inquired into."

In July of 1777, the Massachusetts House of Representatives ordered "that as some of the gunpowder made at Andover had been found defective, arising from want of experience in the new manufacture, all such defective powder should be received back into the mills and good powder furnished the Government instead." Two French experts who had come "to propagate the art of making power in these states," arrived in Andover as advisors and the quality improved.

Phillips even found skilled British prisoners of war and put them to work manufacturing gunpowder. Townsfolk feared treason from these enemies in their midst and Captain Joshua Holt was appointed to keep watch and to report to General Court any "inhabitants dangerous to publick Peace and Safety."

On June 1, 1778, an explosion killed three men and partially destroyed the mill. Many townspeople suspected the British prisoners of espionage and production was ordered to a halt, pending an investigation by the General Court. Deemed an accident, the state then sent Phillips four hundred pounds to rebuild and agreed to pay half the costs of repair should the mill blow up again. Phillips thought highly enough of his British workers to put one in charge of all powder mill operations and protested to military authorities that any prisoner exchange would hamper the success of his powder mill.

With the need for gunpowder decidedly lessened by the end of the war, Samuel Phillips, Jr. shifted the focus of his mill enterprises to the less risky manufacture of paper. ∞

PHILLIPS ACADEMY
OPENS TO "YOUTH FROM EVERY QUARTER"

⚬

"Amid all the terrors of battle I was busily engaged in Harvard Library so that I never even heard of the engagement (I mean the Siege of Boston) till it was completed," Samuel Phillips, Jr. later recalled.

On orders from the Provincial Congress, young Samuel Phillips was in Cambridge packing books while the Battle of Bunker Hill raged. His home town of Andover had been selected as one of the safe places to hide the Harvard Library and the college's important papers for the duration. The books were moved in cart loads to the North Parish homes of Colonel Samuel Osgood (later appointed first U. S. postmaster general by President Washington) and Squire Samuel Phillips.

Eliphalet Pearson, who helped get the gunpowder mill going, attended Harvard College with Samuel Phillips, Jr., who graduated in 1771. Pearson and Junior were in agreement concerning "the loss of traditional virtues and values." Together, they deplored what Phillips wrote was "the neglect of sound instruction of young people and (the) dangerous indifference of parents…" Both were "appalled by the present degeneracy which has increased upon us with such rapidity…the prevalence of ignorance and vice, disorder and wickedness."

These two friends dreamed of founding a school based upon the principles of that eccentric but gifted educator, Samuel Moody who had been their teacher and headmaster at Dummer Academy in South Byfield. This idea received the enthusiastic support and financial backing of Samuel Jr.'s father (the successful North Parish merchant known as Squire Phillips) as well as his uncles, John and William, who had also married wealthy women. Their original plan had been to locate the new educational institution in the North Parish, near the Phillips Homestead, but the final site was eventually determined by the available and affordable land. One hundred and forty-two acres were soon acquired in South Parish, along with Solomon Wardwell's carpenter shop which had to be moved to the location. The new school was within easy walking distance to South Church where Samuel Jr.'s grandfather had served as first minister. The first Phillips Academy building stood on the present site of the Peabody Archaeological Museum.

The Eighteenth Century

Samuel Phillips, Jr. and Eliphalet Pearson were both just twenty-six years old when they drew up the Constitution for Phillips Academy on April 21, 1778. The school's main purpose was to preserve and promote "true piety and virtue." It is still considered one of the most significant documents in the history of American education, since its gates were opened to all qualified boys. Here is an excerpt:

> *He hath blessed us, to lay the foundation of a public free School or Academy for the purpose of instructing Youth, not only in English and Latin Grammar, Writing, Arithmetic and those Sciences, wherein they are commonly taught, but more especially to learn them the great end and real business of living.*

Founded during the turbulent years of the Revolution, just a few months after Valley Forge, Phillips Academy was generated by a concern for the future of the new nation. "The glory or ruin of the state depends upon its youth…," wrote Phillips. "Youth is the important period, on the improvement or neglect of which depend the most important consequences to individual and the community…" The institution would reflect democratic principles as it would "ever be open to youth from every quarter…"

Today the campus covers more than five hundred acres including the Montcreiff Cochran Bird Sanctuary and one hundred and fifty academic and administrative buildings, comprising the National Historic District know as "Academy Hill". The school became coeducational in 1973 when it was merged with Abbot Academy. Phillips Academy now boasts a multi-cultural student body of 1087.

Judge Phillips' original vision remains part of the school's present mission. "Be more covetous of your hours than misers are of gold," Samuel Phillips, Jr. wrote his son, John. "Bar your doors and secure your eyes, your ears, and your heart against all who would rob you of your *treasure*. By your treasure, I mean, of course, your time." ∞

"ELEPHANT" PEARSON:
FIRST HEADMASTER

∾

Phillips Academy opened on April 30, 1778 with thirteen boys in one room. By the end of the first month, thirty were enrolled, some as old as thirty and others like Josiah Quincy, as young as six. Quincy was the nephew of Samuel Phillips, Jr. and later became mayor of Boston and President of Harvard. Since there were no dormitories, students were placed with approved families who lived near the academy. Small Josiah boarded at the parsonage with Jonathan French until he turned fourteen and went off to Harvard.

Eliphalet Pearson, who had been teaching at the Andover grammar school, was the Phillips family's choice for principal. Pearson, whose students called him "Elephant" behind his back, was a harsh disciplinarian. In *The School Boy*, his poem written for Phillips Academy's Centennial, alumnus Oliver Wendell Holmes described Pearson: "…great Eliphalet (I can see him now,—Big name, big frame, big voice, and beetling brow), Then *young* Eliphalet—ruled the rows of boys…"

After being chastised by Headmaster Pearson, one student was asked by friends how he felt, replied, "I pinched myself to know whether I was still alive!" Although the "chief impression he made upon his students was one of unmitigated fear, Pearson was a fine athlete, chemist, botanist and proficient in six languages. He was also an accomplished musician who sang well and played the violoncello. He published a treatise on psalmody and could take an engine apart or construct a violin.

Academy trustees could not have been more pleased with Pearson's perform- ance: "As an instructor he excelled in accuracy, thorough instruction, in preserving order, in forming his pupils to habits of diligence, punctuality and attention to their moral conduct. He was particularly attentive in forming their manners and minds to the love and practice of piety and virtue." Eliphalet Pearson, resigned from Phillips Academy in 1785 to become Professor of Hebrew and Oriental Languages at Harvard College. By 1804, he had become Acting President. Pearson held honorary doctorates from Yale and Princeton, and was secretary of the American Academy of Arts and Sciences. ∾

THE FIRST PRESIDENT PAYS A VISIT

George Washington didn't sleep here but he did stop for breakfast on November 5, 1789, during his tour of the Eastern states as President of the new United States. He traveled in an open carriage drawn by four horses, accompanied by his aide-de-camp, Major William Jackson, and six black manservants, including the coachman. Tobias Lear, the General's private secretary, rode a white horse in advance of the coach.

On his way from Boston to Salem, an entourage from Andover joined the President's escort at Lynn. This company of militia men, in red uniforms faced with green, had rallied at the request of Samuel Phillips, Jr., now President of the Massachusetts Senate. The Andover unit rode with Washington as far as Portsmouth.

Washington had known Samuel Phillips, Jr. since the war years in Cambridge. During sessions of the Provincial Congress, Phillips had been on several committees assigned to confer with the Commander in Chief. Judge Phillips, as he was known, served in the State Senate from 1780-1801 and was elected Massachusetts Senate President in 1785. He later became Lieutenant Governor of the Commonwealth.

The First President recorded his visit in his diary:

> *About sunrise, I set out, crossing the Merrimack River at the Town,*
> *over to the township of Bradford…As we journeyed, I took note of*
> *the surrounding scenery: The country from Haverhill where I had*
> *slept the night before-to Andover is good and well cultivated. In,*
> *and about the latter (which stands high), it is beautiful..*

> *…in nine miles (we) came to Abbot's Tavern, Andover,*
> *where we breakfasted and met with much attention*
> *from Mr. Phillips, President of the Senate of Massachusetts…*

Innkeeper Issac Abbot had been wounded at Bunker Hill and later became an Andover selectman and clerk, as well as a Deacon of South Parish Church. Located on the stage road, Deacon Abbot's house was a licensed tavern and served as the town's first post office in 1795.

Now, acting as President Washington's personal host in his hometown, Judge Phillips accompanied him from Abbot Tavern, past South Church, and to his Mansion House on Andover Hill, where they spent half an hour or so in conversation. The President was particularly interested in the Academy that Judge Phillips had established for "youth from every quarter" in 1778, in the midst of this country's War for Independence. Washington had confidence in Samuel Phillip's educational endeavor and encouraged his nephew, Howell Lewis from Fredericksburg, Virginia to enroll in 1785. The First President's four grandnephews became students in 1795.

According to local tradition, the moment Washington left Mansion House, Madam Phillips tied a piece of ribbon across the chair in the southeast parlor where the great man had sat and there it remained until the day of Judge Phillips' death, when the ribbon to honor Washington was replaced by a black band.

Before departing town, the President, mounted on his white horse, greeted the townspeople and reviewed the militia in formation. Then, still accompanied by Judge Phillips, the cavalcade headed to Lexington.∞

ENDNOTES: THE EIGHTEENTH CENTURY

৵

CHAPTER 16 - THE PARSON WHO RULED
Page 51: Town Meeting Records, 1656-1709, September 9, 1705; May 12, 1707; May 26, 1707; September 15, 1707; October, 1708.
Records of Massachusetts General Court, January, 1709;
See also Juliet Haines Mofford. *And Firm Thine Ancient Vow:History of North Parish Church of North Andover.* 1975, 51-53
George Mooar. *Historical Manual of the South Church in Andover, Massachusetts.* Andover, Mass.: Warren F. Draper, 1859.
Page 52: Sarah Loring Bailey. Historical Sketches. p. 446-447.
George Mooar. Op. Cit. ; see also Sarah Loring Bailey, p. 446.

CHAPTER 17 - ANDOVER'S FIRST ALIENS
Page 53: Town Records, 1745-46; see also Sarah Loring Bailey, p. 246.
Page 54: "Letter to Massachusetts General Court," Massachusetts Archives, vol. xxiii, p. 44; vol xxiv. p. 47. See also Bailey, pp. 247-248.

CHAPTER 18 - "THE PATRIOT'S" SUDDEN DEATH
Page 55: Jean Fritz. *Cast For a Revolution: Some American Friends and Enemies, 1728-1814.* Boston: Houghton Mifflin, 1972.
Juliet Mofford. "The Revolution's Unsung Hero," Lawrence Eagle Tribune, July 3, 1976.
Charles F. Adams, Editor. *Works of John Adams,* Vols. II & X, 1850.
Page 56: "Otis' Obituary." Boston Gazette or Country Journal, May 26, 1783.
Thomas Dawes. Eulogy Poem: James Otis, 1783

CHAPTER 19 - WAR CLOUDS
Page 57: Abiel Abbot. *History of Andover.* Andover: Flagg & Gould, pp. 53-56.
Sarah Loring Bailey, Op. Cit., p. 288.
Dee Liffman. "Change and Conflict Mark 18th-Century Andover." Andover Historical Society Newsletter, Spring, 1996, p. 1-2. page 58.
D. Hamilton Hurd, Editor. History of Essex County, Mass., Philadelphia, PA: J. W. Lewis, 1888, Vol II, p. 1670.

CHAPTER 20 - LATE FOR LEXINGTON
Page 59: Sarah Loring Bailey. Op. Cit. pp. 297-298; 307

CHAPTER 21 - ON THE HOMEFRONT
Page 60: "Symnes' Sermon," 1785. Juliet H. Mofford. *And Firm Thine Ancient Vow: History of North Parish Church of North Andover,* p. 103.
"Change & Conflict Mark 18th-Century Andover," Ibid., Dee Liffman, 2.

CHAPTER 22 - SALEM POOR: "BRAVE & GALLANT SOLDIER"
Page 61: Baptism Records, Journal of Church Matters, 1687-1810. North Andover Historical Society Collections.
Manumission Document, July 10, 1769. Salem, Mass.: Phillips Library, Peabody Essex Museum; see also Andover Vital Records, Marriages and Births
Emily Prigot. Bunker Hill Monument Site Bulletin, Boston National Historical Park.
Massachusetts Soldiers & Sailors of the Revolutionary War, Vol. XII, p. 561.
Sarah Loring Bailey. Historical Sketches…, p. 324.
Page 62: Federal Census, 1790
Maurice Dorgan, *History of Lawrence, Massachusetts*, 1924, p. 9-10.

CHAPTER 23 - CAPTAIN BENJAMIN FARNUM
Page 63: Juliet H. Mofford. *And Firm Thine Ancient Vow: History of North Parish Church of North Andover*, 1975, p. 100-101.
Joan Patrakis. "Andover Captains at Bunker Hill," Andover Historical Society Newsletter, Vol. 13, #2, 1988; also "Many Men Answered the Call to Arms on April 19, 1775." Vol. 19, #1, 1994.
Author's interview with Helen Farnum Doucette, 1975.

CHAPTER 24 - THE REVEREND JONATHAN FRENCH: MUSKET AND MEDICAL KIT
Pages 64, 65: Sarah Loring Bailey, Op. Cit., pp. 453-455
George Mooar, Editor. August, 1859. *Historical Manual of the South Church in Andover, Massachusetts*. Andover, Mass.: Warren F. Draper, 1859; see also South Parish Church Manuscript Records, Andover Historical Society.

CHAPTER 25 - ANDOVER'S GUNPOWDER MILL HELPED WIN THE WAR
Pages 66, 67: Col. Edward Harris. "Our Gunpowder Mill Helped Win the Revolutionary War." Andover Historical Society Newsletter, Vol. 8, #2, 1983.
Andover Advertiser, November 5, 1853
Sarah Loring Bailey, Op. Cit., pp. 342-343; 34

CHAPTER 26 - PHILLIPS ACADEMY OPENS TO "YOUTH FROM EVERY QUARTER"
Page 68: Reverend John L. Taylor. *Memoir of His Honor Samuel Phillips*. Boston: Congregational Board of Publication: Cambridge: Allen & Farnham, 1856
Page 69: Frederick S. Allis, Jr., *Youth from Every Quarter: A Bicentennial History of Phillips Academy, Andover.* Hanover, NH: Univ. Press of New England, p. 37-38; 41-42; 52; 61-62.

CHAPTER 27 - "ELEPHANT" PEARSON, FIRST HEADMASTER
Page 70: Frederick S. Allis, Jr. Ibid., Chapter Four.
Claude M. Fuess. *An Old New England School*. Boston: Houghton-Mifflin, 1917
Oliver Wendell Holmes. *The School Boy.* Cambridge: Riverside Press & Houghton-Mifflin, 1878.

CHAPTER 28 - FIRST PRESIDENT PAYS A VISIT
Page 71: George Washington's Diary Entry, November 4, 1789.
Sarah Loring Bailey. Historical Sketches… p. 401.
Page 72: Frederick S. Allis, Jr., Op. Cit., p. 93

THE NINETEENTH CENTURY

After Andover Theological Seminary was established beside Phillips Academy on the Hill, to train orthodox Calvinist ministers, Andover truly becomes an academic town. The Seminary's missionaries and the *Andover Press* theological publications make the name of Andover known worldwide.

The Essex County Turnpike cut through South Parish in 1807, providing easy access to markets and seaports. Thriving industries, the coming of the railroad, as well as the academies helped make South Parish more populous and the town becomes an active commercial center. In 1855, the town was legally divided into Andover and North Andover and Andover is described at this time as "Hill, Till, and Mill."

By 1837 there were eight woolen mills in Andover, as well as factories producing shoes, hats, tin ware, furniture and machinery. Factories draw workers from Scotland and England, and Ireland.

With the increased leisure time made possible by technological advances, women become active in reform movements like anti-slavery, temperance and suffrage. Andover was a hotbed of abolitionism, with some citizens breaking the law of the land by participating in the Underground Railroad. Local resident, Harriet Beecher Stowe, received famous abolitionist leaders like William Lloyd Garrison, Frederick Douglass, and Sojourner Truth in her home on Andover Hill. With its high number of young men attending schools here, Andover pays a high price in the Civil War. Before the end of the century, the Andover Village Improvement Society pioneered the preservation of green space for future generations. ∞

14. Sojourner Truth.
"It seems only yesterday that Mrs. Stowe sent Sojourner Truth down High Street to our Andover home and we listened to hear the majesty of African womanhood."
—Charlotte Helen Abbott, *Africa to Andover*, Andover Townsman, March 15, 1901.

This image appeared in the first edition of *Narrative of Sojourner Truth: A Northern Slave*, in 1850, and was reprinted in numerous subsequent editions.

(Courtesy of Memorial Hall Library)

15. The Stone Cabin.
Home of Harriet Beecher Stowe and her family from 1852 to 1864.

Originally located on the present site of Andover Inn, it was moved to 80 Bartlet Street. The building once served as a carpentry shop, where theological students fashioned coffins and other wooden items sold for tuition money. It had also been used as a gymnasium and for storage, when Harriet Beecher Stowe claimed it from the Seminary trustees and had it remodeled. From *The Life of Harriet Beecher Stowe* by Charles Edward Stowe, Cambridge: Riverside Press, 1889.

(Courtesy of Memorial Hall Library)

16. **Portrait of Calvin E. Stowe.**
Professor of Hebrew
Literature, Andover Theological
Seminary, 1852-1864.
Stowe claimed he would not
shave off his beard until every
slave was free.

From *The Life of Harriet Beecher
Stowe* by Charles Edward
Stowe, Cambridge: Riverside
Press, 1889.

(Courtesy of Memorial Hall Library)

17. **Temperance
Banner.**

*(Courtesy of Andover
Historical Society)*

18. **Elizabeth Stuart Phelps.**
(1844–1912), famous author and
social reformer who grew up at
189 Main Street, on Andover Hill.
(Courtesy, Andover Historical Society)

"After *Gates Ajar*, it was necessary
to make a change for more quiet in
which to pursue my literary work.
I moved my study out of my father's
house to the next door neighbor's
where I spent the working hours
of the day… There's my blue sky
and King Charles terrier, Daniel
Deronda, at the window." Built by
Judge Phillips in 1791 as a General
Store; Deacon Holbrook Chandler,
Superintendent of Phillips Academy
farm and buildings, lived here 1869-
1880. In 1880, the house was moved
to 54 Morton Street to make space
for Tucker House. Phelps and Dr.
Mary Briggs Harris, Andover's female
physician and the likely model for
Dr. Zay, rented rooms on the first
and second floors.

19. **Miss Phelps' study, Andover, Massachusetts.** From R. H. Stoddard, *Poets' Homes:
Pen and Pencil Sketches of American Poets and Their Homes.*, Boston: D. Lothrop Co., 1879,
page 79. *(Courtesy of the author)*

20. **Ballardvale Mills.** Built after 1836, when John Marland, Daniel Poor, Abel Blanchard, Mark Newman, and Abram Gould formed a woolen company on the Shawsheen River site where Timothy Ballard and Nehemiah Abbott had formerly operated a sawmill and gristmill.
(*Courtesy of Andover Historical Society*)

21. **Home of cotton manufacturer John Aiken.** The house is located at 48 Central Street. Aiken's second wife was the sister of President Franklin Pierce's wife, Jane Means Appleton. Mrs. Pierce died here in 1865. (*Courtesy of Andover Historical Society*)

22. **"Main Street, Looking North."** In this late nineteenth-century view, the Andover Town House appears facing right. Built in 1858, it was the first public building erected after the legal division of Andover and North Andover. Reverend F. B Makepeace, "An Illustrious Town – Andover," *The New England Magazine and Bay State Monthly*, April, 1886, p. 301. (*Courtesy of the author*)

23. **Memorial Hall and Library, 1874.** Original building with Mansard roof. "An Illustrious Town - Andover," *The New England Magazine and Bay State Monthly*, April, 1886, p. 302. (*Courtesy of the author*)

24. **Portrait of Joseph Neeshima.** Andover's first Japanese resident, he later founded Doshisha University in Kyoto, Japan. (*Courtesy of Phillips Academy Archives*)

ANDOVER THEOLOGICAL INSTITUTION & TEACHERS SEMINARY.

Teachers Seminary (Stone Academy)   Samaritan House   Students Workshop   Phillip's Hall   Chapel   Bartlett Hall

25. **View of Andover Theological Institution and Teachers' Seminary.** View of campus circa 1830. The Seminary opened in 1808 with thirty-six students, as a "bulwark of Calvinism against the rising tide of radicalism which threatened Puritan tradition." A century later, it was relocated to Cambridge; and later, to Newton, where it continues to thrive today as the Andover–Newton Theological Seminary. *(Courtesy of Phillips Academy Archives)*

26. **View of Andover Theological Seminary.** From *Harper's New Monthly Magazine,* September, 1877; *(Courtesy of Phillips Academy Archives)*

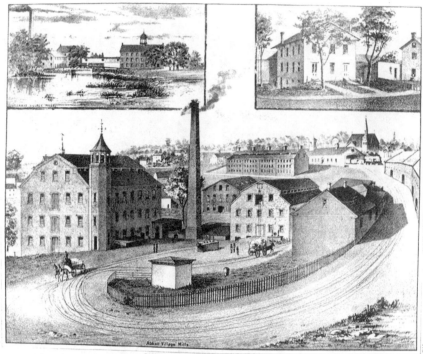

SMITH & DOVE MFG. CO., ANDOVER MASS.

27. Smith and Dove Flax Manufacturing Company. Originally located in Frye Village (now Shawsheen Village), Smith and Dove bought old mills belonging to Pascal and Abiel Abbot, and expanded their business at Abbot Village, downtown near the railroad station. From George H. Walker & Co., *Atlas of Essex County*, 1852. *(Courtesy of Andover Historical Society)*

28. The Old Mark Newman Publishing House, erected 1832. Reverend F. B Makepeace, "An Illustrious Town–Andover," *The New England Magazine and Bay State Monthly*, April, 1886, p. 309.

(Courtesy of the author)

"America" was written in my room at the house of Mrs. Hitchings; while standing before the front window, nearest the front door of the house, in the north parlor. If I remember rightly, I always had my study table in the middle of the room, to guard against being diverted by any objects in the street, as I might have been, if the table had stood near a window.

S. F. Smith

29. *America House*, 147 Main Street. Known as Mrs. Hitchings' Boarding House in 1831 when Samuel Francis Smith, a theological student, wrote the verses beginning *My Country 'Tis of Thee*. President George W. Bush lived here part of the time he was at Phillips Academy.

(Courtesy of Andover Historical Society)

Where America was written

ANDOVER PRINTING ESTABLISHMENT.

J. D. FLAGG,
STEREOTYPER, PRINTER, AND PUBLISHER,
Opposite Phillips Academy, Andover, Mass.

J. D. F. would respectfully call the particular attention of his friends and customers, both far and near, to the unusual facilities of his establishment for manufacturing books of every description, from the smallest pocket edition to the royal octavo; and deriving the advantages of steam in propelling three of the IMPROVED ADAMS PRESSES of the larger size, we feel confident in our ability to manufacture books, for authors and publishers, on the most reasonable terms. It will be borne in mind, also, that we have the "*Improved Dickinson Stereotype Foundry*" connected with the above establishment, as well as a large COMPOSITORS' DEPARTMENT, capable of employing more than twenty compositors, on stereotype or letter-press works, in all the different classical languages. And we would invite the particular attention of scholars to our variety of type in foreign languages.

SPECIMENS OF TYPE.

ⲰⲐⲎ: ⲢⲤⲦⲯⲞⲦⲨ Ethiopic.

ϩⲉⲛ ⲧⲁⲣⲭⲏ ⲡⲥⲁϫⲓ Coptic.

Ⴑⴔⴕⴌⴊⴄⴒ Armenian.

أَحَدَ حَتَّى يَقُولَ إِنَّمَا Arabic.

ܚܕ ܐܚܐ ܩܕܡܝܢ Syriac.

ⵎⵉⵣⴰ ⴼⵎⴼⵣ ⵏ Samaritan.

Rabbinic.

Fünf Bücher gehörten Mose. German.

בְּרֵאשִׁית בָּרָא אֱלֹהִים אֵת Hebrew.

Ἐν ἀρχῇ ἦν ὁ λόγος Porsonian Greek.

Ἐν ἀρχῇ ἦν ὁ λόγος Tauchnitz Greek.

Besides, we have all the different varieties and sizes of English TYPE, amounting to some twenty or more kinds, which are necessary in the execution of work.

30. Andover Printing Establishment. This advertisement which appeared in Vol. I, No. 1 of the *Andover Advertiser* on February 19, 1853, showed the variety of type available at J. D. Flagg.

From Scott H. Paradise, *The History of Printing in Andover, Massachusetts 1798-1931*. Andover Press, 1931.

(Courtesy of Andover Historical Society)

31. Map of Andover, 1830. First actual map showing locations of residents. The population at this time was 4540. The 1831 Tax Lists records 539 dwellings, 49 shops, 19 shops within or attached to dwellings, 3 grist mills, and 6 sawmills. *(Courtesy of Barbara Thibault and the Andover Historical Society)*

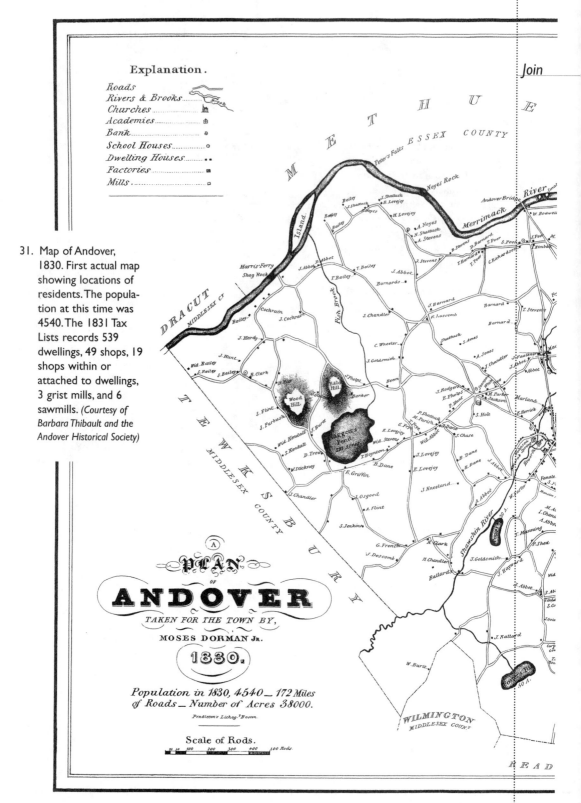

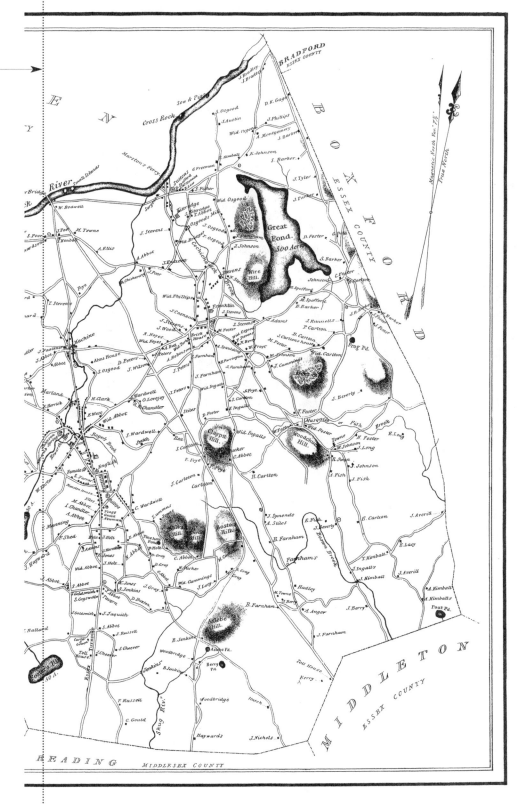

Here is a township of about nine miles square,
occupied by an intelligent, well-fed,
well-clothed, well-housed population.
There are about ten or twelve
neat and commodious places of worship;
twenty of those gems of New England: free schools,
where the sons of the rich and the poor meet on an
even footing, and receive the same useful instruction.
Here too is a classical seminary,
which has long been distinguished for its
ripe and elegant scholars…

DANIEL WEBSTER
FROM A SPEECH GIVEN AT THE ESSEX
COUNTY WHIG CONVENTION

1843

BULWARK OF CALVINISM ON "BRIMSTONE HILL"

⚕

Andover Theological Seminary was founded in 1808 as a "bulwark of Calvinism against Unitarianism, Universalism and all other heresies and errors, ancient and modern…" Here on "Brimstone Hill," as it was nicknamed, Van Wyck Brooks wrote, "the last great wave of the Puritan faith flourished, its final crusade to redeem the world…This faith had begotten the zeal for reform and the passion for education that marked New England for the teaching of the black man and the red man, the education of women, the reform of prisons, and the Andover Theology, with its proselytizing spirit, spread this passion over the West as well."

With Andover Theological Seminary now sharing the Hill with Phillips Academy and Abbot Female Seminary, as well as a teacher's training college, Andover truly became an academic town in the nineteenth century. The Teachers' Seminary, also known as The Stone Academy by its building, existed from 1830 until 1842. Then, lacking sufficient financial support, it was absorbed by Phillips Academy as the English Department. The Stone Academy was destroyed by fire in 1865.

Eliphalet Pearson, who was instrumental in founding Phillips Academy and served as its first headmaster, was now acting president of Harvard University. Religious controversy was sweeping New England and Pearson was dismayed when Dr. Henry Ware was appointed Harvard's Hollis Professor of Divinity. This post'had been established to support a minister of orthodox religion and Ware was a Unitarian. Pearson resigned in protest and returned to Andover, convinced something must be done to defend Calvinist faith and practice. He would establish an orthodox seminary in opposition to the rising influence of liberalism, one "which should maintain the doctrines of the fathers of New England against the threatening apostasies of the times…It came suddenly to mind, as plainly as the sheet let down from Heaven to Peter to establish an institution to train up ministers."

The Reverend Jonathan French, South Parish's second minister, who tutored young men planning to become clergymen, had suggested a school for the training of ministers at the time Phillips Academy was founded.

Religious conservatives at Newburyport were also interested in establishing a seminary and over a period of nine months, Pearson made thirty-six trips by horse and buggy between Andover and Newburyport to raise funds and determine location for the new seminary. Pearson was zealous in fixing its placement at Andover and convinced the wealthy Boston merchant, Samuel Abbot, a cousin of Judge Samuel Phillips and a Phillips Academy trustee, to contribute $20,000. Abbot had planned to leave his fortune to Harvard, but was disturbed to see Harvard "lapsing into Unitarianism," so agreed to contribute over $100,000 to the new institution. Abbot's will already included the support of a professor of theology at Phillips Academy and Pearson persuaded him to donate immediately rather than after his death.

Judge Samuel Phillips, Jr. in a codicil to his will, left his estate to the Trustees of Phillips Academy "to be appropriated to support a theological professor of sound, orthodox, Calvinistic principles of divinity, and for the maintenance of students in divinity." Members of the Phillips family provided for buildings with gifts of $40,000 plus $60,000 more for land and endowment.

William Bartlet was the most generous single donor, contributing funds for the Bartlet professorship, Bartlet Hall (the Chapel), as well as three faculty houses. Besides Bartlet, several other Newburyport merchants also contributed generously. Dr. Pearson, South Parish's pastor, the Reverend Jonathan French and another staunch Calvinist, Squire Samuel Farrar, drew up the constitution for the seminary. Farrar was the first President of the Andover Bank and his likeness appeared on Andover Bank bills. His inspired leadership was also instrumental in founding Abbot Female Seminary in 1829.

The founders realized the need for fine buildings but before construction, the grounds had to be cleared of rocks and bushes. One seminary historian wrote, "It was a frequent spectacle to see the dignified form of Professor Pearson perched aloft among the branches of a tree. From this vantage point he planned and directed the improvement of the grounds." Handsome houses were then erected to attract the finest theological scholars to Andover.

On September 22, 1808, the Seminary was formally launched at South Parish Church. Since the constitution of the new institution stated that no unordained man could serve as a professor, Eliphalet Pearson was ordained the same day and served as Associate Professor of Sacred Literature the first year. He then became president of the board, overseeing both seminary and Phillips Academy until his retirement in 1820.

The founding of Andover Theological Seminary marked a milestone in American church history since it was the first school in the United States devoted exclusively to the training of clergy. Its methods of "raising a learned ministry" became a model for subsequent Protestant theological institutions in the country.

Thirty six students, most already holding college degrees, were enrolled the first year. Throughout the first decade, classes averaged fifty, taxing space at the new school. Average enrollment from 1820 through 1860 was one hundred and ten, and graduates became leaders in their profession, not only as clergy but as college presidents and professors, serving churches and missions all over the U. S. and the world. "In prestige and influence, Andover Theological Seminary was second to none."

Early seminary students lived a Spartan existence. They toted their own water from the outside well, carried fuel from the wood pile to their rooms upstairs and tended their own stoves. "Poverty of the table" was notorious, with cornmeal mush, buckwheat bread, and molasses often replacing meat. Legend has it that when one doctor treated a sick student by blood-letting, all he could draw from the young man's veins was syrup. "Plain living and high thinking" was admired and theologues shivered through hurried meals. Students were expected to mow professors' hay, chop their wood, and tend gardens and grounds.

Historians say that "the health of not a few broke down," and a number died, particularly from tuberculosis. Students nursed each other through contagious illnesses. Chapel Cemetery, established in 1810, has "long rows of graves of early students who died during their course of study."

Faculty members and trustees thought study might be "too sedentary an occupation following a life of farm work. A young man's health was thus, sapped and insufficient nourishment took its toll." Many "suffered from indigestion and proved prey to epidemics." The situation became so disturbing that faculty wives and other Andover ladies formed the Samaritan Female Society "to aid poor students of the Academy and Seminary who were ill and provide for them free bedding, fuel, diet, medicine, nurses, physicians, and comforts, as may be proper for their respective cases." Samaritan House, an infirmary on campus was built in 1824.

For a century Andover Theological Seminary remained the citadel of Congregational Trinitarian orthodoxy. With enrollment dwindling, the Seminary had moved to Cambridge by 1908 and later merged with Andover-Newton Theological Seminary. Its buildings and properties were acquired by Phillips Academy, doubling the size of that school. One local historian summed up nineteenth century Andover as the "Puritan citadel, leader in missions, theology, and religious life…where the tides of intellectual life ran strong and high." ∞

WHAT THEY DID FOR FUN

❧

Zion Hill, as the seat of Andover Theological Seminary was also known, had the reputation of being very straight-laced. A visiting scholar from Germany once asked Edwards Amasa Park, Professor of Christian Theology and Faculty President, "How do you get along without the opera and the theater?"

Park's reply was immediate, "Why Sir, you forget that we have the church and the Sewing Society! And there is always Commencement Day to anticipate."

Author Elizabeth Stuart Phelps, whose father was a seminary professor and headmaster, remembered growing up where "philosophy and theology were elements in the fiber of any bred on Andover Hill;" a place "where little boys played preacher as their chief amusement." Phelps who attended Abbot Female Seminary and later, a private school on Main Street run by the widow of a seminary professor, explains in her autobiography what she and her classmates did for fun:

> *Phillips Academy was across from our girls' school and for young men destined to be ministers and missionaries, there was Andover Theological Seminary…We drew portraits of our favorite Academy boys upon the margins of our books and passed them secretly to our friends. We cut holes in our fans so that we could get a better look at the young men.* ∞

The Nineteenth Century

Temperance Town and the "Cold Water Army"

When Amos Blanchard, a deacon at South Church, built his house and barn in 1819, (now the Andover Historical Society) he credited a portion of construction costs to the purchase of rum for the workers.

Yet Andover Theological Seminary cast its moral values over the entire town. "Demon Rum," so important to early New England economy, was considered by nineteenth century church leaders as the cause of social problems such as Sabbath-breaking, poverty, insanity, and homicide. Although males were considered "the worst offenders and seemed more inclined to drunken behavior, women could also be intemperant, sometimes becoming addicted to medicines laced with alcohol."

The Andover South Parish Society For the Reformation Of Morals was formed in 1814 by the Reverend Justin Edwards. A seminary trustee, Edwards served as South Church minister from 1812 through 1827, when he resigned to devote full time to the temperance movement. His series of papers entitled *Permanent Temperance Documents* had national impact and he traveled through twenty-four states, lecturing on behalf of the American Temperance Society. Doctor Edwards served as president of Andover Theological Seminary from 1836 through 1842.

In 1826, Harriet Beecher Stowe's father, the Reverend Lyman Beecher, some Bostonians, and the Reverend Justin Edwards met at Phelps House on campus to form the American Society for the Promotion of Temperance, which later became the American Temperance Union. Its goal was "to promote abstention from liquor and to persuade states to legislate against the production and sale of alcohol." The new organization received total support from the professors and many students "took the pledge." In September, 1826, one hundred and ninety-eight young Andover men formed their own local temperance society.

The Andover West Parish Temperance Society was organized in 1829 under the leadership of Dr. Edwards, then Secretary of the American Temperance Society. In the 1830s, Andover's South and West Parish Churches passed resolutions "to accept only temperant persons" as members. West Parish Records read that "no person shall, hereafter, be admitted who will not agree to abstain from ardent spirits, except used as medicine, and from all traffic in the same." This resolution was signed in July of 1833 and "for several years, a serious attempt was made to live up to this action." Abstinence was redefined to include beer, wine, and fermented cider. By 1834, reformed drunkards were popular platform speakers in Andover.

The Reverend Justin Edwards, in one annual report of temperance work, happily noted temperance progress here, where "…although some individuals are still reeling to and fro, and some families clothed in woe by this iniquity, yet the evil has been greatly lessened. A few years ago, $15,000 was expended in Andover for ardent spirits in a year, $8000 more than was paid for the support of the gospel, and all the schools, highways, state and country taxes, and all other town expenses. The people now do not expend one third of that sum on ardent spirits which, in the respectable part of the community, are becoming unfashionable and dispensed with in social visits… The practice of taking wine at funerals is almost abolished, and it begins to be understood that ardent spirits, except as a medicine, are not only entirely useless, but ruinous to the bodies and souls of men."

The *Ballard Vale Gazette*, December 25, 1867 praised the Division of the Sons of Temperance, formed in Ballardvale that year, as "…instrumental in taking thousands from the mire and filth of intemperance and placing them where they should be as becomes those formed in the image of God." Ballardvale's organization was committed to "total abstinence and prohibition," stating that "all who may be addicted to the intoxicating cup are urged to help cast intemperance from the land."

Andover youngsters were drafted into the Cold Water Army and paraded for the temperance cause with banners. Decked out in colorful badges and ribbons, these "little soldiers of temperance" learned songs and presented recitations.

For Andover women active in the temperance movement, sobriety was equated with industry. The Village Temperance Sewing Society, founded in 1843, brought women together to produce needlework for local charities and foreign missions.

Women were national and local leaders in the temperance movement because they were usually the ones whose families had been destroyed or who had suffered personal abuse due to alcohol. The Woman's Christian Temperance Union was formed in 1874 and became a national force for social reform, sometimes employing militant tactics in order to realize its goals. Led by local women activists, Andover had formed a WCTU branch by 1880. ∞

MISSIONARY BOULDER

As early as 1810, a number of theological students expressed interest in serving abroad. Four students, led by Adoniram Judson, walked to Bradford and back to ask the Massachusetts Association of Congregational Ministers to "send them as missionaries to heathen lands." The Society of Brethren, organized at Williams College in 1802, was transferred several years later to Andover. Of Andover Seminary graduates in the first quarter century, one in ten was commissioned as a foreign missionary. One hundred and thirty-four served in the mission field in this institution's first fifty years. Many, including Judson, died from disease or in prisons while serving in the Sandwich Islands (Hawaii), India, Ceylon, Burma, China, the South Seas, Africa, Latin America, Mediterranean countries, the Middle East, Eastern Europe, or among Native Americans on the southwestern frontier of the United States. These missionaries made the name of Andover familiar in all corners of the earth. Besides churches, they established elementary and high schools, colleges, several native seminaries, and numerous hospitals.

The missionary effort was enthusiastically supported by local churches, particularly South and West Parishes in the early years. Church records note a charming tradition of missionaries sending sea shells back to Andover congregations upon receiving care packages of clothing, books, educational and medical supplies for their native charges. Numerous nineteenth-century Andover households exhibited exotic shells from foreign seashores in the Best Parlor.

In a wooded area near Rabbit Pond on Phillips Academy's campus is a boulder with a bronze tablet inscribed with the names of the first seven who entered the missionary field from Andover Theological Seminary. This boulder of New Hampshire granite weighing seven tons was found in Andover's Carmel Woods and pulled up Main Street by eight horses, attended by eight men, then up Bartlet Street across the fields and around the pond, the last part on rollers.

Even though the Seminary was no longer based in Andover, the dedication of Missionary Boulder on October 12, 1910 was witnessed by 2000, according to one Boston newspaper. "Five hundred persons arriving by special train from Boston to commemorate the Centennial of the American Board of Foreign Missions…Guides met the Pilgrims at the station and brought them by carriages to Rabbit Rock." After speeches and prayers offered by relatives of those memorialized, the company sang *The Morning Light Is Breaking*, written by Samuel Francis Smith in 1830 when the author of *America* was a student at Andover Theological Seminary.

"In the 'Missionary Woods' once extending to this spot the first missionary students of Andover Seminary walked and talked one hundred years ago," the tablet reads, "and on this secluded knoll met to pray…leading to the formation of the first American Society for Foreign Missions. In recognition of the 248 missionaries trained in Andover Seminary this stone is set up in the Centennial year of the American Board, 1910." ∽

LAFAYETTE STOPS BY

The visit of the Marquis de Lafayette in 1825 marked a memorable event in the lives of Andover residents. Barely remembered by Americans today, Lafayette was then a great hero whose contemporaries credited with helping them win the American Revolution. At the invitation of Congress and President James Munroe, the popular French statesman came to the United States for a triumphal tour of the country.

Born in 1757 into a privileged French family, Lafayette's father was killed fighting the British when he was an infant. Deserted by his mother and raised by his grandmother, young Lafayette dreamed of joining the military to avenge his father's death. He was eighteen years old when the American colonies declared independence from England and he considered the American Revolution his chance for revenge against England, while acquiring military experience on the battlefield. The Marquis was appointed a major general at the age of nineteen, serving under General George Washington and the young man offered much of his personal fortune for the cause. Washington became a surrogate father to the orphaned Lafayette, who often referred to the Frenchman as "my adopted son."

On June 17, 1825, the Marquis de Lafayette was in attendance with Daniel Webster at the laying of the corner stone of the Bunker Hill Monument. On June 21, cavalry from the Andover militia met Lafayette at the Reading-Andover line and led him into town. As he and his carriage companion, Josiah Quincy (who had attended Phillips Academy) were on their way here, the Marquis inquired about the town and what he might say to its citizens. When they arrived at Mansion House on Andover Hill, the former home of Samuel Phillips, Jr. and by then, an inn, Lafayette addressed Phillips Academy and Andover Theological Seminary students. The French hero spoke in impeccable English about "this consecrated Hill, from which light has gone out to the heathen and religion to the ends of the earth," which brought applause and cheers from all assembled there. Phillips Academy's principal John Adams commented later that he "was surprised…I knew in our religious world our school held a very high position, but I was unprepared to find that a man who had spent his days in courts and camps, who had been through the French Revolution, should have known so much about our town and its theological institution."

Esquire John Kneeland, a Revolutionary War veteran and later, merchant, lawyer and member of the Massachusetts Constitutional Convention, greeted Lafayette on behalf of the town, then took the Marquis to his own house at the corner of Central and Chestnut Streets, for a toddy. This house, built by blacksmith Abner Abbot in 1784, later served as the Christ Episcopal Church parsonage, then became a tea-house. Known as Rose Cottage, it is still standing. Here, Lafayette greeted townspeople and personally acknowledged several Revolutionary War veterans.

According to the *Boston Daily Advertiser*, June 23, 1825, "In Lafayette's progress through Andover the windows were generally filled with well-dressed females." The Marquis must have enjoyed his visit for as Thomas Jefferson once remarked, "Lafayette had a canine appetite for popularity and fame."

For some Phillips students the famous Frenchman's stop meant a day out of classes. In a letter home, one student, Oliver Baker, wrote: "LaFayette came through town last Tuesday in triumph; three pocketbooks of much value were stolen, indeed, a general stupor of admiration seized the minds of us all; it broke up all business and all study for the day. May we cherish his memory with gratitude." ∞

AMERICA PENNED IN ANDOVER

❧

Samuel Francis Smith (1808-1895) was a twenty-three-year-old student at Andover Theological Seminary when he penned the familiar verses beginning *My Country 'Tis of Thee*. One blustery February day in 1832, he returned to his board-ing house carrying a stack of musical scores that Lowell Mason had given him. Mason, known as the "Father of Church Music" is remembered for his introduction of music into American public schools. Mason lacked Samuel Smith's ability with foreign languages and had asked the young seminarian to translate some German songs or if Smith wished, to create his own words to the tunes.

America was written in the downstairs north parlor of Blunt House, where Widow Hitchings provided room and board to students from Andover Hill. Since Mrs. Hitchings also made and sold paper dolls, her home at 147 Main Street was frequently filled with giggling girls, hoping for a glimpse of the bookish "theologues."

As Samuel Smith glanced through the sheets of music, one composition in particular, caught his eye. It was a "surging, inspirational melody," and he was "imme-diately caught up in the patriotic air…Led on the impulse of the moment" (he) "seized a scrap of paper…The words seemed to have been dictated, they came to mind so quickly."

There was originally another stanza, deleted by most publishers, although noone really knows why. Historians speculate that the War of 1812 was still too recent a memory for Americans to wish to hear or sing this reminder of war.

No more shall tyrants here
With haughty ships appear,
And soldier bands;
No more shall tyrants tread
Above the patriot dead
No more our blood be shed
By alien hands.

Smith left his scraps of paper inside the books he returned to Mason and was amazed to hear *America* sung the following Fourth of July by the Boston Sabbath School Union at Park Street Church. Smith's name did not appear on the program.

The song was first published in 1832 in *The Choir,* a music primer edited by Lowell Mason and was immediately criticized for being the same tune as the national anthem of Great Britain. The origins of the tune remain unclear. By 1815, this music served as Prussia's national anthem, as well as that of Norway and Russia, and Switzerland. Though classified as a French tune, it has also been attributed to musician Henry Carey, who supposedly composed it in 1742. Others claim the tune was composed by one John Bull of Somersetshire, England in 1562, said to have been as significant to music in his day as Shakespeare was to theater.

Samuel Francis Smith went on to become a Baptist minister in Waterville, Maine, as well as Professor of Modern Languages at Waterville College (now Colby). From 1842-1865, he served as pastor in Newton Centre and Newton Upper Falls and became editor of the *Christian Review,* as well as secretary of the American Baptist Missionary Union. Smith eventually wrote one hundred and fifty hymns and in 1889, for the centennial of George Washington's inauguration, penned an additional verse to *My Country 'Tis of Thee,* which was published in his 1895 anthology *Poems of Home and Country.*

"*America* was the work of a brief period at the close of a dismal winter afternoon…," Smith later recalled. "I did not propose to write a national hymn and did not know that I had done so…Yet I always hoped that the spirit of these simple verses might be the spirit of our people evermore."

Phillips Academy graduate Oliver Wendell Holmes, who was Smith's friend and Harvard classmate, said "When all the poets are gone and forgotten there will live the name of the man who wrote *My Country 'Tis of Thee.*" And the reason for it is very plain to see. He said *My Country!* Not *Our Country.* Every man has an individual interest in the country. That *My* made it a national anthem!" Doctor Holmes immortalized *America's* writer in these lines he wrote for Harvard's 1829 Class Reunion.

And there is a youngster of excellent pith;
Fate tried to conceal him by naming his Smith,
But he shouted a song for the brave and the free:
Just read on his medal—My Country Tis of Thee! ∞

THE INDUSTRIAL REVOLUTION
COMES TO ANDOVER

In 1682, the town had granted "liberty to any approved citizen to sett up a saw-mill, fulling-mill, and grist-mill upon the Shawshin River near Roger's Brooke, to take up twenty acres of land adjoining to the said place, and to enjoy the same forever…" Brothers Joseph and John Ballard, whose names would become prominent ten years later during the witchcraft hysteria, took advantage of this offer in South Parish.

By the mid-nineteenth century there were four mill districts in Andover's South Parish: Ballardvale, Abbot Village, Marland Village and Frye Village, all dependent on the Shawsheen River for water power. An 1837 industrial census shows that Andover farmers were raising more sheep for wool than any other town in Essex County.

Abraham Marland, an English immigrant, learned about the manufacture of textiles in his native land before coming to Andover. In 1807, he began manufacturing cotton yarn at a spinning mill along the Shawsheen River and soon began producing woolen fabric. During the War of 1812 Marland supplied blankets for American troops. He expanded his business in 1820, acquiring the mill privilege that had been the site of Samuel Phillips' earlier gun powder mill and paper manufacturing company. Here, Marland erected brick mill buildings as well as wooden tenement houses for his workers, known as Marland Village. Marland Manufacturing Company was incorporated in 1834 and in 1879, was sold to Moses T. Stevens of North Andover, who continued woolen cloth production. With his two sons and son-in-law, Benjamin Punchard, Abraham Marland established Christ Episcopal Church and the adjacent burial ground.

In 1815, the Abbot brothers, Paschal and Abel, set up a woolen mill, buying wool from local farmers for their spinning machines. Weaving was still done on hand-looms, often by employees in their own homes. The Abbot brothers also produced flannel and cashmere until 1837.

In 1836, John Marland, Abraham Gould, Mark Newman and several other entrepreneurs, bought Timothy Ballard's property and mill rights along the Shawsheen River in the Ballardvale section of Andover. Managed by John and William Marland, sons of Abraham Marland, this enterprise was incorporated as the Ballard Vale Manufacturing Company. The first piece of white flannel produced by the double spinning process in the United States was made here, and as long as white flannel trousers stayed in style for men, business flourished. In 1843, the first worsted goods in the country were manufactured here. John Marland attempted to produce silk by introducing silk worms and planting mulberry trees, but the New England climate was not right. A man of creative ideas, John Marland was less adept at financial management and the company went bankrupt.

Josiah Putnam Bradlee, Marland's former treasurer, took over the mills and by 1866, creditors had been paid off. Ballard Vale flannels became known as "the best in the world," winning awards from the Philadelphia Centennial Committee in 1870 and at the 1893 World's Fair in Chicago. Two hundred operatives were employed here in 1896 and the company provided mill housing for their workers as well as offering them free lectures, concerts, and a variety of sports activities. J. Putnam Bradlee was also generous to the Ballardvale community, establishing a public hall, library, and churches. Operations continued here under other managers, until 1927.

In 1856, Henry G. Tyer, an English immigrant, opened a factory for the manufacture of rubber cement in buildings owned by the Boston & Maine Railroad. Tyer began making rubber shoes, known as the "Compo," then obtained a patent for the manufacture of rubber compounded with zinc oxide to produce water bottles and syringes. The business expanded to include rubber bands and pharmaceutical accessories, although his major product continued to be footwear. Known as Tyer Rubber Company from 1876, it produced automobile tires and tubes after 1909. The old plant was demolished and a new factory built in 1912. Tyer Rubber remained an economic force in Andover until 1977. ∽

SMITH & DOVE
DRAWS THE SCOTS

❧

Smith and Dove became Andover's largest and most successful industry, lasting ninety two years. John Smith had been apprenticed to a millwright in his home town of Brechin, Scotland, where he learned the construction of water wheels and machinery. He said he arrived in America in 1816 with nothing more than "a shilling, a Bible, and machinists' tools." As a journeyman machinist, Smith traveled through the South and worked for several textile mills, then decided he could not live in any slave state. He moved to Plymouth, Massachusetts, where he set up a business for the manufacture of textile machinery with two men from Andover, who soon coaxed him to relocate here. They bought mill privileges on the Shawsheen at Frye Village (now Shawsheen Village) to turn out machinery for cotton spinning. After both partners died, John Smith went into business with his younger brother, Peter and friend, John Dove. As boys, the three had worked together in a flax mill owned by Dove's father in Scotland. It was Dove who convinced the Smith Brothers that they could make a successful business of processing flax in Andover. In 1834, John Dove returned to Scotland to study mill design and production methods. Peter Smith and his wife bleached the first skeins in a bean pot, dyeing them in a brass kettle.

Smith and Dove & Company was formed in 1835 and spun its first flax yarn that August. Their first mill was erected the following year, equipped with machinery they designed and built. This was the first successful enterprise for spinning flax yarn in the United States. Local historians claim John Smith was the director and financial head; his brother, Peter, the preacher and salesman, and John Dove, the mechanical genius.

In 1843, Smith and Dove moved the now booming business from Frye Village to Abbot Village near the railroad station, having bought water power rights and buildings that had formerly been Paschal and Abel Abbot's mill. Unlike other Andover mills that produced fabric, Smith and Dove manufactured linen thread and twines for carpet weaving, shoes, and sail cloth and twine. Shoe factories at Lynn and Haverhill were chief customers. During the Civil War, this company supplied the Union Army with linen thread for making boots and saddles.

Smith and Dove Manufacturing Company was incorporated in 1864 as a joint stock company, with John Smith, president and Peter Smith, treasurer and a year later, they erected a brick mill. By 1896, there were three hundred operatives on the payroll. This company was thriving up to 1927.

Smith & Dove attracted many operatives and skilled workers from Scotland and provided employees with low-cost housing near the mill, as well as playing fields for cricket, soccer, and baseball. Workers enjoyed company sports clubs, a bowling league, and social activities.

The ethnic traditions of Scotland survive in Andover to this day in street names like Brechin Terrace (1906), clubs like St. Matthew's Lodge, in Scottish rites such as the annual Robert Burns Festival, complete with haggis, and in the bagpipe bands of Clan Johnston and Clan McPherson. The latter, a twenty-one member band was organized in 1921 to keep Scottish music and customs alive here. Clan McPherson's piping and drumming, with members in kilts, remain a memorable presence, at nearly every Andover parade or special event.

The Smith Brothers and John Dove serve as excellent examples of nineteenth-century immigrants who worked hard, took business risks on this new nation's rising industrial economy, succeeded financially far beyond expectations, then became philanthropists who gave back ten-fold. Their commitment to the town of Andover still impacts upon the life of the Andover community. They were generous benefactors of schools, including Abbot Female Academy and the seminary, where Peter was a trustee. Andover residents also have John and Peter Smith and John Dove to thank for their local library. ∞

ANDOVER'S ANTI-SLAVERY RIOT

❧

"Anti-slavery is going on well in spite of mobs, Andover Seminary, and rum!" wrote John Greenleaf Whittier, abolitionist editor and Quaker poet.

Andover Theological Seminary and Phillips Academy received financial support from wealthy benefactors and conservative religious organizations. School administrators, trustees, and professors generally believed that controversy over the slavery issue threatened their institutions. The anti-slavery faction on campus represented a small minority, while many students came from southern states or had fathers involved in cotton manufacturing in northern mills. The faculty believed politics only served to distract students from their studies and might even jeopardize chances for securing a good position after graduation, should a student be identified "anti-slavery." Most faculty members opposed slavery on moral grounds, yet stood firmly behind the U. S. Constitution and preservation of the Union.

At a morning assembly in July of 1835, the Reverend Moses Stuart, Professor of Sacred Literature at Andover Theological Seminary, addressed the student body: "I warn you, young gentlemen. I warn you on peril of your souls' salvation, *not* to go to that anti-slavery meeting in Andover Village tonight!"

George Thompson was scheduled to speak. William Lloyd Garrison, editor of *The Liberator*, had brought this militant British abolitionist to New England for a lecture tour. Thompson arrived in Andover soon after being driven out of Boston by an anti-abolitionist mob. Members of local anti-slavery societies hoped that George Thompson "could be quietly heard here. Was not Andover the School of the Prophets, noted for its morality and religious spirit?" one journalist asked.

A group of students had personally invited Thompson and the Englishman was anxious to confront the Academy and Seminary on the slavery issue. Bartlet Seminary Chapel and South Parish Church both refused to allow Thompson on their podiums. The famous orator was finally offered a platform at the Methodist Church on Main Street.

"If you had the power, would you set all the slaves free tomorrow?" one Andover citizen asked Thompson.

"No Sir! I would set them free *tonight!* " Thompson shouted.

Sherlock Bristol, one of the students in attendance, described the event: "A railroad was then being constructed through Andover. The contractor was a pro-slavery character with not a few roughs in his employ. Word got around that a mob planned to break up the meeting and tar and feather Mr. Thompson. Anti-slavery students got wind of this and armed with heavy hickory clubs, were at the church when the doors opened..."

Thompson's lecture ran two hours and according to the newspaper, "fairly raised the audience to its feet. Some students had their minds inflamed. When it was over, every light was blown out and the mob rushed for the podium. About fifty students, most of them farmers' sons—big and strong, closed around Thompson protectively with clubs brandished so threateningly that the mob kept a respectful distance.

Bristol recalled the dramatic details years later: "Our student squad of six guards held the gathering mob at bay. When we sounded the alarm and aroused the dormitories, we heard the tramp, tramp, tramp of a hundred students dashing down Andover Hill... In the still of the night it sounded like the coming of a regiment of cavalry and the mob broke and fled in every direction. Some students remained downtown to patrol the streets until morning with signal whistles, while all the others slept in their clothes, ready for any emergency."

A few days later, Sherlock Bristol was summoned before the entire faculty on charges of "plotting with others to destroy the good name of Phillips Academy." Instead of offering an apology, the student delivered a bold abolitionist speech charging the professors with "the sin of seeking to shield the great crime of slavery" and of "making cowards of young men soon to go forth to help form and reform the opinions of mankind. If we are cowards here, we will be cowards in college, seminary, and in the ministry!"

The faculty resolved to make an example of the young man. They condemned him in front of the entire school at chapel exercises. When he stood and asked to be allowed to defend himself, they ordered him to sit down. "I was cast out," he later wrote. "It was simply decreed that I was no longer a member of Phillips Academy."

Andover Theological Seminary and Phillips Academy then issued an order that "no student shall join any society in the Town of Andover without leave of the principal of the school with which he is connected."

Anti-slavery students from both Phillips Academy and Andover Theological Seminary were furious over Sherlock Bristol's expulsion and scheduled a meeting for July 15 to decide a course of action. Since they had been refused all meeting spaces on campus, they hiked to Indian Ridge where they drafted a written ultimatum stating they would remain at the Academy only if allowed to exercise their "inalienable rights." Otherwise they would request "honorable discharges."

In mid-August of 1835, faculty members denied their petition on grounds that the "principle business for those who come here is to prepare for the ministry...An anti-slavery society would interfere with the spirit of piety among students and with their usefulness in the ministry. It would be taking sides in favor of a particular system of opinions…which a great part of the community looks upon with deep distrust and fear." Fifty students immediately withdrew from school and seminary.

Following his expulsion, Sherlock Bristol's home church canceled his scholarship and he was turned out of his boarding house on Andover Hill and forced to sell all his books. He tried to get jobs around town, "but the brand 'fanatic' was upon me and people were reluctant to employ me." Bristol finally found work mowing hay-fields until the abolitionist John Smith, manager of the Smith and Dove Flax Thread Company, learned of the young man's plight and loaned him tuition money to attend Oberlin College, the new anti-slavery institution in Ohio. Sherlock Bristol eventually did become a minister and returned to Andover in 1848 as the second pastor of Free Christian Church. ∞

THE GRIMKE SISTERS
RAISED EYEBROWS

Angelina and Sarah Grimké were sisters and social reformers from South Carolina. With Angelina's husband, Theodore Weld, a Phillips Academy graduate, they traveled the national lecture circuit on behalf of abolitionism and equal rights for women. They toured Essex County in 1837 at the invitation of the Massachusetts Anti-Slavery Society. In mid-July, the Grimké girls spoke in Andover, sponsored by the Female Anti-Slavery Society. To everyone's amazement, men attended their lecture. In a letter to a friend, Angelina Grimké wrote, "Very hard soil!" one sister wrote a friend. "Great prejudice against women speaking in public!"

An entry in Angelina's *Diary* offers more detail: "At Andover, despite a heavy thunderstorm, the meeting house was full. Eight hundred were present, with many faculty and students. I *never* felt as if I was speaking before such a formidable array of talent and learning *and* prejudice against my womanhood, but *all went well!*"

That the Grimké sisters had addressed a mixed audience seemed to have raised more eyebrows than their politics. The conservative clergy and faculty of Andover Theological Seminary, as well as many citizens, highly disapproved of women speaking from public platforms.

Some members of the "gentler sex" were quick to defend the Grimkés. *The Liberator* of August 18, 1837, published an open letter from the Female Anti-Slavery Society of Andover explaining, "That meeting was designated for Ladies and if Gentlemen attended, they must sustain the responsibility for a mixed meeting!" ∾

THE RAILROAD ACCIDENT THAT AFFECTED THE NATION

America's fourteenth President, Franklin Pierce (1804-1869) frequently visited Andover during the 1850s and 1860s, staying with John Aiken, whose second wife was Jane Pierce's elder sister. A mill agent, Aiken was a trustee of Andover Theological Seminary and a benefactor of Phillips Academy, where his nephew Benjamin Pierce, was soon to be enrolled. The Aiken's house at 48 Central Street is still remembered as the Summer White House, while the President's staff generally stayed at number 47.

A tragic train accident at Andover, following Pierce's election and just prior to his inauguration, changed this man forever and had an adverse effect on his Presidency.

Self-confident and gregarious, with a head of curly, dark hair over fine features, Franklin Pierce was considered quite dashing. According to his biographer, Roy Nichols, "Pierce was master of his voice and could concentrate this ability to the point of hypnotic power." Pierce never lost an election.

A Jacksonian Democrat from New Hampshire, Franklin Pierce was nicknamed *Young Hickory* in deference to Andrew Jackson, who was known as *Old Hickory*. At the age of twenty-four, Pierce was elected to the New Hampshire Legislature and served as house speaker from 1831 to 1833. When he went to Washington he was the youngest member of the U. S. Senate.

He married Jane Means Appleton whose father had been a Congregational minister as well as president of Bowdoin College, Pierce's alma mater. Jane was in delicate health and suffered from depression. She resented her husband's extroverted nature and his fondness for society and alcohol. She hated politics, believing it brought out a man's worst qualities. When their first son died a few days after birth, Jane decided to remain at home in Concord, New Hampshire rather than accompany her husband to Washington. Following the death of their second son from typhus at the age of four, Pierce resigned his Senate seat and opened a law practice back in Concord.

The 1852 Convention was deadlocked when Franklin Pierce was nominated on the 49th ballot as a "dark horse" or compromise candidate, the only choice acceptable to both North and South. Pierce had not sought the nomination, nor did he campaign for the Presidency. He told colleagues that he "gave into the draft for the same reason that I fought in the Mexican War. I believed that having a father who served his country in time of need, would give my son, Benny, great advantages throughout his life."

'I hope Father won't be elected,' Benny wrote his mother from school, 'for I should not like to be at Washington. I know you would not either.' Upon hearing the news of her husband's election, Jane Pierce promptly fainted.

After Christmas with the Aikens in Andover, the Pierces returned to Concord to pack for their move into the White House. On the 6th of January, 1853, they boarded the 1:15 Northbound from Boston. About two miles out of Andover Station, "there came a sudden wrenching and frightful jerking." The bitter cold likely caused the iron works to freeze up and apparently the rail car hit some rocks on the track which broke the forward left axle of the tender. Several cars derailed and toppled off the steep fifteen-foot embankment onto the rocky fill below.

Eleven-year-old Benny had been standing and looking out the window at the time of the accident. He was killed in full view of his parents, the only fatality, although among sixty passengers aboard, several others were injured. According to one eyewitness, the Pierce boy "one minute before so beautiful, so full of life and hope" had been "struck so violently as to remove the upper portion of his head, leaving part of the brain exposed."

John Smith sent his carriages and wagons to take the injured to the nearby alms house. From there, Benny's body was removed to the Aiken's home where a funeral was held several days later with a dozen of Benny's schoolmates serving as pallbearers. Jane Pierce was too devastated to accompany her son's body back to Concord for burial.

It was one the the worst accidents in the history of the Boston & Maine Railroad up to that time. However, Jane Pierce refused to sue B&M for negligence although some passengers did so. The First Lady believed Benny's death was due to Divine Providence and for the rest of her life, remained convinced that their son had to be sacrificed so Franklin could be free from family demands to concentrate on the great political responsibilities that lay ahead. Jane Pierce considered Benny the price for Franklin's ambition and the high honor he had won. Furthermore, her husband had betrayed the promise he made to her years ago—to stay out of politics.

Grief is evident in Franklin Pierce's Inaugural Address delivered on March 4, 1853. "My countrymen: It is a relief to feel that no heart but my own can know the personal regret and bitter sorrow over which I have been born to a position so suitable for others rather than desirable for myself. "

The traditional Presidential inaugural ball was canceled and replaced by a national mourning period. Jane Pierce dressed in mourning clothes for the rest of her life. During the first two years of her husband's administration, the First Lady never once appeared in public and the press referred to her as "the Shadow in the White House." Her husband put up a Christmas tree in the White House (the first President ever do so) not only as a symbol of national good will but to cheer up his wife. Jane finally ventured downstairs in 1855 to attend a New Year's Reception.

Jane Pierce died at the Aiken home in Andover on December 2, 1863, after a long battle against tuberculosis and melancholia. Following her funeral at 48 Central Street, the family boarded a special train for Concord, New Hampshire, where Jane was laid to rest beside her three sons. It was where she had longed to be ever since Benny's death.

Franklin Pierce later said that "the burden of guilt I carried for a public career that destroyed my family will haunt me as long as I live." Roy Nichols, wrote that "Within the space of a few days he lost Benny, rapport with his wife, his self-confidence, his ability to lead and perhaps, his will to succeed…The spark went out and Pierce became known as one of the most ineffectual of all Presidents." He was the only elected President who sought reelection but did not receive his party's renomination.

An ironic footnote to history appeared in the *Andover Townsman*, May 11, 1894. A former Andover resident, Doctor Ezra W. Abbott was traveling in the same rail car as the Pierce family that fateful day in 1853, and rode in the cart that carried Benny Pierce's body from the alms house back to the Aiken's. Doctor Abbott was also at Ford's Theater in April of 1865, when President Lincoln was shot. He was the first doctor to reach Lincoln and remained at the President's side until he died. Though first on the scene at two national tragedies, neither Doctor Abbott's medical expertise nor the instruments in his black bag could help. ∞

THE "MERRIEST EPOCH" IN ANDOVER HISTORY

⌘

What a lovely place Andover is! So many beautiful walks! There is every-thing here. There is no end to the beauty of these trees. Yesterday I was out all the forenoon sketching elms. And last evening a party of us went to ride on horseback down to Pomp's Pond. The other evening a number of us climbed Prospect Hill—a most charming walk. It seems almost too good to be true that we are going to have such a house in such a beautiful place and to live here among all these agreeable people.

—HARRIET BEECHER STOWE,
Letter to Calvin Stowe from Andover, July, 1852

Uncle Tom's Cabin; Or Life Among the Lowly was already the national best-seller when its author, Harriet Beecher Stowe, moved from Brunswick, Maine to Andover in the summer of 1852. Calvin Stowe had been appointed Professor of Sacred Literature at Andover Theological Seminary but the faculty house offered was too small for their brood of six children, as well as for the many friends and family members Harriet planned on entertaining. Mrs. Stowe had her eye on a stone building on campus which had previously served as a gymnasium and was now used for storage. It had been built as a carpentry shop to help theological students meet tuition expenses and contemplate the brevity of earthly life as they fashioned wooden coffins and cradles. When Harriet saw the building, she would accept no other offered and when the trustees shook their heads Harriet simply waved a $10,300 check from her publisher and they allowed her to move in.

The dozen years Harriet Beecher Stowe and her family lived in what she nick-named the "Stone Cabin" would be fondly remembered by local historians as the "Merriest Epoch" in Andover history. She described herself about this time as "some-what more than forty, as thin and dry as a pinch of snuff; never very much to look at in my best days, and looking like a used-up article now."

Mrs. Stowe was the most talked about and most unpredictable character in town. She received so much more mail than anyone else in town that an extra postman had to be hired. Her skills at house decoration and garden design were much admired, and her plants regularly won prizes at Andover's annual Agricultural Fairs.

Stowe lived here at the pinnacle of her career and international fame. She entertained literary lights and abolitionist leaders and threw the best parties. She sailed to Europe three times on speaking tours, arranged by anti-slavery societies in Great Britain and she socialized with the rich and famous. She met Queen Victoria who "wept over her book," and went to Washington to see President Lincoln at the White House. During the Andover years, Harriet published *The Key to Uncle Tom's Cabin, Dred: A Tale of the Great Dismal Swamp, Pearl of Orr's Island*, and *The Minister's Wooing*, and several travel books. She also wrote political, religious, and literary articles for *The Independent* and *Atlantic*, among others, and published short fiction, poetry, and columns in the *Andover Advertiser*.

Harriet found Andover Seminary life much too Spartan for her taste. She was usually in the front pew of the campus chapel each Sunday morning but "saw no reason why religion and long, sour faces must go together...I do not intend to have my children raised in a crushing atmosphere," she told one relative. "I intend to make my home the center of Andover's social life, an open, hospitable place—human, hearty and happy!"

Andover folks disapproved when Harriet attended the theater in Boston to see a stage performance adapted from her book. Proper Victorian ladies did not attend plays and anyway, shouldn't Mrs. Stowe be setting a better example as a seminary faculty wife? At a time and place where Christmas trees were still considered a pagan custom, Harriet put up the town's first Christmas tree and decorated it with painted walnut shells and pine cones. Then she invited the stodgy professors over to celebrate, preparing an appropriate gift for each guest. Instead of souvenirs from her trip to Europe or the hand-made decorative art pieces they expected to receive, Harriet presented each guest with a joke gift!

Night after night the windows of the Stone Cabin blazed with gaslights. There were regular concerts, tableaux, musicals, charades, and much tea-drinking. One particular party, given by the Stowe's two eldest children (identical twin daughters) for their Abbot Academy classmates, went on until "eleven and a half o'clock! So great was the gaiety fostered by Mrs. Stowe that she received a sound scolding from the Seminary fathers."

When the Stowes came to Andover, their youngest child was three. "Everybody wants to know what to do with our Charley. The cook can't have him in the kitchen where he invades the pantry to get flour to make paste for his kite. If he goes into the wood shed, he's sure to pull the wood pile down upon his head...He makes a loco-motive of the work table and a steam whistle of himself..." Harriet's humorous columns on the challenges of raising her very own *Dennis the Menace* ran in the *Andover Advertiser* and later, became a book. Every mother could identify with the antics of this little boy.

Our Charley is rushing in hot haste, hands full of nails, strings, and twine when Mary seizes him and wants to brush his hair. He is interrupted in a burst of enthusiasm and told to wash his hands for dinner. Or greater horror: company is expected and he must put on a clean suit, just as he has made all arrangements for a ship-launching down by the swamp!

There are four hours of school taken out of the best part of every day. Hours in which Charley might move ships, build dams, and run railroad cars, but he must go through what seems to him a useless ceremony of reading and spelling. And when he finally returns home from school, he discovers that the housemaid has swept his foremast into the fire and Mamma has put his top sails into the rag bag and all his affairs are in a desperate situation!

The Stowe's neighbors recalled "there was always some form of dog life about: big and little, curly and straight." There was "a succession and growing multitude of dogs and also, a steady mortality." Passersby wondered at the "curious grassy mounds" in the yard of the Stone Cabin. These were the graves of beloved past pets such as Carlo, Florence, and Rover, the huge Newfoundland which arrived from Maine in a rail car. After each demise, a canine funeral would be held "with pomp and circumstance."

'If horses, cats, and dogs have not souls to be saved,' Harriet wrote, 'what will become of their masters? When it comes to fidelity, devotion and love, many a two-legged animal rates below the dog!'

A fine Italian greyhound was presented to Mrs. Stowe on one of her European tours. According to Harriet, this greyhound "never liked Andover's wet and weary winters. Being Italian, he felt the cold cruelly and usually appeared wearing a blue blanket and shivering. Nor has the cat enjoyed sharing the Stone Cabin with this noble Italian fur-bearer…Our cat has selected a pamphlet closet as her special domestic retreat and makes her lair amid a heap of Calvin's old sermons…"

Charley and his little white dog were inseparable. Chumb was, according to the Stowe's friends, "an affectionate fellow and patient, allowing his furry face to be washed, his hair combed and his tail pulled, but the dog had no aristocratic lineage to boast of."

One day, Charley returned home in tears. A playmate had a bull terrier and another boy with a mastiff, had told Charley that Chumb, "wasn't worth a straw…'tis just a good-for-nothing cur!"

Professor Stowe consoled the sobbing boy. "Son, go directly back and tell those boys that your dog is a full-blooded mongrel and that your father says a better dog cannot be found in all of Andover!" ❧

SOJOURNER TRUTH CAME TO TOWN

In the autumn of 1853, the most famous white woman in America played hostess to the most famous black woman in America. Both were social reformers who campaigned against slavery at a time when ladies were not supposed to be concerned with politics, much less speak in public.

Sojourner Truth took the train from Boston to Andover with the express aim of meeting Harriet Beecher Stowe. The former slave wished to obtain a recommendation from Mrs. Stowe that would help sell her book. Although she could not read herself, the experiences which she had dictated to a white abolitionist, published in 1850 as *Narrative of Sojourner Truth: A Northern Slave*, became a best-seller. Personal stories by ex-slaves were then in high demand and the life of a woman who had been enslaved in the North was something new for readers. William Lloyd Garrison had written the introduction for the first edition and now, he urged the author to get Mrs. Stowe to back the second edition of *Narrative of Sojourner Truth* by penning a "puff" piece.

The famous black reformer was fifty-six, and already had ten years experience on the lecture circuit when she came to Andover with her grandson. Born in 1797 as the slave *Belle* in Ulster County, New York, Sojourner Truth had been sold three times before the age of thirteen. When she was five, she witnessed her brother and sister locked in a box and taken off in a sleigh to be sold.

By New York law, all slaves born before 1827 were to be freed on July 4th of that year. But Belle's abusive master refused to free her, claiming that since her hand had been cut by a scythe, she had not performed her full work load. Realizing she had the law on her side, Belle fled to freedom, leaving her husband and four children behind and taking only her infant daughter.

She found refuge among Quakers and later became a domestic in New York City. In 1843, she claimed to have experienced a revelation from God, directing her to preach against the evils of slavery. Belle changed her name to Sojourner Truth and joined an abolitionist commune in Northampton, Massachusetts, from where she began lecture tours.

Sojourner Truth dropped by the "Stone Cabin" unannounced. A decade later in of April, 1863, Harriet Beecher Stowe would publish her own version of this visit in the *Atlantic Monthly*. Entitled *The Libyan Sybil* the article is filled with racial stereotypes. In fact, Stowe's description of Sojourner Truth's ten-year-old grandson, James Caldwell, might have come from a minstrel show popular at this period: "An African Puck…the fattest, jolliest woolly-headed little specimen of Africa than one can imagine. He was grinning and showing his glistening white teeth in a state of perpetual merriment…" Stowe tells her readers about Sojourner Truth's visit:

> *…our house was filled with company, several eminent clergymen being our guests, when notice was brought upstairs to me that Sojourner Truth was below, and requested an interview. Knowing nothing of her but her name, I went down, prepared to make the interview short…When I went into the room, a tall, spare form arose to meet me. She was evidently a full-blooded African, and though now aged and worn with many hardships, still gave the impression of physical development which in early youth must have been a fine specimen of the torrid zone.*

Stowe wrote that "the African, though dusty from travel" was "dressed in some grayish stuff, neat and clean. On her head, she wore a bright Madras handkerchief, arranged as a turban, after the manner of her race…She seemed perfectly self-possessed…there was almost an unconscious superiority, not unmixed with a solemn twinkle of humor, in the odd, composed manner in which she looked down on me…standing as calm and erect as one of her own native palm trees waving alone in the desert…"

Harriet introduced her father, Dr. Lyman Beecher, "a very celebrated preacher." Sojourner Truth offered her hand and greeted him, "Ye dear lamb, I'm glad to see ye! De Lord bless ye! I loves preachers. I'm a kind o' preacher myself." "Do you preach from the Bible?" Dr. Lyman asked. "No, honey, can't preach from de Bible—can't read a letter."

Stowe wrote that Sojourner Truth was a "welcome guest" for several days. "Her conversation was so strong, simple, shrewd, and with such a droll flavoring of humor, that Professor Stowe was wont to say of an evening, 'I am dull and bored, can't you get Sojourner to come up here to talk with me a little?'"

Harriet wrote the "puff" for the new edition of *Narrative of Sojourner Truth* commenting that the "*Narrative* is in all respects true and faithful, and in some points more remarkable than many which have abounded in late years. It is the history of a mind of no common energy and power whose struggles with the darkness and ignorance of slavery have a peculiar interest…"

Harriet loved retelling Sojourner Truth's visit for family and friends, drawing on her gift for fiction. She particularly enjoyed acting it out in dialect.

Following publication of Stowe's article in the *Atlantic*, Sojourner Truth dictated a letter to the *Commonwealth*, July 3, 1863, enclosing copies of her book where, she insisted, her 'correct history was to be found.' In spite of what Mrs. Stowe had written, Truth had never seen Africa and was not in the habit of addressing anyone as 'honey.'

From the 1840s through the 1870s, Sojourner Truth continued to travel the nation as a social reformer. "I cannot read a book, but I can read the people." she often said. Long after Harriet Beecher Stowe believed her dead at the time she wrote her piece for the *Atlantic*, Sojourner Truth was working for the National Freedman's Relief Association.

Sojourner Truth was no Libyan Sibyl, but she understood the benefits of Stowe's name and fame. Following the *Atlantic* article, hand bills advertising her lectures read: "Sojourner Truth, who has been a slave in the state of New York and a lecturer for the last 23 years (and) whose characteristics have been so vividly portrayed by Mrs. Harriet Beecher Stowe, as *The African Sibyl* will deliver a lecture upon the present issues of the day…She will give her experiences as a Slave Mother and religious woman…" Stowe's article helped turn Sojourner Truth's public appearance into media events. Her visit to Andover proved a wise career move. ∞

THE UNDERGROUND RAILROAD
RAN THROUGH ANDOVER

❧

William Jenkins' gravestone in Andover's Spring Grove Cemetery is a tribute to his political beliefs: 1796-1878, "He lived to see the fulfillment of his great desire—The abolition of slavery in America"

William Jenkins was one of the town's brave citizens who broke the law of the land by aiding fugitive slaves in their desperate run to freedom. Like his friend, William Lloyd Garrison, Jenkins supported immediate and total emancipation for slaves. William Jenkins represented Andover at the Freeman's Convention, an organization dedicated to work for the immediate repeal of the Fugitive Slave Law of 1850.

The William Jenkins house (now 8 Douglass Lane), was built by William's grandfather, Samuel Jenkins in 1765. After inheriting it from his father, William made structural changes in the 1840s that reflected his politics and made the house part of the secret network known as the Underground Railroad. At a time when men like William Jenkins, if caught, had to pay a thousand dollar fine and face imprisonment for helping slaves on their way to Canada, he installed a secret panel in the back of one downstairs closet. Back of the central chimney behind the main stairway, is a place where runaways could hide when the barking of slave-catchers' hounds was heard. In Jenkin's day, there was probably access through paneling in several chambers. When raised, loose boards in the attic floor still disclose a "slave hole," large enough for a standing adult.

Wilbur Siebert, a historian who, in the 1880s interviewed many who had been directly involved, wrote in his landmark book, *The Underground Railroad* that

> *From Reading, the fugitives traveled some 10 miles along the Boston-Haverhill Turnpike, crossing the Essex County line and reaching at length the estate of William Jenkins, who owned hundreds of acres of farm and woodland along the Skug River…His large house, surrounded by commodious barns and outbuildings, was the principal Underground station of the countryside, and in operation from the 1830s. Anti-slavery meetings were often held in his home and Harriet Beecher Stowe was only one among many famous visitors.*

Jenkins' daughter Belle was five years old when one fugitive slave hiding in her home, reenacted a slave auction. George Latimer, "who had an enduring dread of being captured," lifted the little girl atop a table to demonstrate how slave children were sold. Latimer had escaped by steamboat from Norfolk, Virginia in 1842 and had been hiding among free blacks in Boston when pursued by his master who was determined to reclaim his property. On October 20, 1842, Latimer was arrested and held in a Boston jail without a warrant and without evidence of his slave status. Angry protests followed in Boston, where Wendell Phillips and other abolitionists spoke on Latimer's behalf. As a result, Massachusetts passed the Personal Liberty Act on March 24, 1843. Known as the "Latimer Law," it forbid state aid in capturing fugitives who arrived in Massachusetts from other states.

Latimer's freedom was eventually purchased for $400 with funds raised by abolitionists. Before finally settling in Lynn, Latimer stayed at William Jenkins' safe house, where hired help was always welcome at Jenkin's sawmill and soapstone enterprises on the Skug River.

Frye Village, later Shawsheen Village, was a hotbed of anti-slavery activity. Here, John Smith, manager of Smith and Dove, lived and originally located his flax company. Smith, who witnessed a slave auction in the deep South, was a Garrisonian, so zealous in his abolitionism that he named a son after the radical British anti-slavery leader, George Thompson.

Underground Railroad historian Wilbur Siebert wrote:

> *Straight up the pike was the thriving manufacturing center of Frye Village. There William Poor and his sons had a flourishing wagon factory. Elijah Hussey, a sawmill, and William C. Donald, an ink factory…Donald, Hussey, Joseph W. Poor, and others could be counted on to speed black wayfarers on their journey. When Mr. Poor heard a gentle rap on his door, he dressed quickly, went out, harnessed his mare Nellie to a covered wagon and started off with his dusky passengers. Poor was always back in time for breakfast. Underground workers at Frye Village disliked keeping their passengers over for a day or more, preferring to hurry them on.* ∞

FREE CHRISTIAN CHURCH FOUNDED BY ABOLITIONISTS

William Jenkins was among those instrumental in establishing Free Christian Church. He withdrew from South Parish because the church refused to take an active stand against slavery. Abolitionists like Jenkins charged that American churches sheltered slave holders and were sympathizers of the institution of slavery. John Smith, who was treasurer at West Parish, refused to pay his church taxes since, "the majority of the congregation considered it uncharitable to deny worship to any who might be pro-slavery."

William C. Donald also left South Church to join the Free Christian Church. At the fiftieth anniversary observances, Donald, who served as the new church's deacon for many years, recalled its founding:

> We banded ourselves together and took counsel of one another and of God as to how we could honor Him and do something for the liberation of three million of our brethren held in slavery in the South…We came to the conclusion that we must come out from the other churches that apologized for slavery and received slave holders into their communion….We held weekly anti-slavery prayer meetings and though we believed in prayer, we sometimes cried out, "O Lord, how long?…Ministers in those days who sympathized with us were scare. There was not one minister in the town of Andover to wish us Godspeed!

Free Christian Church was established on April 5, 1846. Its founders included fourteen from South Parish, seventeen from West Parish Church, ten former members of the Methodist Society, and three from the Baptist congregation. Services were held in private homes until John Smith purchased the former Methodist Church building. It was moved to Railroad Street, near Abbot and Marland Villages where many Scots, who were anti-slavery, lived and worked in the textile mills. Following renovation, the Free Christian Church building was dedicated on March 8, 1850 and served the congregation until the new brick church was erected on Elm Street in 1908. ∞

POMP'S POND

Few who regularly swim in Pomp's Pond realize that the name of Andover's favorite summer recreation area honors a former slave.

Born about 1724, Pompey Lovejoy was purchased by Captain William Lovejoy and brought to Andover as a boy. Pompey was granted his freedom just before his master died and some eighteen years before slavery was abolished in Massachusetts. On December 26, 1751, he married Rose Foster, the former slave of John Foster. The newlyweds were granted land in the woods near a pond, where they soon built a cabin. At the age of fifty-two, Pomp served one and one half days in the Revolutionary War under Captain Henry Abbot, for which he later received a pension.

Pompey Lovejoy was popular around town, particularly since he and Rose, with her sister, baked cake and brewed root and ginger beers for town meetings and on local, state, and national election days. Of course, as blacks, they were not permitted to vote themselves. Throughout nineteenth century New England, town meeting days were significant occasions for socializing and political bantering. Village dances, rowing boats across the pond and wrestling matches were common and spirits, not always of the political nature, flowed freely. Not far from the center of Andover, such activities often centered in the pine groves near Pompey Lovejoy's cabin. The refreshments served here on election days were as traditional in nineteenth-century Andover as coconuts on Memorial Day would be in the twentieth century.

ORIGINAL RECIPE FOR POMPEY LOVEJOY'S 'LECTION CAKE

1 pound of sugar	*1 pound of butter*
4 pounds of flour	*1/2 pint sweet lively yeast mixed with warm milk*

One half of the quantity of butter and sugar to be put in before raising the dough. The other half afterward, in the dough, raised again in pans or moulded in cakes. This quantity is sufficient for 3 or 4 common-sized pans. It requires considerable kneading. To be spiced with cinnamon and nutmeg. The quantity of flour may be increased to 4 1/2 or 5 pounds, if plums are used.

A letter, written by one of Pompey Lovejoy's contemporaries and now in the Andover Historical Society Collections, describes the baker's musical talent.

> *Many floors have literally groaned under the effects of his fiddle…His services were sought by all classes of society. Pomp was a genuine, undiluted Son of Africa, as his bandy legs, ebony complexion and facial developments testified; but he had music in his soul; and while he shook it off at his fingers' end, those who listened to him could not refrain from shaking it off at their toes.*

Phillips Academy students who enjoyed sneaking off campus on hot days for dips in Pomp's Pond, recalled in letters home that "they always had a smile for you even if Pomp was bad with the rhematiz" or Rose was "laid up for a spell." When Pompey Lovejoy died, he was said to be the oldest man in Essex County. Rose Foster Lovejoy was ninety-eight when she died the next November. His epitaph in the South Parish Burying Ground reads:

BORN IN BOSTON A SLAVE

DIED IN ANDOVER A FREE MAN

FEB 23, 1826

MUCH RESPECTED AS A SENSIBLE,

AMIABLE AND UPRIGHT MAN

For geologists, Pomp's Pond (Ballard Pond in early records), represents one of the best examples of a kettle hole in the area. Kettle holes are reminders of the Ice Age and mark where glacial masses of ice covered by sand and gravel formed holes as the ice melted.

Before electric refrigerators, harvesting ice from ponds was an important local industry and Pomp's was one of several ponds that provided ice for Andover homes in the late 19th and early 20th centuries. On July 16, 1920, the Boston Missionary Society opened Camp Andover for city children at the north end of the pond on land rented from one Homer Foster, a descendant of Rose's former owner. The Malden Boy Scout Camp occupied the south end of Pomp's Pond in the summer of 1921. The *Andover Townsman* of August 19, 1921 featured Camp Manning Stunt Night here. Camp Andover opened its 1922 season with two new dormitories and an infirmary. Two new diamonds were laid out and the facility boasted a new float and diving board. A "hut-shaped house with a log cabin look" served as the administration building. The Boy Scouts also enjoyed six regulation tents and a cook shack. Camp Andover Field Days wound up each season. The following year, Camp Andover opened with two new buildings, including a small house equipped for nature study and an expanded dining room.

Foster offered his property to the town in 1923 and the *Townsman* offered subscriptions to raise funds so that a clearing could be made for a sandy beach. Nine hundred and thirty-one dollars was raised, enough to also purchase a raft, hire two lifeguards and build a bath house. Pomp's Pond opened to the public August 3, 1923 with "supervised swimming assured." Camp Naulauka was also in session that year, while boys and girls continued to attend Camp Andover, although at different times.

In 1947, the town purchased eight additional acres of Foster land and in 1963, bought the former scout camp to create Recreation Park with modern sanitary facilities and tennis courts. The Cross Coal Company cleaned out its open truck each summer and picked up children all over town to take them to Pomp's Pond for a swim, bringing them back home in the late afternoon. This generous community practice continued until World War II gas rationing. Beginning in 1940, the Girl Scouts Council of Greater Lawrence established Camp Maud Eaton here. Pomp's Pond is now part of what is commonly referred to as Rec Park and contains tennis courts, a skating rink, playing fields and a picnic area. ∞

PRINTERS INC.

A small print shop, operated by Ames and Parker, existed in Andover as early as 1798. Eliphalet Pearson's plans for the new theological seminary included the production of theological textbooks, sermons, and religious tracts to disseminate the message of Orthodox Calvinism throughout the world. The Andover Press began when Mark Newman resigned as principal of Phillips Academy to become a bookseller to the school and seminary and built a shop on the academy grounds. Dr. Pearson set up a printing press on the second floor of Newman's "Old Hill Store." From 1813 until 1832, the business was run by Abraham Gould and Timothy Flagg, staunch supporters of the seminary and active members of South Parish Church. Both had served apprenticeships with professional printers in other towns and were committed to using their press to further the Protestant Christian faith. They also provided Phillips Academy and Seminary students with text books and school supplies. Publications of the New England Tract Society, founded in 1814, which in 1825, expanded into the American Tract Society, were produced here. *The Boston Recorder*, the first religious newspaper in the country, originated off these presses.

All of the procedures for writing, type-setting, printing, and bookbinding were done on Andover Hill. "Book Row," the handsome houses of Flagg, Gould, and their bookbinder, Jonathan Leavitt, still stand at 234, 239, and 244 South Main Street.

The *Journal of Humanity* (1829-1833), the first temperance newspaper published in the United States, was produced on Andover's presses. Learned treatises, books on Christian education, and sermons flowed from the professors' pens. Seminary-trained missionaries had to learn to communicate to natives in foreign lands in unfamiliar tongues. Some professors became typesetters since they alone had knowledge of the foreign languages needed. In 1813, Professor Moses Stuart personally set type for his *Hebrew Grammar*, hanging over the compositor day after day to get it right. This is considered the first volume with Hebrew font ever published in the United States.

The Andover Press also printed the first books in the country in Greek. By 1829, books were being printed here in eleven Oriental languages, some of which had never before been seen by Americans. Lexicons, dictionaries and grammars were published so the Bible and religious tracts could be translated into many languages. An ad in the *Andover Advertiser* from the 1850s lists samples of "Specimens of Type Available: Ethiopic, Coptic, Armenian, Arabic, Syriac, Samaritan, Rabbinic, German, Hebrew and two versions of Greek." Missionaries sent from the Seminary to all parts of the world brought back native languages from Asia and Africa, and published more dictionaries and translations. Some developed written alphabets which had not previously existed. By 1878, Cherokee, Choctaw, Tamil, Chinese, Japanese, and Turkish, as well as several African tongues had been added to the bookseller's list.

In 1832, the press moved to a brick building on the Hill. After Timothy Flagg's death, the enterprise was run by Gould and Mark H. Newman, son of the original owner. Warren Draper, publisher and bookseller, ran the business from 1854, later moving it downtown on Main Street. He began publishing the *Andover Advertiser* in 1853.

The Andover Press was twice robbed while Draper was proprietor and he narrowly escaped death at the hands of another burglar. Draper anticipated another break-in and his pistol was on the table, but it was seized by the burglar. A scuffle ensued and the pistol went off, covering the editor's face with gunpowder. The robber was caught and sent to state prison. He was also suspected of having set fire to the Old Stone Academy or Teachers' Seminary on the Hill and Punchard school house.

In 1887, Warren Draper sold the Andover Press to a corporation of local businessmen who named John N. Cole, editor, treasurer and business manager. Cole immediately began publishing the *Andover Townsman*, and since times had changed, his emphasis focused on local news rather than on theology, foreign languages, and temperance. By 1906, the Andover Press had its own building at Main and Chestnut with a bookstore in the front and type-setting and press in the rear. Cole's sons took over the business in 1922. In the early twentieth century and through the 1930s, the Andover Press printed yearbooks for Harvard, Yale, M.I.T., and prep schools throughout the Northeast.

It is estimated that some 400,000 circulars and books by seminary professors were published by the Andover Press, including a number by their wives and daughters, who dared to write fiction. Andover imprints helped gain the town an international reputation for scholarship and made it the recognized center of orthodox religious thought and Biblical research. The most important artifacts remaining of Andover's world renown printing past are the books themselves, published between 1800 and 1840. The religious beliefs, educational philosophies, missionary experiences and accomplishments of their authors are still accessible on printed pages. The books themselves testify to the fervor of the authors and publishers to get their evangelical message into print.

The Andover Press closed in 1960 when Cole's sons sold the bookstore to Jerome Cross of Cross Coal Company, who used the space formerly used for printing to expand their book line. It is highly appropriate that the Museum of Printing was established in North Andover in 2000, since printing and publishing have enjoyed such a long and significant history here. ∞

NIIJIMA JOE—1843–1890
FIRST JAPANESE IN ANDOVER

❧

American visitors to Japan are sometimes greeted by Japanese hosts with the puzzling question, "Niijima Joe? Do you know?"

Shimeta Niijima, Anglicized to Neesima, was born in 1843 at Edo (Tokyo) into the samurai or warrior class and grew up in the home of a prince where his father served as steward. His father also ran a school in the house for boys and girls of the upper class and here, the boy learned to read and write. As a teenager, Niijima served as the prince's scribe. The boy's dream of Western culture first took root when he found a copy of a United States atlas and read a Bible secreted into Japan by Chinese Christian missionaries.

"I read the atlas so many times and I wondered so much as my brain would melt out from my head," he later wrote. His thirst for knowledge, especially of Western ways, seemed insatiable. Even in the calligraphy he produced as a student, the boy's restless nature and hunger for freedom was evident. In sumi-e ink and delicate brush on rice paper, in elegant Kanji, he expressed a "desire to fly away," and said "I want to be a wild tiger in the field rather than a pet cat…I cried out myself: Why does Japanese government not let us be freely? Why let us be as a bird in a cage or a rat in a bag?"

Japan had locked itself away from the rest of the world, forbidding foreign trade, Christianity, and international exchange for over three hundred years. Although the Black Ships of Commodore Matthew Perry had pried the country open for trade by 1854, the country's isolationist laws continued to ban all foreign travel for ordinary Japanese citizens. The penalty for taking a trip outside Japan was death. Signs posted in coastal villages and port towns threatened: 'Anyone who secretly enters into a ship and is later detected will be put to death.' "I was afraid the savage country's law, which if I read the Bible, government will cross whole my family." Yet the young man would soon trade his samurai sword for a copy of the New Testament in Chinese.

Neeshima became the first Japanese to travel to Boston and the first to come to Andover. He was also the first Japanese to graduate from a U. S. college and the first ordained a Christian minister.

The Nineteenth Century

In 1865, twenty-one-year-old Shimeta (his name translates to "lucky," or "you made it!") made his way to the Port of Hakodate in Northern Japan and stowed away on an American ship bound home by way of Shanghai. With Japanese customs officers aboard the vessel, the captain hid the runaway in a cabin stateroom until the brig was under sail. However, the captain was fired from his post for helping a Japanese escape. He was replaced by a Captain Taylor who sailed *The Wild Rover* into Boston Harbor. Taylor gave Neeshima his nickname on the voyage over. When the young man introduced himself as Neesima Shimeta, Captain Taylor replied, "I shall call you Joe."

Captain Taylor taught him navigation skills and the self-exiled young man earned his passage by calculating the ship's position on charts, pulling ropes, and waiting on the captain's table. "I passed through many thousand miles of water very safely, without hurricane, tempest, or any trouble," Neeshima later wrote.

The Wild Rover belonged to Alpheus Hardy, who also happened to be member and chairman of the board of trustees of Phillips Academy and Andover Theological Seminary from 1858-1887. He was also a state senator and board member of the American Board of Foreign Missions. Hardy, who lived in Boston, also had a home at Andover. He was so impressed with the Japanese youth's determination that he became "Joe's" sponsor and sent him to Phillips Academy. Alpheus Hardy and his wife became "Joe's" American father and mother and he soon changed his name to Joseph Hardy Neesima after his patron.

He boarded at 17 Hidden Road with Mary Hidden and her brother, a local architect who was then in poor health. "We find Joseph a gentleman and it is to our shame as a Christian community that we are not more in advance of this heathen brought to our own door…We have made him a regular member of the family…" The Hidden's only other student boarder was Ehraim Flint, Jr., who attended the Seminary. Flint and his wife tutored the Japanese student in English and mathematics. "Although I have taught for years, I have never been so interested in any other pupil," Flint later wrote.

Neeshima completed his studies at Phillips Academy in 1867 and though he still struggled with the English language, went on to Amherst where he became that college's first Asian student. "I was a kind of novelty to them because they had never seen any Japanese. I was invited out to dinners and tea, and was asked by them so many questions." Following graduation from Amherst, Neeshima came back to Andover to attend Seminary with the Class of 1874. By the time he returned to Japan, his native country had relaxed its laws and Christianity was legal. He was no longer "a runaway boy" who felt he had to "hide as law-breaker of government."

In 1875, with $5000 donated by American supporters Neesima established Doshisha Eigokko School in Kyoto with eight students. Doshisha means "shared ideals," or "organization for people who share the same hope." The university's mission was to teach Japanese youth the ways of democracy and Christianity.

Neesima traveled throughout Japan, the United States, and Europe, raising funds for his new college. He frequently met with hostility from fellow Japanese who did not wish to see their country modernized or influenced by Western ways. In 1923, Doshisha became the first college in Japan to admit females and also included a training school for nurses. It remains one of Japan's finest educational institutions.

"Niijima Joe" is revered by Japanese as the initiator of modern education who first brought the freedom of thought to their country. He is the hero who risked his life to learn about democracy in order to teach its principles to his own people. Neeshima's memorial on the Phillips Academy campus quotes his favorite motto, which is also that of Doshisha University, "Come, all exuberant youth who cherish living by your conscience." Japanese who visit New England inevitably make their "Niishima-Joe" pilgrimages to Andover. ❧

A TOWN DIVIDED

On February 15, 1854, the editor of the *Andover Advertiser* noted that "Present movements seen to indicate that the time has arrived, which has been long anticipated, that our large and ancient town should be divided into two…Manufacturing villages are multiplying and the population shifting…so that often a large portion of the people find themselves remote from the place of public meetings."

Since 1781, town meetings had been held alternately in North and South Parishes. When it was the South's turn to host, the crowded meetings were held at the Boston & Maine Railroad Depot or Henry Barnard's furniture warehouse. From 1843, letters appeared in the *Andover Advertiser* complaining of lack of space at these meetings and the need for a town hall, lamenting the good old days when voters could be comfortably seated at meetings held in churches.

> *…we have to stand, bolt upright—5 or 600 men, stowed as thick as stalks in a field of rye, for four or five hours; and in consequence of the noise and confusion occasioned by the moving about and conversation of those who can neither see nor hear or care but little about what is going on, four fifths of the voters are unable to get near enough to the moderator to hear what subject may be under consideration. The result is that most of the town business is generally done up by about forty or fifty citizens who go early and that their stand near the moderator's desk.*

Although having a town high school was a state requirement, citizens could not agree where it should be located and refused to raise the necessary funds. Then, at his death in 1850, South Parish resident Benjamin Punchard left $50,000 for the establishment of a free high school there. North Parish residents were disgruntled because the town would not support a high school in their end of town. Some even went so far as to petition General Court to set off the Merrimack School District to the new City of Lawrence.

At the annual town meeting held March 6, 1854, citizens voted 401 to 102 on the question "Is it expedient to divide the town according to the boundary line between the North and South Parishes?" Apparently this vote was not binding as a group from North Parish subsequently appointed a committee "to further *strenuously* oppose the division of the town." The debate would continue over several years. *Andover Advertisers* during this time are filled with editorials and heated letters, as well as announcements of meetings to discuss the pros and cons of division of the town. "Shouldn't North Parish get to keep the name Andover, since it was the original settlement?…Who should care for the town paupers?…Where should fire-fighting apparatus be housed?"

Gayton Osgood of North Parish, a respected lawyer and congressman, finally stood up at one meeting held at North Parish Church that "the men of South Parish had acted honorably" and that he for one, "liked the name North Andover." South and West Parishes paid North $500 for the right to keep the name Andover.

The Act of Separation to divide the Town of Andover and incorporate the Town of North Andover was passed by state legislature April 7, 1855. The governor appointed a committee to correct any inequities rising from separation."

According to this Act, South Parish "relinquished all right, title, and interest in two fire engines, called the *Cochichawicke* and the *Merrimack*, now located in North Andover, together with equipments and house contained therewith." North Parish also kept *The Lion* (Hunneman #194) owned by Nathaniel Stevens for the protection of his textile mill, while South got to keep the hand tub known as *The Shawshin*.

Students from North Parish would be permitted to attend the South's new Punchard High School at no charge until the time a high school could be built in North Andover. All towns were required by law to maintain facilities for the poor and indigent. Since Andover's alms house was located in the South end, it agreed to house North Andover's paupers until a new poor house could be built.

Since the day of the town's division, citizens have continued to argue over who had rights to the name of Andover. ∞

ANDOVER BUILDS A TOWN HOUSE

❧

Dedicated on December 30, 1858, Andover's Town House was the first public building erected after the division. Theodore Voelchers, a Cambridge architect, designed the Romanesque Revival building, while local builders Abbot and Clement constructed it for a total of $15,500. The local newspaper heralded the new edifice as "substantial, beautiful, and commodious…an honor to the Town."

The first story was divided into rooms for selectmen, town treasurer, a post office and a room "suitable for an office or store." On the second story, there was a "spacious hall" with a gallery and four ante rooms.

The building was in continual use with temperance meetings and political rallies regularly held here. The Hutchinson Family singers performed here, as they had at William Jenkins' House on several occasions. Originally from New Hampshire, these four brothers and a sister, traveled the country singing songs of abolition and temperance. Frederick Douglass lectured at the Town House October 31, 1865 on "The Assassination of Lincoln and Its Lessons." The building was the happening place in town with annual George Washington Balls, Robert Burns Nights, Police and Firemen's Balls, and school graduations. On March 21, 1919, red, white, and blue bunting was draped across the upstairs hall to welcome back Andover's men and women who served in World War I.

For some years, the local police station was located here, as was the school superintendent's office. In 1882, the town voted to add an extension and contracted with Abbot and Jenkins to furnish all materials and do the job for $6,250. Renovations for clubs and parties now included cooking facilities, running water, and stage curtains. The lobby, with its ornamental winding staircase, was designed in 1902, and the mosaic town seal installed at the front entrance.

During the "urban renewal" fever of the early 'sixties, many citizens were in favor of demolishing this building which they considered outdated. Razing this "eyesore" would make way for a mini-mall and widen Main Street. Others, dedicated to preserving Andover's architectural heritage, and led by Andover Historical Society, united in efforts to raise both funds and consciences. In 1987, the people of Andover voted $2.6 million for renovation of the Old Town House and hired Ann Beha

Associates. Saving this building represented a major milestone in Andover's commitment to historic preservation. The Old Town Hall rededication ceremonies took place on Founders' Day, May 6 and May 7, 1989, with a community pancake breakfast, old-fashioned spelling bee, an art exhibit by the Andover Artists' Guild, an art auction and dramatic production—the same sort of activities that took place during the building's heyday of the late nineteenth century. ∾

THE CIVIL WAR CAME
"LIKE A WHIRLWIND"

❧

Partisan politics prompted many an Andover parade. When Lincoln was elected President in 1860, all the church bells rang out and citizens lighted bonfires in their front yards. Lanterns were strung all over town and Lincoln-Hamlin campaign banners, proclaiming "Free Soil, Free Speech, Free Labor, and Free Men" were draped from windows. Letters, strung together to spell *Veritas Vincit—Truth Wins* filled the front windows of Bartlet Hall on the Hill. The *Andover Advertiser*, November 10, 1860, describes the cavalcade of carriages, some pulled by horses decked out in flags, while the Andover Brass Band followed behind six mounted policemen. Roman candles and rockets climaxed these celebrations in "a brilliant display." By going for Abraham Lincoln, Andover made its stand against slavery. Yet it was a bittersweet victory, for as Harriet Beecher Stowe warned, "We are getting ready for a gale."

Andover author and social reformer, Elizabeth Stuart Phelps, was a seventeen-year-old student when, "War came crashing into our normal life, destroying all balance and beauty…It was April of the year 1861 and a dull morning at school. The girls have the Boston newspapers. They are reading the headlines lazily, aware that an educated person must be well-informed. Suddenly, one girl, very young and pretty, grabs the paper and whirls it overhead. She dances around the room, laughing and chanting "War's begun! War's begun!"

In her autobiography written many years later, Phelps explained Andover's intense patriotism. "Andover was no more loyal than other towns, but the presence of so many young men who passed the years from 1861 to 1865 upon the Hill brought the war closer."

According to the *Andover Advertiser* of April 27, 1861, "The largest and most spirited meeting ever held in Andover" assembled at the Town House on April 20. "The Spirit of 1776 was fully aroused…" when the Andover Brass Band played and Professor Calvin Stowe delivered a rousing speech. Smith and Dove Manufacturers John and Peter Smith and John Dove, pledged funds for the cause. Justice Marcus Morton, Jr., a Massachusetts Supreme Court judge who lived in Andover, Oliver H. Perry, son of the naval hero, and John Dove also addressed the crowd.

Before the end of April, 1861, according to the *Andover Advertiser*, Andover women were meeting daily at South Church to make garments and prepare bandages, while Abbot Academy girls got right to work sewing red braid upon blue flannel shirts and making gray caps, as well as flannel drawers, towels, needle cases, and knitted stockings for the recruits.

A committee of twenty-five was appointed to decide on Andover's response to President Lincoln's call for troops. The Andover Light Infantry was formed during the first week of the war. On the 4th of May, Professor Stowe acted as moderator at a special town meeting where "it was voted to provide a uniform for each volunteer; to remit each soldier's poll tax for a year; and to pay $8 per month to the volunteers' families." Enlisted men would earn fifty cents for each day's drill. At the request of Andover citizens, a recruiting office was immediately opened at Town House. On May 19th, Calvin Stowe prayed before the newly-formed Andover Light Infantry Company and delivered a rousing patriotic speech, "Endure hardship as a good soldier."

"A large gathering of citizens" attended the flag raising on Andover Hill June 4th. "...the Andover Light Infantry arrived in their new, very neat and appropriate uniform, and with the Phillips Guards and the Havelock Greys went through a short drill..." Speeches and prayers were presented by several seminary professors and events concluded with the singing of a *Banner Song*, written for the occasion by Harriet Beecher Stowe.

On June 22nd, outside South Church, Phillips Academy students presented a white silk banner to the Light Infantry. Franklin Pierce, in Andover to visit his wife's relatives, attended the ceremony. The newspaper noted that "the former President has now become a staunch Union supporter."

On the 24th, the ex-President joined the citizens' assembly in front of Town House where the Andover Light Infantry, led by Captain Horace Holt, had assembled to depart for Fort Warren in Boston Harbor. The infantrymen were ceremoniously escorted to Andover Railroad Depot by the Ellsworth Guards of Phillips Academy and the Havelock Grays from Andover Theological Seminary.

The Andover Light Infantry was renamed Company H, 14th Regiment, Massachusetts Volunteer Infantry on July 5th and mustered into service for three years with nine other Essex County companies.

By August 7th, the 14th Regiment had departed Fort Warren, ordered to Washington to be stationed at forts along the Potomac River. On January 1st, 1862, the War Department changed Company H Regiment from infantry to Heavy Artillery with an increase of fifty men to each company. On September 20th, 1862 the Regiment was dispatched to Harper's Ferry, for garrison duty.

The *Andover Advertiser* of July 11, 1863 reported that "the Capture of Vicksburg by Union troops on July 3, 1863, following a forty-five day siege, brought jubilation to Andover with the pealing of church bells and ringing of all the bells on the Hill by students...Anyone who possessed a banner put it out and public demonstrations of joy with cannons, guns, and snappers went on into the night. The young ladies of Abbot Female Seminary took turns ringing the house bell and sang patriotic songs until late in the evening, accompanied by hearty applause from the neighborhood."

There was no such joy when the Andover Regiment first confronted the Rebels in combat in the Wilderness and at Spottsylvania, Virginia on May 19, 1864. Townspeople were shocked by the losses and a committee was immediately sent to Virginia to assess local causalities. Of the eighty Andover men who fought in this battle, eight died on the battlefield; eighteen were wounded; three died in the hospital; three were taken prisoner, two of whom died at Andersonville.

Activities on the home front became increasing practical and serious rather than patriotic fanfare. According to the *Andover Advertiser*, "Different religious societies in town have held meetings and have been preparing clothing, lint, bandages, and such articles as are generally used in cases of sickness and wounds. They meet weekly at the Town House where they put together boxes of articles, together with other appropriate things as people are disposed to contribute. Bottles of wine, fruit, jellies, dried apples, pickles, preserves, fans, and any articles that would be used in sickness at home, may be sent."

Five hundred and ninety-nine Andover men served in the Civil War. Fifty served in the Navy and the rest in the Army. Lieutenant Colonel Horace Holt was Andover's highest ranking officer. Fifty-three soldiers from Andover died, many in field hospitals from their wounds or, like sixteen-year-old Walter Raymond, of disease and starvation in Confederate prisons. Charles Barnard was released from Andersonville but died on the way back home to Andover. Robert Rollins served in the 54th Massachusetts Infantry, the "Brave Black Glory" Regiment under Colonel Robert Shaw and is buried in South Church Cemetery.

Calvin and Harriet Beecher Stowe, who had so fervently supported the war effort, learned by reading the *Andover Advertiser* that their son had been wounded in the Battle of Gettysburg. Frederick Stowe had taken shrapnel in his ear and eventually returned to Andover.

In spite of the support of family and friends, Frederick Stowe never recovered his physical or mental health. He returned to Harvard but dropped out and his drunken behavior embarrassed his older sisters. His mother claimed that "Freddie" drank to ease the constant pain in his head. A decade later, after sailing around Cape Horn, Frederick Stowe disappeared forever. It was reported he was last seen along the waterfront in San Francisco. ∞

THE GATES AJAR

"I was hardly the only woman in America then forced to wear life bravely," wrote Elizabeth Stuart Phelps.

> *My grief grew into sympathy for the hundreds of thousands of bereaved women who suffered with me—the helpless, unconsulted women, whom war had trampled down without choice or protest; the patient, domestic women who thought little but loved much, and loving, had lost all. Like those factory girls of Abbot Village and Lawrence, the great mass of American women are powerless to participate directly in the political affairs that governed their lives... I wished to say something that would comfort the women devastated by the deaths of their loved ones, whose misery crowded this land. Into this world of woe, my little book went forth.*

Elizabeth Stuart Phelps was only twenty-four when her book *The Gates Ajar* was published in 1868. Its success "made the author the most astonished girl in North America!" She had actually worked on the book for four years, beginning it after the Phillips Academy graduate and Union soldier she'd planned to marry, succumbed to illness after fighting in the Battle of Antietam.

Phelps' protagonist, Mary Cabot, loses her faith after her brother's death in battle. Like its author, Mary "could not bear the condolences of well-meaning friends" and was "infuriated by the church deacon's pious words." Phelps' fictional character is comforted by an aunt who assures her that Heaven is an actual place where mothers continue to bring up new children, neighbors enjoy chatty reunions, and professors discover celestial libraries.

The granddaughter of Andover Seminary's leading theologian and scholar, the Reverend Moses Stuart, Phelps was raised in the house on Main Street that is still the home of Phillips Academy's Head of School. She was the eldest child and only daughter of Austin Phelps, Professor of Sacred Rhetoric and Homiletics, who later became Seminary president. Elizabeth attended Abbot Academy where she claims she "received a sound education in mathematics, languages, the sciences, and literature." Then she enrolled in Jerusha Billings Edwards' School for Young Ladies which the well educated widow of a seminary professor ran in her home. At *The Nunnery*, (as this school was nicknamed by the Phillips Academy and Seminary students to distinguish it from *Fem Sem*, which was Abbot Academy), Mrs. Edwards' students pursued the same subjects as their brothers at college, with the exception of Greek and trigonometry, considered beyond the scope of the female intellect. Mental philosophy, astronomy, and English literature were Elizabeth's favorites. Her father encouraged her studies, as well as her writing and her first work was published in *Youth's Companion* when she was thirteen years old.

In *The Gates Ajar* the author replaced stern Calvinist theology with a romantic view of the Hereafter where the dead retained their earthly personalities and continued to pursue favorite activities. Phelps offered a vision of the afterlife as a place filled with gardens and dogs; children could still nibble ginger cookies; and pianos waited to be played. There would be crops for farmers to harvest and machines for mechanics to work on and women would enjoy professional opportunities closed to them on earth due to gender.

The Gates Ajar went through twenty editions in its first year of publication, was translated into fourteen different languages and brought Phelps letters from around the world for the next thirty years. Of all the books published in the nineteenth century, only *Uncle Tom's Cabin* by her Andover neighbor, Harriet Beecher Stowe, sold more copies. Hymn writers borrowed the title and before long, there was a patent medicine, a cigar, and a man's collar, as well as a floral design for funeral wreaths, called *Gates Ajar*.

Not all the letters Phelps received were complimentary. The Seminary fathers including her own, repudiated Phelps' personal interpretation of their orthodox theology. Some religious conservatives called *The Gates Ajar* "pure blasphemy" and "waged a religious war over my notions of the afterlife as if I were some evil spirit let loose to destroy the established church. I had dared to challenge the Heaven preached by Calvinist clergy, with my fictional version. I had outraged conventional theology with my crime of heresy."

However, everything Phelps wrote after *The Gates Ajar* was published and eagerly read. She eventually authored fifty-seven books, including fiction for children and poetry, as well as numerous essays on women's issues. Yet nothing else sold as many copies nor captured the public imagination as did her first book, whose appearance clearly coincided with the country's need.

When it was published, the editor of *The Congregationalist* noted, "Miss Phelps has made $20,000 from *The Gates Ajar* and at that rate, she won't be likely to shut them!" ∞

SPIRITUALISM IN SEMINARY TOWN

Seances were a popular parlor activity throughout the mid and late nineteenth century. "Spiritual telegrams," rappings, and other methods of communication with the dead provided proof to believers of afterlife in an era of increasing religious doubt. President Pierce's wife spoke with her dead sons through mediums while staying in Andover, just as Mary Todd Lincoln communicated with her own poor, dead boys in the White House. After the severe losses sustained in the recent Civil War, Spiritualism provided communication with those loved ones who had already "crossed over."

It was not something one talked about publicly, particularly if you lived in the shadow of Andover Theological Seminary. Spiritualists, who often called themselves Societies of Free Thinkers, found theirs a liberating faith without the hierarchy and rigid dogma of established churches. Spiritualists believed that after death individuals merely transformed from corporeal to spiritual beings but maintained their character-istics and earthly interests. Those who had "crossed over" communicated with loved ones left behind if the living would only open the "Gates."

John Russell, an Andover shoemaker, who had lost a son to "the gloomy grave," was one. "You ask me about Spiritualism in Andover," Russell wrote in a letter now in the Andover Historical Society archives.

> *Well Brother I will tell you. You know that old Andover is the headquarters of Orthodoxy and of course, the churches are fervent in strength here perhaps more than in most other places for these officers are quite watchful and not willing there should be any light, only what shines through them. But, there are quite a number of investigators of this new light and of ministering spirits to give us cheer and to comfort all those who have counsel...There are quite a number of mediums here. We meet once in a while but not regularly. But in Lawrence, only three miles from here, they have regular meetings on Sundays and there is quite a large attendance and a good deal of interest manifested and a number of very good trances...Oh, Brother, won't it be blessed to die knowing as we do that after we have thrown off this mortal life, we shall be again united to the loved ones over who have passed the dark river before us, and to have mansions prepared for our entrance into the Land of Souls...Let us keep our lamps trimmed and burn-ing and be as servants waiting for the coming of their torch.*

Harriet Beecher Stowe considered Spiritualism "a reaction to the intense materialism of the present age. My mind remains open to that Other World," she wrote. Harriet was particularly fond of the planchette which was a triangular wooden board on casters with a pencil attached to produce spirit writing that spelled out messages from departed souls. No medium was required to operate the planchette and it was all the rage after the Civil War. "Although I am not able to experience psychic phenomenon as my husband can, I keep my mind open," Harriet said.

Calvin Stowe had been subject to "spiritual manifestations" all his life. He heard voices, saw things that weren't there, and sensed premonitions. "Every house I occupy has a different set of phantoms. I have always seen a multitude of animated objects—even heard them rustle, although I could never touch them. They passed through floors, ceiling and walls. He called them his "aerial visitors" or "blue devils" and while, some were kind, others were quite sinister."

After the children were asleep, Harriet and Calvin would often sit before the portrait of Calvin's first wife and her late friend. The first Mrs. Stowe had died in Cincinnati at the age of twenty-five and Harriet had Eliza Tyler's portrait painted from a photograph as a twentieth wedding anniversary gift for Calvin and it hung in his second floor study in their Andover home. Upon receiving this gift, Calvin had written Harriet appreciatively, "I sit and look at it and feel perfectly satisfied that the doctrine of resurrection must be true and there is already an angel in Heaven looking like this."

After their eldest son, Henry, a student at Dartmouth, drowned, Harriet had his portrait painted too. "Every time I go in or out of the room, Henry's portrait seems to give so bright a smile that I think a spirit dwells within it." There were other spiritual signs from "Golden Henry." The seal ring which was his mother's gift when Henry went off to college mysteriously split across his name on the day he died. And then, there was Henry's guitar, the cords of which would suddenly start strumming as if a hand had been drawn across all the strings at once, when there was no one was in his room.

Harriet investigated Spiritualism more enthusiastically after Henry's death and consulted mediums in order to communicate with her son. She made it clear however, that she would not be convinced "by raps and squeaks and tricks with tables, but would only communicate with the dead through an unquestionable angel." From Europe, where she also heard guitar strings, Harriet wrote her husband at Andover: "What think you? Have you had any more manifestations, any truths from the spirit world?" She suggested "the vibration of that mysterious guitar" in the Stone Cabin might be Calvin's first wife instead of their Henry. "Eliza's spirit has ever seemed to cling to that mode of manifestation, and if you would keep the guitar in your sleeping room, no doubt you would hear from it oftener."

Harriet and the Quaker poet, John Greenleaf Whittier, sat up many a night discussing spiritual manifestations, table-rappings, and trying to encourage the appearance of ghosts. "Much as I have wooed them, they never appear to me," Whittier remarked. "Mrs. Stowe is more fortunate—the spirits sometimes come at her bidding, but never at mine—and what wonder? It would be a foolish spirit that did not prefer her company to that of an old man like me.

Elizabeth Stuart Phelps had grown up hearing family tales of poltergeists in her grandfather Phelps' Stratford, Connecticut parsonage. Spoons, nails, and candlesticks were bent and broken; writing appeared in mysterious languages on the walls; sheets would not remain locked in their cupboard and the minister's clothing was found stuffed with straw. Turnips dropped from the ceiling and were carved with bizarre designs. Phelps would turn this family tale of spiritual phenomena into several short stories.

Her mother, also a published author, died when Phelps was eight. Her baby brother was baptized beside the mother's coffin, according to her wish. "The western sun had stolen into the windows of the sad room and slanting across in one long ray, sought out and rested upon the portrait of the deceased. The little girl was convinced she had seen her mother's soul and remained interested in psychic phenomena for the rest of her life. ∞

MEMORIAL HALL LIBRARY

❧

On a European tour John Smith, founder of Smith and Dove Manufacturing Company was particularly impressed by the public library at Dresden, Germany. He was convinced that such an institution was the means of educating the people of any country. Smith once said he attributed his family's good fortune to his brother Peter, who when a weaver in Glasgow, Scotland "sat beside a good man who lent him books." Smith wrote to his son back in Andover, proposing that a reading room and public library be built on the site where several buildings had recently burned in the center of town, to honor the Andover men who gave their lives in the Civil War.

John Smith put up $25,000 for a public library and reading room with the stipulation that the town match the money. His business partners Peter Smith and John Dove contributed $12,000. John Byers donated $3000 in memory of his brother, Peter the first principal of Punchard High School, on condition that "the library be open at such hours as may be most convenient for working people." Local children collected pennies but funds were still short as the deadline approached. Raising the remainder seemed impossible until someone recalled that the town had set aside $4500 for a Civil War monument. The town then purchased the land from Herman Abbot. Nearly $63,000, raised from pledges, was used chiefly for the purchase of books.

Memorial Hall was built in the popular Second Empire style, complete with Mansard roof. An iron fence surrounded the front of the building to keep out wandering cows and pigs. The watering trough for horses out front even had a faucet and cup for drivers.

The Reverend Phillips Brooks, the well-known Boston clergyman who was a descendent of the town's first minister and regularly summered with his aunts in North Andover, delivered the speech for the dedication of the new building on May 30, 1873. Brooks noted that "the soldier and the scholar came forth together from the culture of our town…A powder-mill and a paper-mill were its two first industries, and the same gentle Shawsheen River turned the wheels of both." This clergyman's words describing Andover were soon adopted for the *Andover Townsman's* masthead: "Everywhere and always, first and last, she has been the manly, straight-forward, sober, patriotic New England town."

One wall of the library contains marble slabs with fifty-two names of those who died for the cause, with the year, place and manner of their deaths. Cemented into the cornerstone is a copper box containing another list naming all the Andover men who served. "They did not merely clear the field of treason," according to the Reverend Phillips Brooks. "By the same labor they built up a new possibility of national character and life."

Memorial Hall Library, both the building and its services, has undergone many changes since it opened. Two canons, once on the lawn, were removed for scrap iron during World War II. As demands for library services outgrew space, four different additions were made in the twentieth century. A Colonial Revival style roof was added in 1927, along with a children's reading room with a separate entrance. This was enlarged in 1961 and a reading room addition was completed five years later. In 1967 the library was designated the Eastern Massachusetts subregional center for thirty-seven cities and towns.

On October 30, 1988, the library was rededicated following three and one half years of major expansion that included a rear wing addition to the renovated original structure. This doubled the space for patrons and allowed the incorporation of the latest in technological equipment. In the 'nineties Memorial Hall Library threw out its old card catalogs and joined the computer age on the "information superhighway," providing its patrons access to the world-wide web and the latest in informational resources. It is an inter-library loan center and the regional reference and research library collections center for three hundred and eleven libraries in fifty-five communities of the Northeast Massachusetts Regional Library System (NMRLS). Memorial Hall Library is the largest library in the thirty-five member Merrimack Valley Library Consortium, an automated network of libraries serving communities in the area. Member libraries use this integrated system for circulation, cataloging, public access catalog, on-line interlibrary loans, acquisitions, and Internet connection to an online periodical database via the Internet.

The most recent innovation is the Teen-Z Room which provides separate space for young people grades six through twelve. This space on the main floor is wired and teenagers can check out laptop computers and young adult novels, log-on, watch films on DVD, listen to CDs, do their homework, or just "hang out." Most teenagers consider Memorial Hall Library "a cool place." John Smith would likely be flabbergasted, but no doubt, quite pleased. ∞

THE ANDOVER VILLAGE IMPROVEMENT SOCIETY PIONEER IN CONSERVATION

❧

The rapid industrial progress that brought financial success to entrepreneurs and industrialists as well as labor-saving conveniences to the lives of Americans in the nineteenth century also created disturbing side effects. Some Andover residents wondered if all this new technology was really worth the loss of the town's pastoral character. They considered the natural environment a basic human need; a walk along a wooded path, essential to the mental and physical well-being of all.

The birth of the Andover Village Improvement Society in 1894 was Andover's response to the growing national outcry over the loss of the natural environment in the race for material progress. Abraham Marland, founder of Marland Mills, said he came to Andover so that "I might have elbow room for my children." That "elbow room" was fast disappearing.

At the turn of the twentieth century, building codes and zoning laws were non-existent. Careless dumping of garbage and waste from back porches into yards or beside roads, was commonplace. Droppings of horses and oxen cluttered streets and sidewalks were few and far between. Broadsides and bill boards covered store fronts and public buildings and littering was rampant.

"Does Andover care to preserve its natural beauties?" Sarah Nelson Carter asked in a letter to the *Andover Townsman*. As former innkeepers at Mansion House, then at the Stowe House hostelry, she and her husband heard complaints from out of town visitors who said, "We don't want to go to Andover now. You have spoiled all those charming drives that we loved so well…Roadsides have been so mutilated that they are noticeable for unsightliness rather than beauty.'

A public announcement to organize a Village Improvement Society appeared in the *Andover Townsman* on April 27, 1894.

> *An effort is being made to form in Andover an organization, the object of which shall be the planting of shade trees, the protection of those already planted, the reclaiming and care of unsightly spots. No one who feels an interest in this work may be deterred from becoming a helper.*

> *(signed) IMPROVEMENT.*

Seventy citizens joined to found the Andover Village Improvement Society at the meeting held two days later. Represented were local businessmen, clergy, publishers, professors from Phillips and Abbot Academies, the Theological Seminary, public school teachers, as well as manufacturers from Andover's textile and rubber factories. Women had a prominent role from the beginning, holding offices in this new organization. All seemed eager to sign up as volunteers for "spade and shovel work."

From its birth, the Andover Village Improvement Society was committed to the preservation of the environment for future generations. "To have a beautiful town is not just a passing whim, a mere fad of this generation to be discarded in the next," said George Eaton, the Phillips Academy math teacher and AVIS president for thirteen years.

Society members and its volunteer work force have always been prepared for hard work and dirt under their fingernails. The involvement of students from Phillips Academy and Andover's public schools as well as scouts, has been ongoing and AVIS properties have long served teachers as outdoor classrooms. Throughout its history, AVIS has counted on energetic, enthusiastic young people to participate in town clean-ups, recycling efforts, bridge-building and trail-blazing. In the early years, youngsters were provided with seed packets to plant gardens and trees, competing for prizes. In 1913, the first prize went to a boy who "ever-so-carefully transplanted every single flower from his garden to the other side of town when his family moved."

Early AVIS members fought the brown-tail moth annually as those pests menaced local trees. Children collected nests and brought them to school to be counted and burned, receiving ten cents per caterpillar tent. A total of 159,000 tent caterpillar belts were turned in by Andover youngsters in 1909.

Throughout the 1920s, 30s, and 40s, AVIS efforts continued to focus upon beautification and cultivation. Roadsides, public buildings and squares, including the "unsightly" area around the railroad station, were planted with flowers and shrubs. Storekeepers and mill managers were encouraged to dispose of their debris, boxes, and barrels "anywhere except right outside their establishments." The Society organized periodic town clean-ups, inviting citizens to join in picking up litter. School children designed *Do Not Dump* and *Civic Pride* posters for roadsides and new rubbish barrels. In 1920, questionnaires entitled *Do You Love Your Town?* were mailed to every household in Andover.

As early as 1901, AVIS secretary Emma Lincoln wrote in her *Annual Report*: "The village improvement idea has made gratifying growth in our country in recent years. Americans are beginning to realize that the heritage of natural beauty which we have received must be passed on unimpaired. Hence the desire to secure woodlands, parks and other natural places for the benefit of posterity."

With the building boom that followed the Second World War, it became evident that green space was fast disappearing beneath concrete. In the mid-1950s, the Andover Village Improvement Society redefined itself. Saving open space for future generations became the organization's priority.

In 1956, AVIS established a Land Committee to: 1) acquire land for park and recreational use and 2) to acquire wetlands and marshes for the conservation of wildlife and life plant life in their natural state. This Land Committee would also prioritize parcels, concentrating on obtaining areas deemed particularly desirable for conservation, such as wetlands which were not practical to build on and thus, were less expensive and would not present as much competition from developers. Wetlands were also ecologically significant as natural flood control areas.

In March of 1957, AVIS' original charter was amended by state legislature to allow the Society to buy land. The Andover Village Improvement Society now went into the business of land acquisition. The following announcement was posted in storefronts and public buildings, delivered door to door or mailed to local homes:

DO YOU OWN WETLANDS, BACK WOODLANDS, OR ROCKY SLOPES?
ANDOVER VILLAGE IMPROVEMENT SOCIETY IS INTERESTED IN
BUYING SUCH LANDS TO KEEP PERMANENTLY FOR CONSERVATION.

In September, 1958, the Andover Village Improvement Society acquired Baker's Meadow, long revered by naturalists as a bird and wildlife sanctuary, as its first reservation under its new land acquisition program. "Andover Leads the Way to Land Protection," announced the *Christian Science Monitor*. With such public recognition AVIS became a model for other communities to preserve their own open spaces and natural habitants.

The town followed AVIS' leadership. At the 1957 town meeting, citizens appropriated $25,000 for the purchase of conservation lands, a number of which are presently linked to AVIS properties. On March 12, 1960, a town warrant was passed that created the Andover Conservation Commission. In March of 1967, the town voted to appropriate $250,000 towards the purchase of land for conservation.

An Ecological Action Committee, started by AVIS in the early '70s, focused on recycling, as well as organizing petitions and a letter writing campaign to get federal, state, and local environmental legislation passed.

The Society's warden system, an idea of committed board member, Claus Dengler, was established in 1971, whereby each AVIS reservation has a volunteer overseer who lives nearby and assumes responsibility for maintaining trails and public access points. Trails are maintained for passive recreation, often by students or scouts, who learn stewardship of the land, as did their young predecessors. As volunteers, whether earning scout badges or community service hours for their schools, young people continue to assist wardens, trustees, and volunteer AVIS members at cutting trails, building bridges, and laying walkways across swampy areas. Volunteers also periodically join community efforts to clean-up the Shawsheen and Merrimack Rivers, wading in to clear out muck and debris tossed there.

The Andover Village Improvement Society now maintains some twenty-three reservations encompassing more than 1,000 acres, with over thirty miles of trails, which belong to the people. AVIS' current goal is to make these lands more accessible to visitors by offering a range of activities relevant to the unique natural features of each property. The Society regularly sponsors walking tours, community cross-country ski trips, snow-shoeing treks, and canoe races on the Shawsheen River. Emphasis is on opening up the reservations for public enjoyment of wildlife and flora on a diversity of terrain ranging from granite cliffs, glacial eskers, to rivers and marshlands. ∞

HOW FOUR DETERMINED LADIES
SAVED INDIAN RIDGE

The winding, forested ridge in the center of South Parish that had been created by glacial deposits formed by the ice sheet that once covered the northern part of the continent, had long been a favorite Andover retreat. The name *Indian Ridge* dates back to the eighteenth century when arrowheads and other evidence of Native American presence was uncovered.

"It is broad and level at the top…Its sides are thickly covered with trees. As children, we firmly believed it to be a great mausoleum within which reposed the bones of vast Indian tribes," wrote Sarah Stuart Robbins, daughter of a seminary professor, who recalled playing there as a child. "Their dusky ghosts, we thought, haunted their resting place, and looked down frowningly upon us palefaces from the high tree tops, or stealthily glanced out from behind the old moss-covered trunks. I doubt whether you could have induced one of us to remain there after the shades of evening crept over the Ridge."

Physicians prescribed daily walks up Indian Ridge for healthy constitutions of their patients. Samuel Farrar, trustee and treasurer of Phillips Academy and Andover Seminary, called Indian Ridge "a panacea for every ill that flesh is heir to." Asked how he remained so vigorous into his 90s, Farrar replied, "I saw all my own wood. I work in my garden an hour every day and I have walked twice a day around Indian Ridge for fifty years." According to local historians, Farrar's strolls were so regular that townspeople set their clocks to the minute by his passing particular places. Indian Ridge's proximity to the crowded mill housing of Abbot and Marland Villages offered factory families the opportunity to retreat to nature.

By the mid-nineteenth century scientists were hotly discussing the new theory of glaciation. Many traveled to Andover to study glacial evidence in kettle holes and this 500-foot-high moraine created by the glacier's retreat at Indian Ridge. The British geologist, Sir Charles Lyell, visited Andover to study evidence of kames. President Hitchcock came from Amherst College while preparing his geological survey of Massachusetts in 1846.

The Reverend G. Frederick Wright, a former Free Church minister, a leading geologist and later, Professor of Harmony of Science and Revelation at Oberlin College, called Indian Ridge "the mesh which lifted the whole glacial net in North America."

Then, in 1896, as the town prepared to celebrate its 250th anniversary, developers threatened to destroy Andover's beloved hiking spot. Their plan called for the cutting of trees and use of the area for a sand and gravel pit. The Andover Village Improvement Society, formed just two years before, called an emergency meeting and rallied to save Indian Ridge. Voters at the November 17, 1896 town meeting failed to put a stop to the destruction of trees and digging of gravel here, to be used for roads. Alice Buck, Susan Blake, Salome Marland, and Emma Lincoln, refused to take "no" for an answer.

The fight to save this twenty-three acre glacier esker known as Indian Ridge, was led chiefly by these four determined women and represents Andover's first organized campaign to protect its green space from development. They organized door to door canvassing, published pleas for preservation in regional newspapers, sponsored a lawn party benefit, and challenged Andover children to collect pennies for the effort. "Cannot Indian Ridge be given to Andover as a fitting memorial, for all time, on her 250th Anniversary?" their Appeal read.

Due to the site's recognized geological significance their campaign to preserve Indian Ridge was not merely a local matter. The cause made *Harper's Weekly*, the *New York Evening Post,* as well as Boston newspapers.

G. Frederick Wright dispatched letters from Ohio, noting that "Maps of Indian Ridge are found in every important scientific library. It is the great object lesson of the world touching a certain department of glacial geology. Its preservation would be a gilt-edged investment."

Andover author Elizabeth Stuart Phelps Ward wrote that the "emphasis for purchase should be based upon present and especially future advantages. Now is the chance to save it from the hands of despoilers!"

By November 18, 1897, $3,500 had been raised by public subscription to purchase Indian Ridge and preserve it as a town forest. Nearly two hundred and fifty individuals donated to its conservation, in sums ranging from 25 cents to 400 dollars. Public pressure and conscience finally inspired the Abbot heirs to reduce their original asking price.

In subsequent years, Alice Buck led squads of school children up Indian Ridge, where she had students recite the Gettysburg Address and sing *My Country 'Tis of Thee.* "Each May, (perhaps the most charming time on the Reservation)," she wrote, "I take school children there to show them its wonders, play woodland games, and teach them to respect the trees and flowers...always to preserve and never to destroy." Buck's avowed goal was "to impress upon the children that they were future guardians of this land we saved from steam saw and shovel." In her notes for the Indian Ridge Association, Buck wrote: "With the coming of the snow all unsightly things are covered, even the scattered newspapers, those silent reminders to the old trees of what their fate might have been had a saw mill been set up among them."

Children dutifully collected the caterpillar nests of brown-tailed moths and were rewarded with pennies for each tent they brought to school where the tenacious, destructive insects were burned. Gypsy moths ravaged the Ridge so thoroughly in 1910 and 1911 that the State Forestry Commission had to be hired to spray. However, the moths won, since by 1916, the records read, "the oak trees so attractive to gypsy and brown-tail moths, were all dying and had to be cut down to save the pines."

In April, 1907, a granite boulder with a bronze tablet was placed atop Indian Ridge honoring Alice Buck, the prime mover in saving Indian Ridge. The reservation is now owned and maintained by the Andover Village Improvement Society. ❧

THE WOMAN'S HOUR

One of the nineteenth century's most popular American authors, Elizabeth Stuart Phelps (1844-1911) is barely remembered today except by feminist scholars, although recent reevaluation has inspired new editions of some of her novels. Critic Michael Sartisky described Phelps as "a novelist whose works offer enormous insight into the social and cultural history of the late nineteenth century United States, especially into issues of the nature of the family, gender roles, and the changing position of women in middle class American society."

Phelps marked her true beginnings as an author when her short story about the Civil War, *A Sacrifice Consumed* appeared in the January, 1864 edition of *Harper's New Monthly Magazine.* Its theme was close to heart of the young author, for her intended life partner, Samuel Hopkins Thompson (Phillips Academy, 1862) died of diphtheria after the Battle of Antietam. The twenty-five dollar check attached to the editor's acceptance letter made the prospect of financial independence as a writer seem possible.

Phelps left school at the age of nineteen, then did reform work and teaching among factory families employed by the Smith and Dove Manufacturing Company at Abbot Village in Andover. Her work with these tenement dwellers helped inspire her lifelong commitment to improve conditions for working class people. Phelps' novels, *Mercy Glidden's Work, Up Hill,* and *Hedged In* were based on her Abbot Village experiences.

"I saw that I might do for these mill hands, with my pen, what my former Andover neighbor, Mrs. Stowe, had done for the slaves." Phelps claimed that reformer's blood ran in her veins. "The books that our family made had a purpose beyond mere entertainment. I was raised with the idea that the reason for literature was to teach, so writing became the way to express my views about society."

In *The Silent Partner* (1871), one of her most significant and enduring novels, set in a textile mill, Phelps brought a new realism to American fiction. With this book, one literary historian considered her "the first American novelist to deal with themes of urban industrial problems."

In 1871, Elizabeth Stuart Phelps wrote her mentor, John Greenleaf Whittier, that she "was now invested in the woman's cause. It grows upon my conscience, as well as my enthusiasm, every day." In her autobiography, *Chapters From A Life*, Phelps wrote, "It is impossible to understand now, what it meant when I was twenty-five, for a young lady reared as I was on Andover Hill, to announce that she should forthwith approve and further the enfranchisement and elevation of her own sex. I was reared in circles which did not concern themselves with those whom we called agitators." Phelps had always found it difficult to keep her opinions to herself. She wrote,

> ...*tea parties where theologues came in alphabetical order and the professor told his best stories. The ladies of the family were expected to keep quiet while the gentlemen talked. I recall the shocked expressions upon the faces of the men when I, a mere female, dared to join in the conversation.*
>
> *Andover is every bit as male-dominated as a Western town—living amongst the Phillips Academy boys and future ministers as we do, with their splitting of theological hairs over ordination, predestination and all those other 'ation words that buzzed like mosquitoes around these informal conventions. Women are excluded from the debates and the posturings of the Theological Seminary.*

Elizabeth Stuart Phelps used the name recognition and popular success she gained from her first book *The Gates Ajar*, to challenge existing social customs and soon became recognized as a pioneer feminist. She intended to shock her readers to a new awareness of wrongs against women and to bring about social change. At a time when females were brought up to believe that personal fulfillment came through husband, hearth, and family, Phelps challenged the notion that the woman's place was in the home. While society then viewed a woman as an "angel in the house" and domestic pursuits her "natural sphere," Phelps alerted women to the "corroding cares and drudgeries inherent in marriage and motherhood and the toll it exacted on her self-development and personal ambition." She believed that women's intellectual potential disappeared in domestic pursuits. This feminist author, far ahead of her time, attacked "the protection and dependence theory of the masculine oligarchy which was responsible for keeping one half of the full grown human race eternal minors." Phelps boldly wrote that "all women, rich or poor, were bound by a system of dependence upon men."

This author shocked both male and female readers with articles published in *The Independent* and other quality journals of the day. She championed such radical beliefs as a wife's right to keep her own name after marriage; women taking responsibility for financial decisions; and equal rights, including equal pay, for women. What Elizabeth Stuart Phelps advocated was nothing short of radical reorganization of late nineteenth-century society.

An address she presented in 1869 before the New England Women's Club in Boston on the topic of dress reform was later published as *What to Wear*. Phelps believed dress reform a major step towards women's self-fulfillment. "I believe that the methods of dress practiced among women are a marked hindrance to the realization of their possibilities and should be scorned or persuaded out of society." She spoke out against corsets and stays that constricted waists and endangered women's health in order to achieve a stylish hour-glass shape.

> *Why does a man wear a linen collar and a cloth coat, and his wife wear corsets and a muslin waist with low linings? Why does he clothe himself in flannel from head to foot and neck to wrist, and her under (if not her outer) clothing requires she bare neck and arms in the freezing but 'becoming' fashion on a winter's day?*
>
> *...One half the world ought not to be called upon to influence the other half by its physical beauty....The methods of dress practiced among women today are a marked hindrance to the realization of their mental possibilities. Fashions make women appear to have camel humps on their backs and market gardens on their heads!*

Elizabeth Stuart Phelps also condemned heavy trailing skirts that restricted exercise and walking outdoors or upstairs as "bondage," writing that 'dressed to kill' had "ceased to be a metaphor." Until women were "unshackled," society would never take them seriously.

Phelps fought for woman's self-development and economic independence. She urged women to pursue education in a time when higher education was considered detrimental to a woman's health, injurious to the female brain, and a threat to social order. She protested the education of girls in her era which she said "focused its curriculum on the science of scrubbing the hall floor and held out the promise of a diploma in gingerbread." Phelps told young women to "dream and dare".

"Choice is the main thing. I believe in women and in their right for their own best possibilities in every department of life." In *What Shall They Do?* published in the September, 1867, issue of *Harper's New Monthly Magazine*, Phelps wrote, "Women need to lead productive and independent lives and financial independence is the first step!" In *A Talk to the Girls* published in *The Independent*, Phelps asked young women, "Why do your parents mean one thing for you, another for your brother?...Why do they fling open to him the gates of active usefulness, which they close and bar to you?"

Using the power of her pen, Phelps was a constant crusader for gender equity, advocating wider career choice and "meaningful work" for women. She passionately believed in a woman's right to choose her own profession and to earn her own wages at a period when females had few vocational options beyond sewing, factory work, and teaching, all which offered low wages.

"Whether for self-support, or for the pure employment's sake," Phelps wrote, "the search for work is at the bottom of half the feminine miseries of the world." She continually urged women to get more business experience so wives and daughters would not remain perpetually financially dependent upon men. Her short stories and novels often depict women succeeding in professions traditionally open only to males such as business, sales, the ministry, art, and medicine.

Although Phelps prepared and submitted numerous petitions to state legislature, she was not an active participant at women's suffrage or social reform meetings. Instead, she preferred to present female characters in fiction to serve as role-models for a generation of young women.

Doctor Zay, published in 1882, is considered the first American novel to depict a successful woman physician. It is based on Andover's successful homeopathic physician Dr. Mary Briggs Harris, with whom Phelps shared office space. Dr. Harris, whose brother taught at Andover Theological Seminary, slashed her skirts in order to facilitate house calls by foot and horse.

After her purchase of a summer place in Gloucester, Phelps was moved by poverty and alcoholism among the fishermen's families of Cape Ann. Several of Phelps' novels focus on their plight and she also became active in the temperance movement.

Literary critic Walter Fuller Taylor called Elizabeth Stuart Phelps "the first American novelist to treat the social problems of the Machine Age seriously and at length." ∞

ENDNOTES: THE NINETEENTH CENTURY

❧

CHAPTER 29 - BULWARK OF CALVINISM ON "BRIMSTONE HILL"
Page 87: Elizabeth Stuart Phelps. *Chapters From A Life.* 1896, p. 30; 33
Van Wyck Brooks. *New England Indian Summer, 1865-1915.* NY: E. P. Dutton, 1940,
pp. 80-82.
Henry K. Rowe. *History of Andover Theological Seminary.*Newton, Mass., 1933, 7; 59.
Pages 87, 88:
Juliet H. Mofford. *And Firm Thine Ancient Vow: History of the North Parish Church of North
Andover,* p. 125-126.
___. "Eliphalet Pearson, Puritan Incarnate." Eagle Tribune, July 3, 1976.
Page 89: Henry K. Rowe, Ibid. p. 30, 31
Claude M. Fuess. Chapter XVI "Citadel of Orthodoxy."

CHAPTER 30 - WHAT THEY DID FOR FUN
Page 90: See Claude M. Fuess. Chapter XVI "Citadel of Orthodoxy."
Elizabeth Stuart Phelps. *Chapters From A Life.* Boston: Houghton-Mifflin, 1898, p. 30.

CHAPTER 31 - TEMPERANCE TOWN AND THE "COLD WATER ARMY"
Page 91: Journal of Humanity; And Herald of the American Temperance Society,
November 11, 1830.
South Parish Church Manuscript Records. Andover Historical Society.
Pages 91, 92: Eleanor Campbell. *West of the Shawsheen.*West Parish Church, 1975,
p. 22-23.
Susanna E. Jackson. *The West Church,* Andover, 1906, p. 24.
Journal of Humanity, Ibid., November 11, 1830.
The Ballard Vale Gazette, December 25, 1867.
Marsha Rooney. "We Trust in Israel's God & Drink What He Has Given,"
Andover Historical Society Newsletter, Vol. 4, #2, 1979.

CHAPTER 32 - MISSIONARY BOULDER
Page 93: Clippings from various Boston newspapers, October, 1910.
Phillips Academy Archives
Henry K. Rowe, *History of Andover Theological Seminary,* "Andover Men in Foreign
Missions," Chapter VI. Newton, Mass. 1923

CHAPTER 33 - LAFAYETTE STOPS BY
Page 95: Claude M. Fuess. *Andover: Symbol of New England,* 1959, p. 271-272.
Boston Daily Advertiser , June 23, 1825
Page 96: Oliver Baker. Student Manuscript Letters, Phillips Academy Archives

CHAPTER 34 - *AMERICA* PENNED IN ANDOVER
Page 97: Juliet H. Mofford. "Smith Wrote a Classic in 30 Minutes."
Lawrence Eagle Tribune, July 3, 1976.

The Nineteenth Century

Reverend Samuel Francis Smith. *Poems of Home & Country*. Boston: Silver, Burdett & Co., 1895, p. xvii.
Page 98: Samuel Francis Smith, Ibid., xvii
Juliet H. Mofford. " A Man and His Song." Andover Historical Society Lecture, March 20, 2002
Oliver Wendell Holmes. Class Reunion Poem, Harvard University, 1829

CHAPTER 35 - THE INDUSTRIAL REVOLUTION COMES TO ANDOVER
Page 99: Sarah Loring Bailey, *Historical Sketches of Andover...* p. 579, quoting Town Meeting Records , 1682; also pp. 592-594.
Business History of Andover. Anniversary Souvenir Number of the Andover Townsman, 1896. "Marland Mills" p. 8-10;
Page 100: Ibid., *Business History of Andover*, 1896. "Ballard Vale Manufacturing Company" p. 12-15; "Tyer Rubber Company," p. 20-21.

CHAPTER 36 - SMITH & DOVE DRAWS THE SCOTS
Page 101: Eleanor Campbell, Elizabeth Gorrie and Margaret Roberts. *A Red Cloak for Mother: The History of the Smith Family in Andover*, April, 1992, pp. 5-8
Sarah Loring Bailey, Op. Cit ., pp. 595-597.
Pages 101, 102: Florence Feldman-Wood. "A Long Line of Thread: Smith & Dove in Andover." Andover Historical Society Newsletter, 1999, Vol. 23, Number 4.
Op. Cit., Business History of Andover , 1896, p. 16-19.

CHAPTER 37 - ANDOVER'S ANTI-SLAVERY RIOT
Page 103: (Juliet H. Mofford) The Anti-Slavery Movement and the Underground Railroad in Andover & Greater Lawrence, Massachusetts. The Greater Lawrence Underground Railroad Committee. Punchard Trustees Fund, Andover, Mass. 2001.
Reverend Sherlock Bristol. *The Pioneer Preacher: Incidents of Interest and Experiences in the Author's Life*. NY/Chicago: Fleming H. Revell, 1887, pp. 40-55. See also "Auld Lang Syne: Anti-Slavery in Andover Fifty Years Ago," Andover Townsman January 27, 1888; February 3, 1888.
Page 104: Park's Letter, December 5, 1896. Phillips Academy Archives; *see also* Andover Townsman , December 25, 1896.
Frederick Allis, Jr. Youth From Every Quarter , 1978, pp. 137-139
Phillips Bulletin , October, 1913, p. 21-22
Report of the Faculty on the Proceedings Respecting Anti-Slavery, September 1, 1835. Phillips Academy Archives

CHAPTER 38 - THE GRIMKE SISTERS RAISED EYEBROWS
Page 106: Gerda Lerner, *The Grimké Sisters from South Carolina*, Boston, 1967.
Angelina Grimké. Diary Entry, July 3 and July 10, 1837
William Lloyd Garrison. The Liberator, August 18, 1837.

CHAPTER 39 - THE RAILROAD ACCIDENT THAT AFFECTED THE NATION
Page 107: Roy F. Nichols. *Franklin Pierce: Young Hickory of the Granite Hills*. NY: Charles Scribner's, 1931.
Dumas Malone, Editor. *Dictionary of American Biography*. NY: Charles Scribner's, 1936, Vol. VII, pp. 576-580.
Juliet H. Mofford. "Presidents Who Passed Our Way." Script for First Person Performances

adapted from letters, diaries, autobiographies, and news accounts for Andover's 350th Anniversary Celebrations, May, 1996.

Page 108: Claude M. Fuess. *Andover: Symbol of New England*, 1959, p. 279-280

Page 109: Andover Advertiser, January 22, 1853

Lawrence Courier, January 11, 1853

Lowell Daily Advertiser, January 10 & 11, 1853

Lowell Daily Journal & Courier, January 7 & January 11, 1853

New York Times, January 7, 1853

Andover Townsman, May 11, 1894

CHAPTER 40 – THE "MERRIEST EPOCH" IN ANDOVER HISTORY

Page 110: Harriet Beecher Stowe. "Letter to Calvin Stowe, June, 1852." *Life and Letters of Harriet Beecher Stowe*. Annie Fields, Editor. Boston: Houghton Mifflin; Cambridge: Riverside Press, 1897

Susan E. Jackson. Reminiscences of Andover. Andover Press, 1914, p. 167.

Page 111: Op. Cit. *Life and Letters of Harriet Beecher Stowe*. Annie Fields, Editor.

"Mrs. Stowe in Andover." *The Andover Magazine*, Andover Press, pp. 35–37

Harriet Beecher Stowe. *Our Charley and What to Do With Him*. Philadelphia, Penn.: Lippencott, 1869.

Page 112: Ibid.; See also Sarah Nelson Carter. *For Pity's Sake: A Story For the Times*. Andover Press, 1897, pp. 107-109.

CHAPTER 41 – SOJOURNER TRUTH CAME TO TOWN

Page 113: Juliet H. Mofford. "Sojourner Truth Visited Stowe in Andover in 1853." Andover Historical Society Newsletter, Vol. 22, No. 3, 1997.

Page 114: Harriet Beecher Stowe. "The Libyan Sybil." Atlantic Monthly, April, 1863.

CHAPTER 42 – THE UNDERGROUND RAILROAD RAN THROUGH ANDOVER

Page 116: Wilbur H. Siebert . "The Underground Railroad in Massachusetts, 1898" (Juliet H. Mofford) "The Anti-Slavery Movement and the Underground Railroad in Andover & Greater Lawrence, Mass." The Greater Lawrence Underground Railroad Committee. Punchard Trustees Fund, Andover, Mass, 2001.

Page 117: Bessie P. Goldsmith. "The William Jenkins House ." The Townswoman's Andover, Andover Press, p. 21.

CHAPTER 43 – FREE CHRISTIAN CHURCH FOUNDED BY ABOLITIONISTS

Page 118: Church Manuscript Records and Histories of South Parish Church and West Parish Church, Andover Historical Society, 1830s through 1850s.

Letters of Reverend Samuel Jackson to his parents, Andover Historical Society.

Page 118: Kathryn S. Daniel and Martha H. South, Editors. *The History of Free Christian Church*, 1996

Ibid., "Address of Deacon William C. Donald." Fiftieth Anniversary Observance, 1896.

CHAPTER 44 – POMP'S POND

Page 119, Vital Records of Andover, Marriage

Charlotte Helen Abbott, et al. Lovejoy Files, Andover Historical Society

Page 120: Student Letter. Phillips Academy Archives.

Bessie P. Goldsmith. "Pomp's Pond." Townswoman's Andover, 1964, pp. 22-24
James Batchelder. "Pomps Pond Timeline History." Andover Townsman, 1920-1924.

Chapter 45 – Printers Inc.
Page 122 : Scott H. Paradise. *A History of Printing in Andover, Mass., 1789-1931.*
Andover Press, 1931.
"The Andover Press." Business History of Andover. Anniversary Souvenir Number
of the Andover Townsman, 1896.
Page 123: Frederick S. Allis, Jr. *Youth From Every Quarter*, 1978, p. 129-130
Eleanor Richardson . A Century of Change, Andover Historical Society, 1996,
p. 136, 137.

Chapter 46 – Niijima Joe
Page 124: Arthur S. Hardy. *Life & Letters of Joseph Hardy Neesima.* Boston: Houghton,
Mifflin & Co., 1891.
Phebe Fuller McKeen. *A Sketch of the Early Life of Joseph Hardy Neesima.* Boston: D.
Lothrop Co., 1890
Page 125: Emi Nakatsukasa. "Joe Neesima Was the First Japanese to Visit Andover."
Andover Historical Society Newsletter. Vol. 25, # 4, Winter 2001

Chapter 47 – A Town Divided
Page 127: Claude M. Fuess. *Andover: Symbol of New England*, 1959, pp. 301-307
Andover Advertisers February 15, February 25, 1854; January 20, 1855.
Records of Andover Town Meetings, March–April, 1854. March 5, 1855. North Parish
Church Records, North Andover Historical Society Collections.
Page 128 : "Act to Divide the Town of Andover and to Incorporate the Town of North
Andover." Chapter 150 of Massachusetts Acts & Resolves of 1855; Act of Separation
approved April 23, 1855

Chapter 48 – Andover Builds A Town House
Page 129: Bernice Haggerty. "Town Hall Was An Administrative and Social Center."
Andover Historical Society Newsletter, Vol. 09, Number 1, 1984.
Eleanor Richardson. A Century of Change. 1996, pp. 43, 55.
Page 130: Norma Gammon & Charlotte Smith. "Andover Rededicates Old Town Hall."
Andover Historical Society Newletters, Vol. 14, #1, 1989, 4/28; 5/6 & 5/7.
Charlotte Smith. "Rededication of Town Hall Was a Historic Success." Ibid., 1989,
Vol. 14, #2.

Chapter 49 – The Civil War Came "Like a Whirlwind"
Page 131: Lincoln's Election, Andover Advertiser, November 10, 1860
Elizabeth Stuart Phelps. Chapters From A Life, 1896, pp. 67-87
Page 131-133: Joan Patrakis. "Andover Contributed 599 Men to Help Win the Civil
War." Andover Historical Society Newsletter, 1989 Vol. 14, #4.
Joan Patrakis. "A Soldier Describes the Realities of the Civil War." Ibid., 1990, Vol. 15, #2.
(Calvin's Stowe Speech). Andover Advertiser, April 27, 1861
(Flag Raising Ceremony) Ibid., June 8, 1861
(Vicksburg) Ibid., July 11, 1863

CHAPTER 50 - *THE GATES AJAR*
Page 134 Elizabeth Stuart Phelps, *Chapters From A Life*, 1896.
_____ _____ ___. Preface to *The Gates Ajar*, 1869.
Page 135: Juliet H. Mofford. "The Nunnery Was a School With a Wide Reputation."
Ibid., 1997, Vol. 22, #1.

CHAPTER 51 - SPIRITUALISM IN SEMINARY TOWN
Page 136: John Russell, Manuscript Letters, Andover Historical Society Collections.
Charles Beecher. Spiritual Manifestations. Boston, 1879, pp. 25-36.
Harriet Beecher Stowe. "Who Shall Roll Away the Stone?" The Independent,
September 1837.
Forrest Wilson. *Crusader in Crinoline*. NY: Hutchinson & Co.1942, p. 167-168
Page 137 Annie Fields, Editor. *Life and Letters of HBS*, 1897. Letter to Duchess of
Sutherland, August 3, 1857; Stowe's Letters to Annie Fields. October 29, October 31;
December 1, 1884.
Page 138 : Van Wyck Brooks. *Indian Summer*, p. 336
Elizabeth Stuart Phelps. *Chapters from a Life*, pp. 6-8.

CHAPTER 52 - MEMORIAL HALL LIBRARY
Page 139: Mary Smith Byers. "The Founding of Memorial Hall." Essex Institute
Historical Collections, Vol. 79, 1943, pp. 246-255.
Sarah Loring Bailey. *Historical Sketches of Andover...*p. 531-532
Reverend Phillips Brooks. An Address Delivered May 30, 1873 at the Dedication of the
Memorial Hall, Andover.
Page 140: Karen Herman. "Library Has Served Town 125 Years." Andover Historical
Society Newsletter, 1996, Vol. 21, #2
Judy Wakefield. "A Room of Their Own." Andover Townsman, October 10, 2002

CHAPTER 53 - ANDOVER VILLAGE IMPROVEMENT SOCIETY: PIONEER IN CONSERVATION
Page 141: Juliet H. Mofford. "AVIS: A History In Conservation." 1980
Sarah Nelson Carter. Andover Townsman, January 15, 1897
Ibid., April 27, 1894
Page 142: George Eaton. Story of the Andover Village Improvement Society,
December, 1922
Page 143: Juliet H. Mofford. Op. Cit., p. 99; 116, 117

CHAPTER 54 - HOW FOUR DETERMINED LADIES SAVED INDIAN RIDGE
Page 145: Sarah Stuart Robbins. *Old Andover Days: Memories of A Puritan Childhood*.
Boston: Pilgrim Press, 1908, p. 135-136
Bessie P. Goldsmith. Townswoman's Andover, p. 16
Page 146: Juliet H. Mofford. Op. Cit., Chapter 2; p. 24
Page 147: Deed acquired, December 16, 1897; Indian Ridge Association incorporated by
Massachusetts State Legislature, Act 169, Chapter 90, February 24, 1898: "for the purpose
of maintaining a public park or forest reservation in said Town of Andover.
Juliet H. Mofford. Op. Cit., p. 32-33; Chapter 8: Public Land by Public Demand.

The Nineteenth Century

CHAPTER 55 - *THE WOMAN'S HOUR*

Page 148: Michael Sartisky quoted in *Doctor Zay*, Introduction, Feminist Press Reprint, 1987.

(Samuel Hopkins Thompson, Phillips Academy, 1862) Claude M. Fuess. *An Old New England School: A History of Phillips Academy.* Andover Press, 1917, p. 295

Mari Jo Buttle & Florence Howe, *Silent Partner*, Afterword. Feminist Press, 1983, pp. 356–371.

Mary Angela Bennett. *Elizabeth Stuart Phelps*. Philadelphia, Penn.: University of Pennsylvania Press, 1939

Page 149: Elizabeth Stuart Phelps. *Chapters From a Life,* 1896, XII "Art for Truth's Sake."

Pages 150: Joan Patrakis. "19-th Century Author Speaks to Modern Women." Andover Historical Society Newsletter, 1992, Vol. 17, #4.

Elizabeth Stuart Phelps. "What to Wear?," The Independent, 1867; "What Shall They Do?" *Harper's New Monthly Magazine*, September, 1867

_____ _____ _____. "The True Woman," October 12, 1871; "A Talk to the Girls," January 4, 1872; "Female Education of Women," 1873 all published in The Independent

_____ _____ _____. "How Shall Women Dress?" North American Review, June, 1885

Page 151: Walter Fuller Taylor. *The Economic Novel in America.* Chapel Hill: University of North Carolina, 1942, p. 58.

*"We stuck our necks out
and they dragged us in
and we formed
a land company."*

∞

HAROLD RAFTON
ANDOVER VILLAGE IMPROVEMENT SOCIETY

THE TWENTIETH CENTURY

The modern era arrived at the turn of the century. In 1890, the town got a water system and the following year, the electric trolley line was put through to Lawrence. There were electric lights downtown in 1897 and the telephone exchange system opened in 1899. By the year 1906, autos were "scorching down Main Street at sixteen miles per hour, terrifying horses and creating dust clouds." Movies previewed at the Wonderland Theater in 1909, although never on Sunday.

Andover's rural character changed. In 1920, Andover had two hundred farms. By 1947, there were seventy-seven. One farmer said, "Industry offered more money for land than any farmer could hope to earn in a lifetime." Many farms, particularly in West Andover, were now run by new immigrants from Armenia, and provided vegetables and dairy products to mill workers in Andover and Lawrence.

Phillips Academy underwent dramatic growth when Andover Theological Seminary moved to Cambridge, leaving its buildings to the academy. The campus was redesigned, buildings were relocated and new ones erected in the 1930s. Abbot Academy merged with Phillips in 1973.

Andover suffered the worst flood in its history in 1936 and hurricanes hit the town hard in 1954 and 1956.

The Merrimack Valley experienced unprecedented growth and change in the 1950s, with the nation's material progress and national prosperity that followed the Second World War. Development of high tech firms along Route 128 brought families to the suburbs, resulting in unprecedented construction. Andover's population increased by 37.8% between 1956 and 1960 and its school population quadrupled between 1945 and 1970. Raytheon took over the American Woolen Company's former Wood Mills at Shawsheen Village in 1956. As Route 93 cut through Andover in 1959 and Route 495 intersected Andover in 1965, the town and the Andover Village Improvement Society fought to preserve conservation lands. A plan to raze the historic downtown for urban renewal was defeated by town vote in 1962.

New residents brought increased diversity to Andover, which was now home to some twenty-six different religious groups. ∞

159

PHILLIPS ACADEMY
ANDOVER, MASS.

32. **View of Phillips Academy**, 1911, by W. Tuttle. This view shows the campus after the departure of Andover Theological Seminary, but before it was redesigned and old buildings were razed or moved and new ones erected according to plans of alumnus Thomas Cochran and his architects, 1921–1933. (*Courtesy of Phillips Academy Archives*)

33. **The Deacon Amos Blanchard House and Barn.** Located at 97 Main Street and built in 1819. Since 1911, it has been the headquarters of the Andover Historical Society. Sketched by H. Winthrop Pierce, about 1908. The elm tree on the left was blown down by Hurricane Carol, August 31, 1954 and the maple tree was taken down in 1959.
(*Courtesy of Andover Historical Society*)

34. William Madison Wood (1858-1926)
President of American Woolen Company.

Illustration from *Andover: Symbol of New
England* by Claude M. Fuess, 1959, p. 320.

(Courtesy of the author)

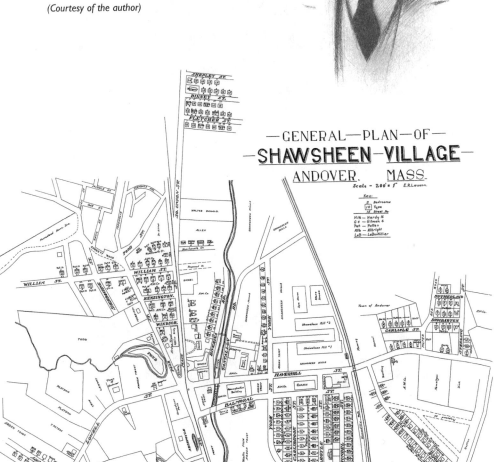

35. General Plan of Shawsheen Village, Andover, Mass., for the American Woolen Company, 1922.
(Courtesy of Andover Historical Society)

36. **President Calvin Coolidge with First Lady, Grace.**
Headmaster Alfred Stearns is seen at the right. Photographed at Phillips Academy's
Sesquicentennial, May, 1928. *(Courtesy of Phillips Academy Archives)*

37. **Andover Press delivery truck.** As well as publishing the *Andover Townsman* weekly,
this press published magazines and books, as well as academic catalogs and yearbooks
for schools and colleges all over New England. *(Courtesy of Bernice Haggerty)*

38. **Artist's rendering of nineteenth-century Lucy Foster house.** From *Historical Archaeology at Black Lucy's Garden, Andover, Mass.*, by Adelaide and Ripley P. Bullen. Published in 1945. *(Courtesy of Andover Historical Society)*

James Leno
32 Clark Road
Jay
Possible Future Career:
Retired Millionaire

Funniest
Lyn Deyermond
Jay Leno

39. **Jay Leno's high school days.** Andover High School Yearbook, 1968.
(Courtesy of Andover High School)

163

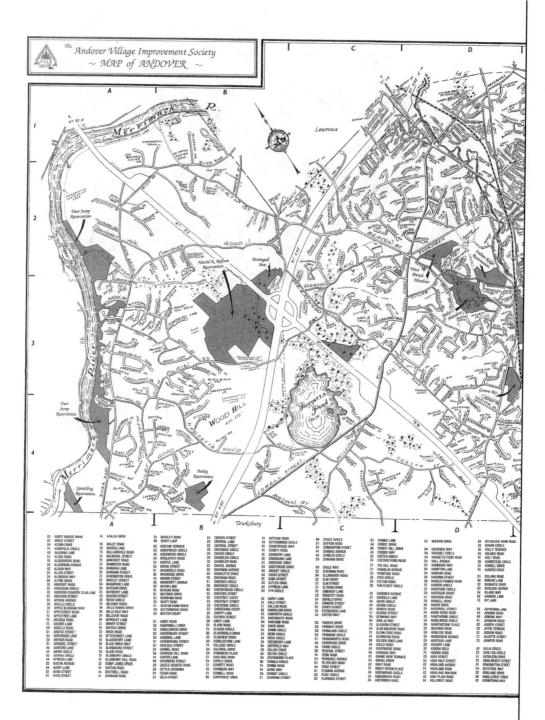

40. **Andover Village Improvement Society (AVIS), map of Andover, 1994.**
Maps available for purchase. Contact AVIS at P.O. Box 5097, Andover, MA 01810

Join

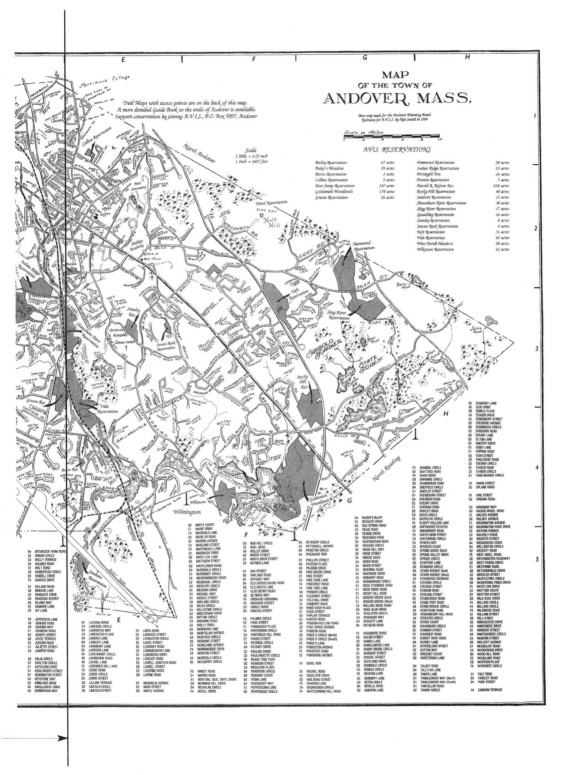

MAP
OF THE TOWN OF
ANDOVER, MASS.

Base map made for the Andover Planning Board
Redrawn for A.V.I.S. by Nija Smith in 1994

Scale in Miles

AVIS RESERVATIONS

Bailey Reservation	67 acres	Hammond Reservation	38 acres
Baker's Meadow	59 acres	Indian Ridge Reservation	23 acres
Burns Reservation	3 acres	Pettingill Ave.	16 acres
Collins Reservation	5 acres	Purdon Reservation	5 acres
Deer Jump Reservation	147 acres	Harold R. Rafton Res.	226 acres
Goldsmith Woodlands	170 acres	Rocky Hill Reservation	40 acres
Greene Reservation	26 acres	Sanborn Reservation	15 acres
		Shawsheen River Reservation	30 acres
		Skug River Reservation	37 acres
		Spaulding Reservation	16 acres
		Stanley Reservation	8 acres
		Sunset Rock Reservation	4 acres
		Tofts Reservation	31 acres
		Vale Reservation	45 acres
		West Parish Meadow	28 acres
		Wilkpoon Reservation	23 acres

Trail Maps with access points are on the back of this map.
A more detailed Guide Book to the trails of Andover is available.
Support conservation by joining A.V.I.S., P.O. Box 5097, Andover

Scale
1 Mile = 3.25 inch
1 Inch = 1625 feet

THE SUFFRAGE MOVEMENT IN ANDOVER

The national movement for the female vote, formally organized at Seneca Falls, New York in 1848, declared it "the duty of the women of this country to secure to themselves their sacred right to the elective franchise."

Andover women seem to have been first inspired in 1873 when a day-long convention brought famous suffrage speakers Julia Ward Howe, Lucy Stone and Henry Blackwell to town. This event resulted in the formation of the Andover Woman's Suffrage League. Some of the same Andover women active in anti-slavery and temperance also campaigned to secure for women the right to vote. Elizabeth Stuart Phelps was elected the Andover Woman's Suffrage League's first vice-president and remained an honorary member from 1887, after she had relocated to Gloucester and then to Newton Center.

Not all local women supported suffrage, believing that a woman's place remained in the home rather than the political arena. Although many Andover men actively supported women's suffrage and even submitted petitions to state legislature, others argued that "women's lack of worldly experience and their sensitive, emotional nature would hamper their political decisions." In 1913, when five women came to Andover to speak in support of their right to vote, the program was, according to the *Andover Townsman*, "canceled due to lack of an audience."

An Andover anti-suffrage group worked to block the state referendum and the battle continued to be fought in the local newspaper.

> *Remember that every Socialist and every Feminist is a Woman Suffragist. Remember that the great majority of women do not want the ballot thrust upon them by the fanatical minority! Vote against Woman Suffrage…the average woman, your wife, sister, mother, is busy enough already with natural, congenial and necessary duties and ought not to be loaded against her will, with political responsibilities…your best way to help Massachusetts Womanhood is to vote against the amendment.*

Andover citizens voted against the proposed 1915 amendment two to one. Nevertheless, the local Equal Suffrage League continued to rally for the vote and regularly spoke from open automobiles draped with *Votes For Women* banners. Andover school children competed for prizes for the best essays on a woman's right to vote.

After all American women achieved the franchise with the 19th Amendment, the Andover Equal Suffrage League evolved into the League of Women Voters in 1921, with an original membership of three hundred and twenty-six.

In the elections of 1920, 1,557 Andover women registered to vote. The first to cast her ballot was eighty-two-year-old Nancy Jenkins. All Andover women, but one hundred and ten, voted. The majority voted for the Republican ticket of Coolidge and Harding and against the referendum allowing the sale of beer and wine in Andover. ∽

INDIAN ROGER'S REVENGE

Cochichawicke River became known as the Shawsheen River in the seventeenth century and the name of Indian Roger, to whom Andover's first English settlers had granted fishing and settlement rights, was memorialized in the brook that ran through the center of South Parish. In the late eighteenth century, Nathaniel Swift had operated a tannery here with power provided by this "never-failing stream of water," where he turned out leather goods.

Yet Roger's Brook proved to be a recurring nightmare to residents of downtown Andover and was a source of concern to town fathers for over a century. This bothersome brook refused to be tamed. Drainage problems increased along with Andover's population. In 1900, Roger's Brook overflowed onto downtown streets, nearly isolating the busy railroad station. A sixteen-inch drainage pipe was installed in 1902. The town purchased land from Richardson for a playstead in 1904, and planted trees and ornamental shrubs, enhancing The Park at the corner of Bartlet and Chestnut Streets with gravel walks. The following year, a stone bridge was built over the brook, which was damned to create a pretty pond. The bandstand, with a tool shed underneath was built in 1913, but Roger's Brook still would not behave. During the 1938 and 1954 hurricanes, it flooded over again. In March of 1968, Roger's Brook went on another rampage, turning The Park into a lake. Nearby streets could only be reached by rowboat or canoe and many families had to evacuate their homes. With the help of state funds, the town finally took drastic action to prevent further flooding by draining and enclosing Roger's Brook in seven-foot high concrete pipes burying it some twenty feet underground. Today, that early twentieth-century stone bridge remains in the middle of The Park. It crosses a well-maintained flower bed but leads nowhere. ∞

COCONUTS

Andover may be the only town in America with a tradition of eating coconuts on Memorial Day. It used to be a more common sight to see spectators picking and gnawing fresh coconut out of shells while watching Memorial Day parades. Local historian Bessie Goldsmith recalls one year when a local clergyman who was the keynote speaker for this solemn occasion, stood at the podium with a bouquet of flowers in one hand and a small American flag and a coconut in the other.

For Andover citizens, Decoration Day coconuts are "as obvious an association as fireworks on the Fourth of July" or trees at Christmas. Older residents believe that coconuts made their local debut in the 1880s at Mrs. Basso's fruit and vegetable market on Main Street, due perhaps, to a shipping error. Children were soon spending their pennies on these exotic imports, along with bananas and peanuts in the shell. George and Peter Dantos continued the custom when they opened their grocery store, now the Spa, on Elm Street, in 1921. Three hundred and thirty coconuts went for twenty cents apiece in 1951, although they charged twenty-five cents during the Second World War. Phidias Dantos claimed that in 1969, the last year he ran the Spa, he sold 1,600 coconuts before noon. Current owners continue this time-honored tradition.

With nails and hammers or ice picks, children pounded holes in their coconuts to suck out the sweet milk with straws, then smashed them on rock walls, against buildings, or broke them open on tombstones. Some citizens thoroughly disapproved. In a letter to the editor of the *Andover Townsman*, Charlotte Helen Abbott, the town genealogist, said that she for one, "did not wish to see the graves of our veterans of war service used for nut crackers, nor be subjected to the ugly, disgusting sounds of the cracking of the nuts on the memorials of my dead." ∞

THE "HORRIBLES"

❧

Nobody knows when the first parade of "Horribles" on the Fourth of July marched through Andover, although this custom goes back to the nineteenth century, if not before. Considered unique to New England, the origin of Horribles Parades relates to the carnival parades of New Orlean's Mardi Gras or Philadelphia's Mummers. At least four other Massachusetts towns are known to celebrate Independence Day with this tradition which may have begun as a way for the working classes to parody local social and political elites who marched in other town parades. An article published in Andover's earliest newspaper in 1853 says residents donned wigs, dressed in Colonial costume and rode through town in horse-drawn carriages on the Fourth.

It was common in Horribles parades to poke fun at ethnic minorities. Irreverent marchers charcoaled black faces and mocked Irish immigrants. Photographs from the turn of the twentieth century show citizens on floats or horseback, wearing papier maché masks that brutally mocked prominent national figures and town officials. Others dressed as hoboes, rode atop wagons decorated with junk and dragging pails or tin cans.

In the early 1900s, a ten-dollar prize was awarded to the "Most Truly Horrible Horrible." Policemen, public works employees, and selectmen were regularly lampooned. Firemen were singled out as targets in 1912, when many Andover citizens considered the proposed purchase of a new fire truck an unnecessary expense. "What's the matter with our town fathers to approve of such junk?" asked one sign on the side of a broken down vehicle filled with people dressed as firefighters. Another wagon labeled the fire truck Andover's "new white elephant."

A ladder was carried through a parade in Ballardvale and put up against houses along the route, its marchers pretending to be "Peeping Toms." In one parade, during Prohibition, several men dressed as policemen, carried a sign that read, "Moonshine taken in recent raids for police use only!" Ballardvale was the place to be on the Fourth. According to ninety-one-year-old Ruth Sharpe, Ballardvale's retired librarian, "The Vale always had the best Horribles, the biggest bonfires and you got a prime view of the fireworks from a canoe on the Shawsheen River." The traditional midnight bonfire to mark the opening of Andover's Fourth of July celebrations, was built at Ballardvale with railroad ties, stacked as high as a house, then set afire.

Trains from Boston arrived filled with people who had heard of these famous festivities at Ballardvale. Streets were closed off for block parties and dancing. "Tilting" was especially popular, when those in one canoe attempted to tip another canoe into the Shawsheen.

Al McKee, who operated Campion's Grocery, won most of the Horribles Parades in the 1920s and '30s. He received the prize by gathering all the tin cans he could find from the town dump, then tying them together to be dragged up Main Street by the family horse, while his family strutted alongside in clown costumes.

The Horribles Parade fizzled out during the Great Depression and World War II. Apparently, citizens dressed as hoboes no longer seemed funny. However, prizes for "Most Horrible," "Antique" and "Local Hit" were still awarded in Ballardvale in 1937. Games for all ages like the fifty-yard dash, tugs-of-war, pie-eating contests, and sack-and-potato races became the focus for fun on the Fourth. Town baseball games crossed generation gaps.

The Andover Service Club revived the Fourth of July parade in 1970 but "The Horribles" truly made a successful come-back in 1982, when more than 3,000 specta-tors turned out to watch, with 600 marching. "Decorate your husband, wife, son, daughter, cat, bicycle, baby carriage, car, or make a float!" urged posters put out by the Committee for Patriotic Observances. According to the *Andover Townsman* of July 8, 1982, some residents said it was "the best parade they had ever seen in Andover…There was a lot of imagination and a lot of fun." "Uncle Sam" marched on tall stilts; the "Keystone Kops" arrested surprised bystanders, and a group of children dressed as gypsy moths carried a banner that read, "The Only Good Caterpillar Is A Dead Caterpillar." Following the Horribles Parade, everyone gathered in The Park for pie-eating and greased pig contests and the dunk tank. Entertainment included a mime and a juggler, as well as a concert from the bandstand.

These days, Horribles parades avoid political commentary. Now, under the leadership of Andover's Department of Community Services, boys and girls of all ages decorate bikes and scooters and parents push small children in strollers decked out in red, white and blue. In one recent parade, an eighty-year-old marched, dressed as a skate boarder. Selectmen and other town officials flip pancakes at a community breakfast. There is usually a firefighters' muster featuring antique engines pumped by hand. One recent Fourth of July celebration featured over one hundred and fifty firefighters on fifteen teams competing to see which team could pump water the furthest, using hand tubs. ∞

THE ROBERT S. PEABODY
MUSEUM OF ARCHAEOLOGY

Located on the spot where Phillips Academy's first classroom building once stood, the Robert S. Peabody Museum is dedicated to the study of prehistoric and historic archaeology and Native American cultures.

In 1901, Robert S. Peabody of the Class of 1857, gave Phillips Academy money to establish an archaeology department and build a museum at 180 Main Street to house his collection of nearly 40,000 artifacts.

The Peabody collection now numbers some 500,000 items and primarily represents the New World from "the Attic to Argentina," according to the curator. There are also ancient Peruvian textiles as well as Paleolithic stone tools from Europe which are between one and three million years old.

The outreach of this small museum has been phenomenal. Since its founding in 1901, the Peabody has been recognized as a premier source for archaeological fieldwork, research and publication. The Society for American Archaeology was founded here in 1935. Public lectures, are regularly cosponsored with the Massachusetts Archaeological Society which was inaugurated here in 1940.

Robert S., Peabody's son, Charles, was a paleo-archaeologist and served as the museum's first director with Warren K. Moorehead as first curator of collections, then director from 1924. He conducted excavations all over North America, adding some 200,000 artifacts to the museum collection. President Teddy Roosevelt appointed Moorehead to the Board of Indian Commissioners in 1909. Moorehead subsequently investigated Indian claims of fraud, exposing illegal seizure of reservation land by lumber companies and land speculators. The appreciation expressed by the Native American tribe is visually documented at the museum.

Alfred V. Kidder from Harvard University, remembered as the "Father of Archaeology," worked out of the Peabody Museum in Andover. Between 1915 and 1929, he excavated sites in the Pecos Valley of New Mexico. Pecos is considered the first site to be scientifically excavated with artifacts cataloged stratigraphically. It also offered the first full chronology of Southwestern culture, demonstrating different time periods from the 1300s to the 1800s. The Pecos excavations recovered more than 25,000 artifacts, which became part of the museum collection. Field studies by archaeologists connected with the Peabody Museum have become an essential part of the recognized methodology and science of archaeology.

Archaeology was finally recognized as a true science in the 1940s when Peabody's Ripley P. Bullen developed a cultural chronology based on the stratigraphic positioning of different styles of projectile points in New England. Dr. Bullen's excavations in the Merrimack Valley revealed the culture and daily lives of Northeastern tribes before the arrival of the Europeans. His work proved that the indigenous occupation of this region went back much further than previously thought.

In the 1950s, Curator Fred Johnson collaborated with anthropologists on Carbon-14 dating in archaeology. Johnson and Director Douglas S. Byers were national leaders in research and publication from 1938-1968. The Robert S. Peabody Foundation for Archaeological Research updated the cataloging and storage of artifacts. Fieldwork focused on New England stratigraphy.

Peabody Museum is also famous for the "A-Maizing" studies of another director, Richard "Scotty" MacNeish, who investigated the origins of agriculture in the Americas, focusing on corn and its significance for American cultures. Working with geologists and botanists in the '50s and '60s, MacNeish identified the domestication of plants and animals and the beginnings of settled village life in the New World. MacNeish was internationally recognized for heading up the Tehuacan Valley project in Mexico and tracing the evolution of corn over thousands of years.

Through the efforts of recent director, James Bradley, who was appointed by the Secretary of the Interior to the Review Committee for the Native American Graves Protection and Repatriation Act, the Peabody Museum has received national recognition for its repatriation efforts. NAGPRA mandates that institutions receiving federal funds must document their Native American collections and provide for the return of certain ceremonial artifacts. The Peabody Museum in Andover now serves as the national model for compliance and partnerships with Native American tribes. Dr. Bradley, who saw NAGPRA as a new opportunity for museums, archaeologists, and Native People to work together, explained that "Native people are now equal partners in the process of determining how their material heritage will be treated." The museum returned artifacts, many of which had been acquired by Warren Moorehead in the 1930s, to Pecos Pueblo in New Mexico. Since 1999, Phillips Academy students have been directly involved in learning partnerships with Pecos Pueblo natives at Jemez archaeology sites. The Peabody Museum continues to maintain close links with North American native peoples, fostering the exchange of artifacts and multi-cultural understanding. ∞

ANDOVER HISTORICAL SOCIETY
KEEPER OF ANDOVER'S PAST LOOKS TO THE FUTURE

On April 14, 1911, sixteen townspeople met to organize the Andover Historical Society, "For the purpose of cultivating and encouraging an interest in historical and antiquarian research, to collect and treasure significant historical matter and antiquarian relics, and to found and maintain a museum where such collections shall be presented and exhibited, thus making a valuable, interesting feature in the life of Andover." Dr. Charles E. Abbott was the first president.

The earliest meetings of this new organization were held in members' homes, then in rented rooms at 71 Main Street which were outfitted with shelves and cases to exhibit artifacts donated or loaned by individual members.

The Society's first public fund-raising event was "Mr. Jarley's Wax Works," a stage production presented at town hall in 1915. A historical pageant held the following year involved a "majority of town residents." Other early activities featured more pageants, historical lectures, loan exhibitions, Washington's birthday ball, and the ever-popular whist tournaments.

The members' long search for permanent headquarters was finally realized in 1929 when Caroline Underhill offered her house to the Society on the condition she would be allowed to remain there during her lifetime. Underhill had inherited the house at 97 Main Street from her sister, Julia Underhill Robinson in 1924 and the Society had voted to purchase the property in 1926, but could only raise $800 of the $18,000 asking price.

Three years later, Caroline Underhill agreed to sell the Blanchard House and Barn for an annual payment of $420, with the stipulation of life tenancy. Trained as a librarian, Underhill then became the Society's first curator, painstakingly cataloging its infant collections, enlarging the library, undertaking research on Andover history, and hosting school groups for tours. Andover Historical Society's new headquarters opened to the public in time for the celebrations of Massachusetts' Tercentenary in 1930.

Amos Blanchard, born in Wilton, New Hampshire, built the house in 1819. He attended Phillips Academy and became administrative assistant to Judge Samuel Phillips, Jr., surveying and managing land transactions for the academy.

Later, Blanchard ran a paper manufacturing mill in Andover, served as moderator, treasurer and deacon at South Parish Church, and became cashier at Andover Bank. A man rising in responsibility and fortune required an appropriate house downtown. Blanchard originally had several acres of land and his barn, raised the year prior to the house, remains relatively unchanged. The eight room, federal style house and two story, attached barn that faced Essex Turnpike, cost Blanchard $4100. The house had an indoor fresh water source, quite modern for that time. Remains of his spring well can still be seen in the cellar. There is also a dove cote above the second story of the barn where pigeons were apparently raised for food.

The Blanchards took in boarders who attended Phillips Academy and the seminary, which was customary for upstanding local citizens who lived within walking distance to these schools. Families were licensed by the trustees to provide room and board, with strict schedules for prayers, study and chores, around the students' classroom hours. Most parents of students, who ranged in ages from seven to twenty-eight, preferred to have their sons live with local families rather than in dormitories with meager meals. The usual cost was $1.26 per week for board and "washing and sweeping."

Edward Taylor bought the house in 1849 and resided here until his death in 1893. He had been a boarder with the Blanchard family at the age of twenty-two while a student at Andover Theological Seminary. Taylor followed Blanchard as cashier at Andover Bank, then became bookkeeper for Marland Manufacturing Company until 1868, when he was appointed treasurer of Andover Theological Seminary and Phillips Academy. He served as town treasurer, town clerk and tax collector and represented Andover and North Andover in the state legislature in 1866 and 1869 and served as South Church deacon for some forty years.

In 1860, Taylor salvaged the stairs from South Parish Church for his barn when the 1778 meeting house was demolished to make way for a new church. In 1870, he enlarged the lot and added apple orchards. A memorial tribute called Edward Taylor "a power in the community and a blessing to the world."

Taylor bequeathed the property to his niece, Adelaide Taylor Merrill. Her husband was the Reverend Selah Merrill, who taught Hebrew at the seminary. Dr. Merrill had worked as an archaeologist with the American Palestine Exploration Society and from 1894-1907, served as U. S. Consul to Jerusalem.

The Merrills remodeled the house in 1894, installing hot and cold running water, soapstone sinks and redesigning the kitchen for turn of the century efficiency. A verandah and Georgian vestibule were added in the early 1900s.

Further construction in the 1960s provided an extension to the side of the building and opened the dining room for a meeting area. This also provided a new exhibit room upstairs, donated by Fred E. Cheever. The Susanne Smith Purdon Wing was added in 1977-78, through the generous legacy of a longtime member who was the granddaughter of Peter Smith, a manager of Smith and Dove Manufacturing Company. Her gift also included antique furniture and paintings. Climate-controlled, the Purdon Wing houses the Caroline Underhill Research Library and archives with some two hundred feet of materials.

When Emily Walton Taft died in 1997, she left two outbuildings located on her family property on Salem Street to the Andover Historical Society. One was David Gray's blacksmith shop, listed in the 1740 Gray Farm inventory, where shoes and barrels had also been made in the eighteenth and nineteenth centuries. These two small buildings are rare survivors of Andover's agricultural past and a collection of blacksmith tools came with the Taft bequest. Working with a contractor from First Period Colonial of Windham, New Hampshire, volunteers painstakingly dismantled these outbuildings, piece by numbered piece, and moved them onto historical society grounds where they will be reconstructed and used for interpretive programs.

According to the By-laws, Article II, Andover Historical Society's mission was redefined in 1993: "to maintain a museum and library where artifacts of local historical significance are collected, preserved, exhibited and interpreted. The Society provides a wide range of educational programs and services for individuals and groups of all ages in order to encourage a greater appreciation for and understanding of local history and related preservation issues."

There is a working nineteenth-century wood shop in the barn where classes are regularly offered using period carpentry tools. The Contemporary Andover Artists' Series provides exhibit spaces and programs for local artists working in a variety of media. Over one hundred and thirty volunteers donate more than 9,000 hours annually for various programs, special events and collections management. The Society collaborates with other cultural institutions and schools in the area on specific programs and events. Several educational programs have become integral to the Andover public school curriculum. The Underhill Library is constantly busy with researchers working on histories of their houses, genealogies from the "Family Files," or studying historical photographs from the Society's prize collection of more than 17,000 photos of local significance. Changing exhibits, as well as period furnishings, showcase items from the museum's collection of some 55,000 items.

The Andover Historical Society has become a first-class community museum. It was accredited by the American Association of Museums in 1982 and reaccredited in the mid-1990s. The Blanchard House is on the National Registry of Historic Places and the Essex National Heritage Area. There have been many changes since the Society began but the early purpose of the founders pervades. It remains an educational institution that teaches about Andover's past, yet its motto is "history is happening now." ∞

The Twentieth Century

Letters Home from Andover Boys "Over There"

❧

Three hundred and fifty Andover men enlisted to fight in the First World War, the "War to End All Wars." Sixteen would never return. Thirty-two Andover boys, including J. Everett Collins, enlisted immediately. "I was only fifteen and wanted to see the world," one soldier told a local reporter, "so I lied about my age."

Six Andover men joined British and Canadian forces before America entered the war on April 6, 1917. Most were immigrants who had come from Scotland to work in the Andover mills. "I was from Scotland and felt it was my duty," one explained. William Rae from Arbroath, Scotland, employed by Tyer Rubber Company, enlisted in the Black Watch Regiment in 1915 and was killed in France. David Croall, also from Arbroath and working for Tyer Rubber, enlisted in the Black Watch Regiment and became another local casualty. William Pert left Andover to become a private in the British Army and was killed in September of 1916.

The town's first fatality was a native of Dundee, Scotland, Charles Aitken Young, a Smith and Dove employee, who died of blood poisoning following a hand wound. Most of these Scots were members of Clan Johnson, which had thirty-eight Andover men in uniform, who through World War I saw action in France, Egypt, Siberia and the Near East. The first Phillips Academy student to die in action was a French foreign student, Antoine Henri Engel, on July 3, 1915.

Phillips Academy raised funds for the purchase of an ambulance and formed its own ambulance unit, sending some twenty-two volunteers, (the only prep school known to have done so). This Academy Ambulance Unit sailed on April 28, 1917. One soldier wrote home to tell of his trip across the Atlantic, saying he had seen a pal from Andover on another ship near his own. "We exchanged greetings with delight and new-found courage."

Phillips Academy introduced military training and drilled its students. Historian Frederick Allis wrote, "The boys, erect and khaki-clad; the flags flung out from windows along the street, the flare of bugles and the roll of drums were, throughout the springtime of 1917, outward and obvious signs of change." Archie Roosevelt, Phillips Academy Class of 1913, a son of former President Theodore Roosevelt, was wounded

177

by shell fire on March 11, 1918. The French government honored him with the *Croix de Guerre* for "conspicuous gallantry in action."

Andover's home front efforts were also heroic. "Packages of cheer," as the doughboys called boxes received from the Andover Comfort Committee, ranged from clothing to "smokes," and were dispatched to such places as Brechin, Scotland, from where so many Andoverites had immigrated, including mill owners John and Peter Smith and John Dove. Tyer Rubber Company produced gas masks and hot water bottles which were sent to British hospitals. Local mills also turned out bandages. To its sister city in Andover, England, the town wrote, "Our boys are enlisting; our people are contributing; our committees are second to none in preparedness."

Pleas from England and France for relief and surgical supplies led to the organization of the Andover Red Cross in 1916. Sessions for rolling bandages were held regularly at local churches. The Red Cross organized school and women's groups into the Women's Relief Corps for knitting and letter-writing. Volunteer aid committees directed Liberty Bond drives and organized volunteers to make surgical dressings. Girl Scouts collected prune pits to be used for the production of poison gas. Phillips and Abbot Academy students raised Victory Gardens, while school children were inspired to think of the vegetables they produced as "Allies, winning the war against weeds which represented the Kaiser's troops who must be vanquished."

The sinking of the *Lusitania* by German U-boats and the loss of American lives prompted a special resolution at the March, 1917 Andover town meeting, commending President Wilson for severing relations with Germany. Thirty-one Andover men immediately joined the heavy artillery battery formed in Lowell. The Andover Committee of Public Safety was organized with a call for a Home Guard Unit.

Throughout 1917 and 1918, letters sent home by Andover men in the U. S. Army and Navy serving "over there" were published by the *Andover Townsman* and read from church pulpits. The men wrote of guard duty, billets, the food they ate, and compared the French countryside, weather and cuisine to Andover's. Often, under the heading "Somewhere in France," letters were limited to two per week per soldier and were strictly censored.

"We are very glad to hear news from Andover," wrote Joseph Dagdigian. "I am sorry I am not allowed to tell anything about where we have been or what I have seen...I am not allowed to send any post cards with any views of any cities..."

Herbert W. Auty wrote that "All the Andover boys seem to be in good spirits after our trip across the briny deep." John M. Erving asked "My Dear Ma" to "Slip me a muffin in your next letter, if possible."

W. G. Rice, Jr., Phillips Academy, Class of 1910, serving with the American Ambulance Corps in France, wrote: "My close friend and classmate, both in Phillips Academy and in Harvard College, John Radford Abbot, and I sailed from New York on July 8, 1916, on the steamship *Rochambeau*. At that time, she had one gun, a French seventy-five, mounted aft...On arriving at Bordeaux, those of the passengers who were going into the service of the American Ambulance found large red and yellow paper tickets giving free railway transportation to Paris. The trip by railroad, through Aquitaine and Touraine was as uneventful as the sea voyage. We rarely saw Frenchmen of military age. The work in those rich fields was being carried on by women, old men, and children. Occasionally we saw German prisoners building roads…At Neuilly, a squad of American ambulance drivers attached to the American wounded was there to help unload from sanitary trains the men who had been sent for treatment. It was there that I first appreciated the fortitude and gentleness of the wounded. I had often heard of their wonderful bravery, not only in the battle but through the suffering which succeeds the battle, but now I met and felt it…"

Julius H. Preston, Phillips Academy Class of 1914, sailed for France on February, 1916 and was a member of the Andover Ambulance Corps sent to the Allied Front. An excerpt from his letter home to Andover says, "I was called out at ten o'clock to go up to one of the dangerous posts for four seriously wounded men. We drove for eight miles in sight of German trenches. The road is used only at night, and then we have to go without lights, and on stormy nights someone has to walk ahead of the car so that we won't run into a shell hole. I got these four men, but one of them died in the car before I could get him to the hospital, and one of them bled nearly all the way and filled the car full of blood, which, considering it was about three o'clock in the morning before I got back, gave me a sort of eerie feeling."

J. Everett Collins wrote he expressed "extreme happiness" for "reaping our harvest" of mail from Andover. "Among the packages I received was a good sized khaki bag, full of all kinds of good things from Christ Church…On the front are embroidered my initials, over which, beautifully laid in with sort of a criss cross stitch is the American Flag…truly a very pretty thing. It contained all manner of things, including cake, smokes, pipe, tobacco, and pouch; tooth-brush, khaki handkerchiefs, heavy knit stocking, face cloth, comb, dental floss, a small volume of short stories and oh, other things! Can you imagine how pleased I was when I found that 'treasure bag' waiting for me?"

Paul Cheney reassured the folks back home on December 4, 1917 that "All the Andover fellows are well and happy…There are many temptations thrown in our way, and for a fellow who hasn't had a good home training, it would be easy to yield to these temptations. However, lay aside your fears for the Andover boys as we are holding our heads just as high as when we left Andover."

On December 13, 1917, J. Everett Collins wrote that "Cold rains have made soldiering very disagreeable…the wet weather has made life miserable. Many days I have seen us going around in mud and water to our knees. Can you imagine me doing that at home? It is purely the marvelous physical condition that we are in, that makes it possible for us to endure it…" He would, "just love to drop into Andover and see what it looks like at this time. From reports, all the young men are out doing their duty."

"Well, it's a noble duty," Collins' letter continues, "and a duty which in years to come will mean your happiness and mind, and the world at large. It is a duty which will make our lives easier and living will be more free. In this spirit of duty these boys have gone into this that my nation and your nation and their nation may enjoy a greater degree of liberty and happiness. God will guide and protect us. We are right. Do not fear about our return; it is simply a matter of time and it is His will and way, that the end will come as soon as He sees that civilization is ready for peace."

Andover men serving in the Allied Forces were thrilled to receive Christmas packages. "Somewhere in France, December 23, 1917. To the Andover Comfort Committee: Thanks ever so much for that box of peanuts you so kindly sent as a Christmas gift. They arrived in fine condition, and as you may imagine, anything American tastes good over here!"

On February 20, 1918, Corporal Ted Lawson told the folks back in Andover that he had arrived at the front. "We have fired many times at the enemy. We have had the experience of ducking shells ourselves, our position is very secure. The dug-outs you have often read about are marvels of construction. They are much more comfortable than one would suppose. Recesses, far beneath the ground, are easily ventilated and afford easy access. The gun crew in our section that fired the first shot against the enemy was composed entirely of Andover boys: Partridge, H. Larkin, Symonds, Buss, Lindsay, and Lawson (me). Weather very good here. Nights are cold but days mild for this season. I wish you could enjoy the beautiful sunsets we are able to witness. It's then that everything seems calm and peaceful…at such a moment when one sits looking at the sinking sun and wonders what it is all about. Oft times, one does not have long to enjoy this meditation for the shrill whistle and the crack of a shell brings him to… The fireworks we see at night is a Fourth of July on a large scale: rockets and star shells bursting in air."

On January 8, 1918, still "Somewhere in France," J. Everett Collins wrote: "Dear Mother" about joining other Andover boys "gathered around the campfire, talking of home, club-doings, and missing the Fireman's Ball. Some were writing home; others were sewing on buttons, or fixing the lining on their coats. All in all, it was really a home-like scene…The one thing that we have to look forward to now, is mail from home. We haven't seen a *Townsman*, for quite a long while and you know how much they are in demand when they reach this side." J. Everett Collins was engaged in action on the front lines on November 11, 1918, when "…all loading guns as fast as they could be fired when there came a sudden stillness as the guns stopped and were replaced by cheers for Armistice."

Lieutenant William B. Wheeler, stationed in Marseilles, on November 11, 1918, wrote: "It is twelve o'clock, and the armistice has been declared for one hour. A few moments ago, I was standing in the large square where our band was playing the French national hymn. Thousands were singing, and I joined in with the rest, never realizing what I was singing until behind me, I heard another voice singing the same words. I looked around and saw another officer standing there, and we were both singing with all our strength *Old Andover is Champion*." ∞

WILLIAM MADISON WOOD

Andover's most famous resident in his day was an immigrant's son whose driving ambition made him one of the richest men in America. One obituary called him a "strange mixture of despot and philanthropist." American Woolen Company, which he created and served as president 1905-1924, became the world's largest textile corporation. Yet unlike most mill owners of his day, William Wood was not a Yankee descendant of New England's earliest, wealthiest and cultured families. His biography represented the "rags to riches" American dream of self-made success, mythologized by Horatio Alger, Jr.'s popular novels of that day.

Born in 1858, Wood was one of ten children of a Portuguese fisherman and his wife who emigrated from the island of Pico in the Azores to Martha's Vineyard. His father's Portuguese surname cannot be ascertained, but it was likely Silva which translates to "Wood."

When he was eleven, his father died and William left school for a job as an office boy at $4 per week in a New Bedford cotton mill. "That was when my good fortune began," he told an interviewer many years later. He met the city's "big whigs" and got to go into the mills where he observed production. "I asked questions of everybody: superintendents, foremen, operators…From the very beginning, I was curious about the cost of things…"

While still a teenager, William Wood reinvented himself by adding his mother's maiden name, Madison. His mother was the daughter of a Portuguese girl and an Englishman and young Wood knew his Anglo heritage would serve him better in the business world.

Wood moved to Lawrence in 1885, to help save the cotton manufacturing branch of Frederick Ayer's Washington Mills. Before the age of thirty, Wood became treasurer, then assistant manager. He married the boss' daughter and in 1889, directed the consolidation of twenty-six mills to form the American Woolen Company. Wood became president upon Ayer's retirement. Four of AWC's textile factories were located in Lawrence and the Company had offices in Boston and New York.

The Wood Mill, built in 1905, became the largest producer of worsted cloth in the world with 1,470 looms requiring some 10,000 workers during the peak season. Standing six stories high, encompassing thirty acres of floor space under one roof and stretching a third of a mile along the Merrimack River, the Wood Mill represented only one of the American Woolen Company's manufacturing concerns, which the *New York Times* referred to as "the $65 million wool trust." By 1910, the American Woolen Company employed more than 30,000 workers, 75% of whom were foreign-born. Always in need of a supply of cheap labor for his factories, Wood supported open immigration policies.

For many unskilled, immigrant workers, William Madison Wood was the villain of the Strike of 1912, remembered as the "Bread and Roses Strike." It erupted after a new state law went into effect which cut the working hours of women and children from fifty-six to fifty-four hours per week. Wood and other mill owners cut their employees' wages accordingly. Upon receiving reduced paychecks, the operatives stopped their machines and left the mills in droves, calling upon out-of-town union leaders from the Industrial Workers of the World to lead the strike.

Boss Wood refused to meet with either his workers or union representatives to negotiate their grievances. At first, he would not even admit that a strike was underway. "There is no strike in Lawrence—just mob rule—intent upon destroying private property in Lawrence," he told the local press.

Later, as leader of Lawrence's mill owners, Wood was determined to break the strike, calling the strikers "ignorant and irresponsible men who are unaware of the hard economic fact that employers cannot pay employees for fifty-six hours work when they labored only fifty-four hours." Wood was also guilty of strike-breaking tactics. Only after the strike dragged on for sixty-three days and gained national sympathy for the workers and management, worried that its factories would be unable to produce its Spring orders, did William Wood agree to the striker's demands.

The strike remains a landmark in American labor history, and following its success, Wood showed more concern for his employees. His son, William Junior, who had majored in sociology in college, was known for the enlightened labor-management policies he brought to AWC. Wood's biographer explains that he was so obsessed with building his empire that he "lost touch with people on his payroll." The lives of his 25,000 operatives, most immigrants from Southern Europe, were simply unfathomable to their employer. The crowded, dark tenements in which they lived had likely never been viewed by their boss who resided in Arden, his large and lovely rural estate in Andover.

William Wood learned a hard lesson and under his son's supervision, day-care nurseries were provided for working mothers and summer camps, social and athletic clubs were organized for AWC workers. A Homestead financial office was established to help employees purchase co-owned houses on the installment plan. Medical benefits and life insurance were also provided.

In the early 1920s, the American Woolen Company owned and operated sixty mills and employed a work force of 40,000. With sixty mills in eight states, it was the world's largest textile corporation. Yet it was constantly faced with stiff competition.

The Twentieth Century

With a decline in demand as well as profits following World War I, the corporation faced financial loss. This, coupled with a series of family tragedies, left William Wood hopelessly despondent.

The youngest of his four children died at the age of twenty-four in the flu epidemic. Her father erected a granite trough in tribute to Irene's love of animals which still stands at Shawsheen Square. Then on August 15, 1922, thirty-year-old Billy Wood, Jr. was killed when his Rolls Royce wrapped around a telephone pole on Route 28. The old man lost all interest in business and indeed, in life. "Life isn't worth living," Wood was heard to comment.

The roaring twenties brought a new informality to fashion. Women wanted shorter, looser frocks suitable for dancing the Charleston and market demands for wool and worsted changed. By 1924, AWC was losing money. Wood suffered a stroke and at his physician's insistence, resigned, a disillusioned, broken man.

On February 2, 1926, while vacationing in Daytona, Florida, sixty-eight-year-old William Madison Wood suddenly ordered his chauffeur to stop along Flager Beach. He got out of the car and disappeared behind the trees where he put a .38 caliber revolver into his mouth and pulled the trigger.

William Madison Wood, the would-be-Yankee millionaire, built mills and mansions and created an entire model village to compensate for his humble beginning in a fishermen's cottage. The poverty stricken immigrant son always had to prove that he was worthy of belonging to the ruling social class. He smoked the finest Havana cigars and sported a fashionable cane. He belonged to the Algonquin Club of Boston, Manhattan's Metropolitan Club and several yacht clubs. He served as a director of several national banks, including Chase National, then the largest in the country. His children were sent to the finest private schools and studied abroad. He liked to tell how he could trace his heritage back to Martha's Vineyard's early whaling families.

William Madison Wood was generous to town and church. In 1908, for example he had West Parish Cemetery landscaped as a garden cemetery with an arched granite gateway and erected a charming chapel with Tiffany windows on the grounds. Devotion to community beautification inspired him to support the Andover Village Improvement Society. A workaholic, he enjoyed earning and spending money, and the power that money brought. He climbed all the way to the top but in the end, found little that was really worth having. ∞

WONDER VILLAGE

In the early twenties, Andover citizens watched the transformation of Frye Village into Shawsheen Village with great interest.

> *Like a sunrise in summer, so fair to be seen*
> *Rose the Queen of the Valley, Bonnie Shawsheen.*
> *With its streets and its homes all modern and grand*
> *And its buildings the peer of any in the land;*
> *Each forming a part of a wonderful plan*
> *That was born in the brain of a remarkable man,*
> *A prince of industry of national fame*
> *Who in building Shawsheen adds luster to his name.*

From *Arden*, the hilltop residence which John Dove, partner in the Smith & Dove Manufacturing Company had built in 1846, William Wood dreamed of a self-contained, self-sufficient company town for his managers, agents, and white-collar employees. Attractive homes with up-to-date conveniences, efficient schools, and recreational facilities would surely inspire company loyalty and increase employee efficiency. The headquarters of American Woolen Company were here 1923-1925.

For years, this Empire Builder had been buying up land around Frye Village. Sparing no expense, Wood hired some of the most highly regarded architects and landscape designers and proceeded to move eighteenth-century buildings he deemed worth keeping. He laid out new streets and personally directed every detail of Shawsheen Village.

One employee told how in the summer of 1921, Mr. Wood returned from a trip to Europe to discover an entire street laid out and a row of houses erected in the wrong spot. "Move those houses! Eliminate that street!" ordered Wood, and within weeks, the buildings had been relocated and the street had vanished.

Mr. Wood determined that everything that went into the creation of Shawsheen Village would be top rate. He bought the best bricks from a New Hampshire brick yard. Architectural elements like fanlights and interior woodwork, hardware for plumbing, kitchen equipment, and electricity, all exemplified the highest quality of products available. It was an incredibly expensive project and one not with-out controversy in Andover. Some Frye Village residents did not take kindly to having an outsider like Wood change the time-honored name of their neighborhood. Others simply refused to sell, while some townspeople expressed fear that Andover would be annexed to Lawrence, where most of the textile factories were located.

Furthermore, Shawsheen Village was elitist. Executives, overseers, mill agents, managers, clerks, secretaries, and accountants could live here. A company brochure extolled that "Here children have the advantages of education and association with boys and girls of their own type and breeding, where under ordinary conditions the child of the average office worker is denied such advantages."

"White Shawsheen" was created for middle management and clerical workers while "Brick (or Red) Shawsheen" was designed only for upper management. The mill operatives, chiefly recent immigrants, remained in crowded, company-owned three-decker tenements in Lawrence, catching the train or street railway to work in the new factory in "Wonder Village," as it was called in the local newspaper. Cornelia Yancy Lawrence remembers that blacks were not permitted to dance in the Crystal Ballroom even though her brother played in the orchestra. She and her friends danced to his music outside the building.

Ever the Anglophile, Wood designed his village to reflect Colonial Revival, Tudor and Georgian architectural styles. Business, recreational, and private buildings complemented the few eighteenth-century houses that had been preserved. Streets were given English and Scottish names, the latter also to honor Wood's private secre-tary, Wallace, who came from Scotland and oversaw the development of Shawsheen Village with Wood. The dormitory built for unmarried, female office workers at 48-58 Balmoral Street was christened Martha Washington's Lodge.

William Wood liked harmony. Green shutters and blinds adorned each white house. He did not permit fences in residential areas. Screened-in side porches were allowed but not front porches. He selected designs for street light fixtures and decided what particular shrubs and trees should be planted. Grand old elms and maple trees were painstakingly dug up and replanted where he decreed, if they interfered with Wood's grand design. Unsightly telephone and electric wires were installed under-ground. Monthly rental fees, arranged and paid through the village's Homestead Association, even included the cost of sunken metal garbage containers located behind each house. This Homestead office also provided residents with fresh plants in bloom.

There was decidedly a feudal nature to William Wood's environmental endeav-or. It was like the lord of the manor looking down from his castle and overseeing every aspect of the lives of happy workers toiling for him.

There were paternalistic rules to live by since Billy Wood knew what was best for his employees and their families. Seeing laundry hanging in back yards irritated his aesthetic sensibilities. The central Shawsheen Laundry had been built for that purpose. You couldn't park your car in the driveway and since Wood did not like the look of garages attached to houses, employees were required to leave their automobiles at the large brick Colonial Revival community garage built in the Village center. Company chauffeurs drove the executives back to their brick homes, while those from White Shawsheen found their own way.

Shawsheen Village was indeed self-contained. American Woolen Company employees could find everything they needed for the good life right here. The model village had its own meat market and general store in the post office building which also housed a common meeting hall. Here stood the barber shop and beauty salon. AWC offspring attended the kindergarten and then, went to school here. The village had its own boy's club and women's club. Dairy products from company-owned farms in West Andover were trucked into Shawsheen Village's own creamery.

Since residents had everything they needed within walking distance, except churches, many Shawsheen Villagers seldom ventured downtown or mixed with the rest of Andover's citizenry.

John Smith's former mansion on North Main Street was remodeled into Shawsheen Manor and served as a hotel for visiting businessmen. Wood bought the old brick alms house from the town and had it remodeled into a dormitory for single male employees.

One million square foot of mill, (now Brickstone Square) employed 2,700 hands and nearby was the dye plant, warehouse and power plant. The handsome Executive Administration Building (later Sacred Heart School and now, private condominiums) became AWC headquarters. It was decorated with the company symbols: cast stone rams' heads, American eagles, and Native American faces.

For many Andoverites, dancing at the Balmoral in summer and the Crystal Ballroom in the winter remains a precious memory since they were in operation until 1957. The Balmoral Spa was a drugstore complete with a soda fountain, while dances, movies, and theatricals regularly took place in Balmoral Gardens, an outside pavilion. Young people rode the train from Boston and from many towns around to Shawsheen Village Station to dance under the stars to the ten-piece orchestra known as Roland Russell's Ramblers. Louis Armstrong, "King of Trumpet Players" performed here in 1932. When the weather got too cold, they danced inside under flickering lights cast by the huge crystal ball hung from the ceiling. The lights were dimmed and the rotating ball reflected facets of light throughout the room.

Shawsheen Village's social scenes took place during Prohibition and there is some evidence that a few residents flaunted the 28th Amendment, along with other Americans. Residents complained of "loud noise, swearing and howling" as cars left late in the evening.

In July of 1925, the *Andover Townsman* noted that the selectmen decreed that "two dancing parties per week in Balmoral Gardens were not to exceed the hour of eleven p.m.; no minors under seventeen admitted, and grounds policed after the dance in order there be no loitering…In deference to the residents of Shawsheen Village, who have complained about the noise and quality of the music, the sounding board must be faced toward the east."

There were tennis and bowling tournaments and winter skating parties. Shawsheen Village also boasted a bowling alley with bowling-on-the-green and baseball outside, as well as a children's playground on the Balmoral playing field. Wood purchased Hussey's Pond, which once powered sawmill operations. He had it drained and laid with a concrete bottom, built bathhouses and hired lifeguards. He bought one hundred and seventy-five acres for an 18-hole golf course that was designed by the same man credited with creating Pebble Beach in California. This is now the Andover Country Club. In 1925, the Shawsheen Athletic Association won the American Soccer Championship.

Wood envisioned his employees living in contentment in cozy dwellings among their American Woolen Company colleagues. Enjoyment of daily life here would make them want to contribute more toward the company's financial success. Apparently, Billy Wood failed to realize that he could not personally direct the lives of his employees. People who worked together were not necessarily interested in living and socializing together right under their boss' nose.

In 1924, Wood resigned due to failing health and mounting depression over family tragedies and business problems. The Executive Administration Building at Shawsheen was closed that same year. Company headquarters were moved back to Boston, then to New York. Many managers had considered the concept of Shawsheen Village sheer folly anyway, costing the company unnecessary expense. Wood's wishes had been AWC's mandate, but now it was out of the old man's hands. The attractive houses soon became prime real estate and were sold off individually.

William Wood created Shawsheen Village between 1919 and 1924 as one of this country's first corporate model communities and it remains a sterling example of twentieth-century suburban planning. In 1979, Shawsheen Village was added to the National Register of Historic Districts. ∞

CALVIN COOLIDGE CAME TO TOWN

✖

Phillips Academy Headmaster Al Stearns invited the thirtieth President of the United States to deliver the keynote address on the occasion of the school's Sesqui-centennial. He and Calvin Coolidge had been friends and classmates at Amherst College. Coolidge's second visit to Andover was May 19, 1928. In August of 1919, as Governor of Massachusetts, Coolidge addressed the town's World War I Victory Banquet.

Coolidge almost didn't make it in 1928. He thought he really should attend his son's Amherst graduation and didn't really see how he could justify two trips away from Washington so close together. Yet it seemed to mean so much to his old friend, Al Stearns, who said local newspapers were already heralding the President's visit as "the most notable occasion in the history of the town."

As the Academy made Sesquicentennial plans, President Coolidge hedged on dates, not knowing exactly when Congress would adjourn. "Why not just bribe some long-winded Senators to filibuster?" Al Stearns suggested.

Coolidge's White House secretary finally assured Phillips Academy Headmaster Stearns that "it was all sewed up for the 19th," and that the President would require an amplifier for broadcast. After all, Coolidge had written his own speech and wanted it broadcast over the air waves, so the nation could tune in on their radios. Always one for protocol, the President insisted that all guests and speakers were to be seated before he and the First Lady entered *any* room.

Colonel Starling, head of the Secret Service, accompanied the Coolidges to Andover, along with three army officers, seven other members of the secret service, seven newsmen, five photographers and a messenger.

The Coolidge Special pulled into Andover Station at nine o'clock in the morning. Along with Headmaster Stearns, Phillips Academy dignitaries, and town officials, in spite of pelting rain, a large crowd was on hand to greet the President and First Lady. The First Couple dutifully waved from the platform at the back of the train and posed for the photographers. Newspaper reporters noted that Grace Coolidge was "smartly dressed in a black frock, bordered in gold and wore a wide black hat and she had a yellow rose pinned on her coat." And the President sported a top hat.

Members of Battery C, 102nd Field Artillery met the train, assigned to serve as military escort. Sixteen Calvary officers from the National Guard drew their sabers and were performing an elaborate equestrian maneuver when two members of this honor guard toppled off their horses to the ground. "Those two fellas surely were surprised to see us!" the President remarked.

At the head of the procession to Andover Hill was the American Legion's Weymouth Post Band, all in red coats, led by a drum major with a silver baton. Behind the band, came the Calvary with sabers drawn, followed by an open car bearing the Coolidges. As the entourage reached Chapel Avenue, a twenty-one gun salute was fired and the President waved his hat. Four bands were stationed at various points of the campus. Stone jars filled with apple blossoms lined the front steps of Headmaster Stearns' house on Andover Hill. Massachusetts Governor and Mrs. Alvin T. Fuller met the President and First Lady at the door and presented them with medals bearing the profile of the school's founder, Samuel Phillips, cast for the occasion. President and Mrs. Coolidge both immediately put the commemorative medals around their necks and wore them the rest of the day.

Then everyone donned academic robes for the procession across campus. With his black, ankle-length robe, the President wore a purple scarf around his neck and a mortar-board on his head. The procession was headed by the color guard from Andover Post number 8, American Legion, and Grand Marshall General Marlborough Churchill, and followed by the Phillips Academy Trustees, the Governors of Massachusetts and New Hampshire with their wives, thirty college presidents, the robed representatives of some forty other prep schools, and finally, Phillips Academy faculty members, all in academic robes. Academy students, wearing blue jackets and white pants, lined both sides of the path, cheering.

"The Governors must be in the front row! It is protocol!" President Coolidge reprimanded Headmaster Stearns, as the dignitaries were seating themselves on the platform. He did express his appreciation upon seeing the loud speakers in place. After all, he had spent one hundred hours studying the history of Phillips Academy and writing his own speech and he intended to have it amplified for the benefit of the great throng here present.

"It is more than the passage of time that brings us here to observe and celebrate this anniversary," President Coolidge began. "The significance of this occasion lies not in the number of days but in the importance of purpose and the magnitude of accomplishment."

The Sesquicentennial speech stressed the need for quality in one's endeavors. "The world will have little use for those who are right only part of the time. The world is not content with a musician who can strike only ninety percent of the notes. Of what use is a baseball player on the diamond who catches only eighty percent of the balls?" The President paused now and then to wait out audience applause.

"Our determination to make sacrifices necessary for the common good ought to be strengthened. We may be certain that our country is altogether worthy of us. It will be necessary to demonstrate that we are worthy of our country…"

As the dignitaries proceeded to Case Memorial Building for the alumni luncheon, carillon bells pealed from Memorial Tower above the old parade ground where so many young men of Andover had been mustered for war and where former U.S. Presidents George Washington and Andrew Jackson once reviewed the militia.

The Coolidge Special pulled out of Andover promptly at one o'clock in the afternoon, headed for Northampton. The President's special train had to leave ahead of the Boston and Maine number 183 Express, which was scheduled to steam into the Andover Depot at 1:14 PM. "Certainly wanted to avoid a collision if we could!" quipped President Coolidge. ∾

BLACK LUCY'S GARDEN

❧

In 1943, Harvard archaeologists Adelaide and Ripley Bullen were excavating a Native American site on Woburn Street in the Ballardvale section of Andover, when they uncovered a wealth of artifacts that revealed the daily life of an African-American woman who lived here a century before. These precious pieces of material culture are now housed at the Robert S. Peabody Museum of Archaeology at Phillips Academy. Eugene Winter, an archaeology scholar, museum volunteer, and honorary curator of Black Lucy's Garden collection, said, "This represents one of the earliest archaeological projects ever carried out to give historical context to a black American." The Bullens also uncovered a root cellar and a fallen brick and mortar chimney, still filled with charcoal.

An article by Alfred Poor in the *Andover Advertiser*, August 29, 1863, tells us that "Lucy, daughter of a slave in Boston, was given to Mrs. Job Foster, who married second, a Chandler, and who left Black Lucy an acre of land about twenty rods from the Brook. Lucy's house was built about 1815 and she resided there until 1845."

Charlotte Helen Abbott, writing at the turn of the twentieth century claims that "Lucy had a wonderful singing voice that would carry her songs half a mile." Church, Probate, and Vital Records help piece together Lucy's life. On July 14, 1771, the Reverend Samuel Phillips recorded Lucy's baptism in the *South Church Record Book*. Job Foster, a yeoman with one hundred acres, died of smallpox in 1782. Since Lucy was not listed among assets in his probate inventory, we can assume that she had already been granted her freedom or that she was still the property of his widow, Hannah. In 1791, Lucy "formerly servant of Job Foster" was warned out of town for failing to provide permission to reside in Andover. The *South Parish Records* of October 20, 1792 note the birth of "Peter, son of Lucy Foster, negro woman." Since no father's name is listed, the child is assumed to have been illegitimate. The following year "on profession of faith," Lucy became an official member of that church. And records show that she could read and write.

Hannah Ford Foster married her second husband, Philemon Chandler in 1789. Lucy was bequeathed, along with Chandler's stock of cattle, pewter, household goods and wooden utensils… "my negro maidservant, my horse and tackling, sheep and swine, corn, grain and cider that shall be still in my house." In December of 1812, the Widow Chandler died, leaving a will that reads, in part: "I, Hannah Chandler of Andover, Widow, give to Lucy Foster, the black girl who lives with me, and her heirs, one cow and the sum of $126.15. I also give to Lucy one acre of land." Yet Mistress Chandler left heavy debts, so that Lucy could not live as comfortably as she previously had, yet she did have a place to call her own.

Neighbors collected funds and pitched in to build a cottage for Lucy on her acre where she lived for the next thirty years. Lucy may have worked as a domestic for local families and she received a yearly dole from South Parish Church that ranged from one to five dollars.

Gun flints, knives, a brass belt buckle, as well as a shaving mug uncovered in the archaeological dig suggest that her son, Peter, continued to live with his mother. Shards of quality imported Staffordshire, Chinese export porcelain bowls, Delft ware, and willow pattern plates discovered in Black Lucy's Garden testify to this ex-slave's love of pretty things. Perhaps Hannah Foster Chandler and others gave Lucy decorative pottery pieces when they became chipped or out of fashion. One plate has a view of a castle in Portugal. Another shows archaeological ruins in Europe being viewed by several men.

Archeological evidence unearthed at Black Lucy's Garden offers many other clues about her daily life in mid-nineteenth century Andover. She probably smoked these clay pipes and once wore the spectacles that were found. Lucy likely cooked in this redware pottery and served meals in pewter. Her salt-glaze jug probably held cider. There is an iron padlock and a tin candle holder. Green glass bottles were used to hold her patent medicines. Pieces of a parasol were found, along with shell buttons and what was probably once her most treasured brooch in a tiny brass frame. Lucy Foster's sewing scissors, thimble, and pins were also uncovered. Clam shells, fish bones, and pig knuckles told archaeologists and historians what she and her son often ate for dinner.

A U. S. penny, dated 1827, which Lucy must have treasured, was found among these artifacts, along with a ceremonial plate of General Lafayette landing on American shores in 1824.

According to *Andover Infirmary Records*, seventy-eight-year-old Lucy Foster was "indigent" and a "state ward" when admitted on October 22, 1845 to the alms house, ten days before her death. Charred remains found in Black Lucy's Garden suggest her cabin may have burned down prior to her hospital admission.

This historically significant site was bulldozed by developers in the 1970s. ∞

HAROLD RAFTON:
"THE CONSCIENCE OF ANDOVER"

"Mr. AVIS", as Harold Robert Rafton became known to Andover, was born in Boston, December 21, 1890. A sickly child, he was inspired by the early life of Theodore Roosevelt and exercised diligently. He entered Harvard at the age of fifteen, graduating with highest honors in chemistry in 1910.

Years later, on a canoe trip in Maine, Harold was horrified by yellow foam from paper mills polluting pristine waterways. He decided to dedicate his career to industrial research, applying his chemical training to the recycling of waste products from the manufacture of paper. He was associated with Champion-International in Lawrence, then in 1916, started his own company, Raffold, which produced quality paper for National Geographic Society, among others. Later, he founded Rafton Laboratories. Harold was also an inventor and received some one hundred and fifty patents during his lifetime. He and his wife, Helen, a Ph.D. chemist, moved to Andover in 1928.

Following World War II, Andover experienced unprecedented growth, becoming a popular suburb from where fathers commuted along the new highway systems to their offices in Boston or along Route 128, where so many high tech and engineering companies were now located. In 1955 alone, there were two hundred and sixty-three applications for new building permits in Andover. Route 93 cut through West Andover in 1958.

On December 22, 1955, a letter signed "Helen and Harold Rafton" appeared in the *Andover Townsman* in response to one previously published, advocating Andover's rapid development as "inevitable due to the increase of population and rapid pace of construction."

The Raftons' letter urged that "provisions be made for publicly owned areas for recreation...so we will not become merely a town of rows of houses...Park areas are vital and should not be an afterthought, but an integral part of community planning...and can never be replaced once they are gone." They proposed Andover citizens donate towards the purchase of lands and urged quick action since development was proceeding at an accelerated pace and the town would soon lose its opportunity. The Andover Village Improvement Society rose to meet the Raftons' challenge and Harold became known as the "conscience of Andover."

"We stuck out our necks and they dragged us in," Rafton said, "and we formed a land company...Ever since man first scraped a wooden stick to use a plow, he's been changing his environment, and that's progress. But we can't constantly strain our resources without consequences..."

The Raftons were also watch dogs when it came to pollution. "People are beginning to realize that they came to this town to see some trees and get some fresh air. Good clean air has become almost as scarce as marshland and unpolluted water. We can't just keep pouring waste products into the atmosphere and water and filling in our wetlands..." Harold also insisted that "intelligent waste disposal should be a major concern of industry. It is not the privilege of private industry to dump waste. This is an infringement on the right of the public."

Following his retirement in 1958, Harold went to work full time to increase the land holdings of the Andover Village Improvement Society. When Raftons joined AVIS efforts in 1955, the Society owned a mere twenty-three acres. At the time of Harold's death in 1982, AVIS held nearly eight hundred and fifty acres.

Rafton did his homework on any parcel of land that he thought might be obtainable. Before the advent of photocopy machines and computers, Harold put in endless hours studying maps, researching wills, and undertaking complicated title searches at the Registry of Deeds in Lawrence and Salem. He understood the legal processes of land procurement. He walked the lands, matching his exhaustive deed research and map studies with boundaries in the field.

Rafton's power of persuasion at getting landowners to sell or bequeath their properties, became legendary. There were rumors around town that Harold would actually show up at the bedsides of the dying. It is true that he dedicated much of his time trying to convince people to place their land in public trust and keep it forever wild as a legacy for future generations, rather than selling out to developers. AVIS trustees grew accustomed to late night phone calls from Harold Rafton when he had finally persuaded someone to sell and required votes from board members to purchase some particular property.

According to AVIS president, Nathaniel Smith, a math teacher at Phillips Academy, "Harold was a bulldog when he thought a piece of property was attainable...There is no opponent so formidable as a man totally and tirelessly dedicated to a cause, particularly if that man is Harold Rafton."

Harold's genius was in obtaining a piece of land for AVIS, then building on it with a series of small parcels to link sites together. Deer Jump, one hundred and forty-seven acres situated along the Merrimack River, is a shining example of how Rafton was able to link lands owned by different parties into one large reservation. Purchased between 1960 and 1973, Rafton considered Deer Jump "the most ambitious and rewarding" of all the AVIS properties.

Harold Rafton and AVIS received citations from the Massachusetts Department of Natural Resources, the Massachusetts Audubon Society and in 1978, the

Environmental Award from the Massachusetts Conservation Council for "most valuable service to conservation through the preservation of land." In 1973, Harold and Helen Rafton were awarded the Outstanding Conservationist Award from the Massachusetts Department of Natural Resources.

After twenty-seven years of acquiring land for AVIS, Harold retired and AVIS presented him with an antique snowshoe, a symbol of all the miles he had trekked over the years on behalf of their organization. When Harold Rafton died in 1982 at the age of ninety-one, he was credited with saving nearly nine hundred acres of wetlands, woodlands, and meadows from developer's bulldozers. Society president Nat Smith said, "Harold Rafton has been the conscience of this town. Without him we wouldn't have what we do. Harold had the long vision and a sense of what the town will be like eighty to one hundred years from now." ∞

THE MULTI-MILLION DOLLAR BUSINESS THAT STARTED ON ROSE'S STOVE

A television commercial that played in 2002, opened with the *Entering Andover* sign opposite Merrimack College, then faded to interior shots with Bob and Alice Colombosian. "It started on a kitchen stove," Bob explained on TV, as a vintage portrait of his parents appear on the screen. "There was a farm, a barn, a couple of cows."

Columbo, America's first yogurt company, was the product advertised. It began in Andover in 1929, when Bob's mother, Rose, put to practical use the extra milk produced by family cows.

Although yogurt had been a staple in middle-eastern diets for 6,000 years, it was unknown in this country, except among Turkish and Syrian immigrants who settled in this country from the 1870s. Rose and Sarkis Columbosian came to the United States in 1917 fleeing the genocide perpetuated against the Armenians by the Ottoman Turkish Empire.

The couple moved to Argilla Road in Andover in 1927. They had cows and chickens and grew vegetables on their five acre Wild Rose Dairy, but it was difficult feeding four children, especially during the Depression. Sarkis delivered milk to Lawrence and to grocery stores in ethnic neighborhoods in Boston by horse and wagon. Rose had been making cheese and yogurt on her wood stove for the family with left-over milk, using Armenian recipes she remembered from childhood. Syrians, Greeks, Lebanese, and Armenians throughout the Merrimack Valley were soon asking for Rose's homemade yogurt.

On March 2, 1939, a major fire took their house and barn but with the help of relatives and friends, they not only built a new place to live, but a second building for yogurt production. This remained a neighborhood cottage industry until 1951 when an article by health advocate Dr. Gaylord Hauser appeared in *Reader's Digest*. Entitled "Look younger, Live Longer" Hauser's article heralded the benefits of yogurt as one of the best sources of protein and the secret to good health and longevity. Soon, the Columbosians were selling to supermarkets and Sarkis and his sons were driving a pick-up truck filled with Rose's yogurt and her traditional braided cheeses to middle eastern settlements in Brooklyn and New Jersey. The family enlarged operations with more refrigerator space, added a yogurt room with tile walls and an incubator room with electric heaters, pasteurizing vats and a homogenizer.

Sarkis died in 1966, and in 1971, in need of more space, operations were relocated to Methuen. Since Columbosian seemed too difficult to pronounce, the product became known as Columbo Yogurt and soon become a million dollar business. It was sold to Hood and Sealtest who added fruit. The business was bought by Bon Grain S. A., of Versailles, France in 1977, who later sold out to General Mills.

Columbo also became the largest player in the billion dollar frozen yogurt business and products continue to be sold worldwide in food outlets, hospital, business and college cafeterias, convenience and health food stores and supermarkets. The Old World recipe that Rose Colombosian recreated on her cook stove in Andover is America's earliest yogurt dairy and now, the largest manufacturer of yogurt in the world, with annual sales of $100,000,000, offering sixty different flavors. In 1989, a Colombo University Training Center was established in Atlanta, Georgia to train personnel for this highly competitive, global market. People attend from all over the country for training in the operations, management, and marketing of yogurt. When Rose Colombosian prepared yogurt for her family she did not realize she was pioneering the country's first yogurt company. ∞

ANDOVER'S MUSIC MAN

ॐ

With his shock of white hair, mustache and raised baton, J. Everett Collins was Andover's own Arthur Fieldler, the famous Boston Pops conductor. Collins was also "Uncle John" to three generations of students and parents.

Born in 1894, John Everett's musical career started as boy soloist at Christ Episcopal Church in 1906, and he sang for several Boston church events. He was the bass soloist at Punchard High School until his graduation in 1913. He grew up in the center of town, where his father took care of horses for T. A. Holt, the grocer whose store was located in the basement of the Baptist Church at Elm Square. On Halloween, Mr. Collins used to cover the delivery wagon with sheets and then hold one sheet up with a broom as if a ghost were driving. Then through town and across The Park he'd race his wagon, scaring all the children.

From 1912-1923, with a hiatus as a doughboy with the Yankee Division during World War I, Collins served as South Church soloist and then choir director from 1923 to 1929. For fifty years, he also directed the choir at First Calvary Baptist Church in Lawrence.

J. Everett Collins was a star athlete. He played baseball and was a paid catcher for one Manchester, New Hampshire team. "All my life I've worked, worked, and worked to get where I wanted," Collins said, "whether it was sports or music." He seldom missed an Andover High School football game and at the age of ninety, was awarded a Varsity A and inducted into the school's Athletic Hall of Fame. This made Collins the first and only individual inducted into both Andover's Sports Hall of Fame and Fine Arts Hall of Fame. He was also a cricket coach.

Collins was founder and director of the Andover Male Choir in 1926, first known as the Square and Compass Glee Club. In 1930 this became affiliated with the New England Federation of Men's Glee Clubs and won the Federation contest for eight consecutive years. "We are just a bunch of guys singing out because we love music," Collins explained. Members made annual Christmas visits to sing carols to patients at Lawrence General Hospital. In 1929, Collins founded the Andover Choral Society, a community group that included all ages and occupations. For fifty-three years, the maestro conducted Handel's *Messiah* every Christmas season in Andover.

The Twentieth Century

J. Everett Collins was elected representative to state legislature in 1941 and served fourteen years. An Andover selectman for twenty-one years, he also served on the school committee for six. "My philosophy has always been to help people. Help organizations." Collins claimed. "Join up! Get in and do!"

Retired from his day job as an auditor and insurance adjustor, "Uncle John" signed on as a consultant for the Andover School Music Department in 1963. He directed *A Capella Choir* madrigal singers and girls' chorale at Andover High School and West Junior High. "One of the greatest joys in life was getting young people to sing," Collins said.

Andover Selectmen declared April 27, 1983, J. Everett Collins Day in Andover. In 1983, Andover's Endowment for the Arts named the new $4.1 million facility *The J. Everett Collins Center for the Performing Arts* and the guest of honor spoke at its inauguration, which concluded with a concert by the Boston Pops. Built with town tax money, it is meant to be a cultural mecca and performance center for the entire Merrimack Valley, as well as a stage for high school productions and a television studio.

Big names performed at the center but a few years later, the Center suffered financial set-backs. Ten years after its opening, it was used for little else but a high school auditorium. Many thought the facility lacked the seating and money to draw famous and expensive talent. Today, however, the Center is an active venue for the arts.

Andover's beloved maestro who filled the town with the sound of music for more than half a century, died at the age of ninety-two in August of 1986. His obituary noted that "He gave generously of his time and talent to encourage many in the Merrimack Valley to know the gladness of singing together." ∞

OUTWARD BOUND OUT OF ANDOVER

❧

Joshua Miner was born in Andover and so was Outward Bound, which he founded in the United States. According to the Reverend Calvin Mutti, minister of South Church, who was Miner's good friend and neighbor, "For Josh, the name *Andover* meant both the school he worked for and the town he lived in."

In 1952, Joshua Miner was invited to Phillips Academy to teach science and physics and to coach. "But be careful not to make changes," warned Headmaster John Kemper. Miner later served as dean of admissions for thirteen years, where he "opened the doors to minorities, special needs students and young people from other countries. He built the diverse student body we have today." Yet Josh Miner's greatest legacy is Outward Bound, USA.

Rock climbing, rope ladders, hiking, orienteering, crawling through nets-these were the teaching tools of Outward Bound. "We put kids through twenty-six days of abject misery," Miner said. "You are challenged to compete against yourself. The individual sets, then raises the limits, of his or her endurance…Outward Bound is a life-changing experience where the wilderness becomes a classroom to develop self-esteem, teamwork, community and environmental concerns, and commitment."

Born at Phillips Academy and parented by Josh Miner, the first Outward Bound school in this country opened in Colorado in 1961 with forty students and changed the face of education. By 1991, Outward Bound USA had 30,000 enrolled nationwide and six hundred schools with their own programs. Many other institutions have adopted aspects of Outward Bound to their curriculum and numerous businesses have developed similar self-reliance wilderness programs for their employees. Outward Bound has enriched and turned around countless lives. Six hundred thousand people, including former President Jimmy Carter, have taken the course. The program also helps troubled teens to develop a sense of confidence and a new outlook on life by teaching them to master personal challenges and the need for teamwork.

Miner graduated from Princeton University in 1943, then served in France and Germany during World War II. He received the Purple Heart, Bronze Star, five combat stars and the *Croix de Guerre* for bravery. After the war, he began his teaching career at the Hun School in New Jersey.

The Twentieth Century

"I accidentally backed into education and found it very rewarding…I liked the classroom. I liked the kids. I liked the coaching. I couldn't believe life was so good that I could get paid for something that was so much fun." Hun School operated on a tight budget so all students were expected to help with maintenance of the plant and grounds. The new teacher observed how these campus jobs developed teamwork among the students and gave them a sense of responsibility to the school community.

Josh Miner observed that most teenagers were bored. "Many didn't fit the mold they were poured into but learned in less traditional ways. Students today may be entertained by the Internet and video games, but are not being challenged." Miner believed education was "a total life experience…Learning is not about absorbing facts to throw back on a test. Real education means asking questions, not reciting the answers. The teacher's job is to lead students to the thrill of discovery. That is the essence of the Outward Bound method."

It was while teaching at Gordonstoun School in Scotland in the early 'fifties that Miner got to know German educator Kurt Hahn, who founded Outward Bound in Europe during the Second World War. Miner was inspired and became determined to model a program for Americans after Herr Hahn's. "The idea is to challenge yourself to be more than you thought you could ever be-emotionally, physically, and mentally…testing one's limits and commitment to service."

It had already been demonstrated in Europe that students with Outward Bound training were better prepared in life skills. Yet it wasn't easy to change tradition at Phillips Academy in the 1950s. For Miner, it was a frustrating ten-year struggle to get his program accepted. "Selling the program to the headmaster and faculty was not easy. Then the Soviet Union shocked Americans by launching Sputnik and the educational climate changed," Miner explained. "Then young President Kennedy challenged the nation with 'Ask not what your country can do for you, but what you can do for your country,' and the Outward Bound philosophy sold like hot-cakes." The Peace Corps, which Joshua Miner also helped launch, adopted the Outward Bound philosophy and outdoor training program for its new recruits.

In 1973, Miner was awarded an Honorary Lifetime Membership in the Appalachian Mountain Club, "in recognition of his role in education." He also served on the White House Conference on Youth and the State Advisory Committee for the U. S. Commission on Civil Rights. The Joshua L. Miner National Outward Bound Center, "a non-profit organization dedicated to building character in the individual by experiential programs in wilderness settings," was dedicated in Garrison, New York in June of 1995.

In Andover, Miner was considered a "model of dedicated community service." Until his death, he received letters from all over the world, many which began, "You don't know me, but you changed my life." When Josh Miner died on January 30, 2002, the Reverend Calvin Mutti honored him as "The resident philosopher of Andover… A folk hero, not just for Andover or the Merrimack Valley, but for the entire country."

∾

THE ANDOVER BOOKSTORE: "A SPECIAL PLACE"

The town's oldest continuously operating business is the Andover Bookstore, whose roots and history are entwined with the Andover Press. This bookstore is also the second oldest continuously running bookstore in the United States.

In 1963, Jerome and Ethel Cross moved the bookstore off Main Street into Olde Andover Village. The building, where the bookstore remains today, was a former barn that had been used for community dances, roller skating and once, even boasted a trapeze. Cross and architect Lincoln Giles renovated the barn to include a balcony and fireplace. During the thirty years it was owned by the Crosses, there was a lending library and patrons could borrow books at five cents a day.

William and Carolyn Dalton bought the Andover Bookstore in 1990 and added a lower level. They also brought in overstuffed chairs, a sound system and computers and added a dumbwaiter to deliver books upstairs. In 1992, Robert Hugo of Marblehead, who owns several other bookstores, became the owner.

The bookstore has always maintained close ties with Phillips Academy and continues to purchase textbooks and supplies for the students. The store once sold ink, pens, stationery, cards, and all paper products imaginable, including toilet paper. It continues to offer t-shirts and mugs with the Phillips Academy logo, blank books, calendars, tapes, and greeting cards, but no more toilet paper.

The Andover Bookstore is a community center and a cultural mecca. People drop in to relax, browse, help themselves to a cup of coffee and cookies, then settle onto a sofa for a good read. One employee calls it the "Brigadoon Bookstore," because one can step back in time. "There's a sense of being in a different time and place. In fact, there's not even a noticeable clock around."

The bookstore serves as an ideal small event venue. Just ask Robert Pinsky, former Poet Laureate of America, who read here a few years ago as part of the regular Poetry Series. A weekly children's story hour, book discussion groups, authors' signings, and storytelling crowd the calendar each month. Town Tales is a favorite event, when different residents are invited to share stories of growing up in Andover, or tell some fascinating historical happening.

According to storyteller Susan Lenoe, a children's book specialist who runs the storytelling events, "Andover Bookstore is bigger than the books and the people. It has a spirit of its own; a spirit that has been there throughout its long history." ∞

THE HIGH COMMISSIONER OF STICKBALL

❧

"He turned senior year into a frolic for all of us," exclaimed one of George Walker Bush's Phillips Academy 1964 classmates. "A very popular fella; Tweeds was a natural leader," other prep school pals recalled.

Unlike his father, former President Bush, Class of '42, George W. would not be remembered for academic achievement or athletic distinction. The sons had a tough time following in the footsteps of a father who had been voted most popular student, senior class president, secretary of the student council, and a member of the editorial staff of *The Phillipian*. Father Bush was also captain of the varsity baseball and soccer teams and considered the campus baseball champion of his time.

In the early 'sixties Phillips Academy was still a jacket-and-tie place. Even though Abbot Academy was a few blocks away, the boys led, for the most part, a celibate, isolated, ivory tower existence. They got together with girls only on weekends, usually at well-chaperoned dances. Daily or evening chapel services were mandatory and academics, difficult and demanding. Later, George W. Bush would say, "I can remember trying to figure out how to catch up...I learned to read and write there." One picture in *Pot Pourri*, the 1964 Yearbook, caught him yawning and lying over an open book in the library. There is another shot of him with a group of fellow students trying to squeeze into a phone booth—a favorite campus prank of that day.

George W. had grown up in Texas and Phillips, Andover was not his first choice. He had not been accepted at St. John's, near home. Andover seemed "cold, dark, faraway" to him. It was a world apart from Texas and he would recall his years at Phillips Academy as a balancing act of the eastern preppie elite and the down-home Texan. His nicknames at Phillips Academy were "Tweeds" and "Lip." He resided in America House where *My Country 'Tis of Thee* had been written.

George W. placed second in his class for BMOC (Big Man On Campus) and third for "Wit". Chief among the achievements listed under his senior yearbook photograph is "Head Cheerleader." There is a picture of him wearing his A-letter sweater and cheering the troops on with a giant megaphone. Being such a successful head cheerleader earned him the nickname, "Boss Tweed." In fact, he was so good that staff members and several administrators warned George to "cool it, or keep his cheers more low-keyed" as his squad was diverting attention from the football team.

Yet it is as "Stickball Commissioner 3, 4" and "High Commissioner of Stickball" in his senior year that he is best remembered by classmates and faculty. Indeed, it is said that George W. Bush founded stickball at Phillips Academy. This usually urban street game, played with broomstick and tennis ball in sneakers or bare feet, started as something to do while waiting for the dinner bell or to be played after supper. George W. organized the boys and their dorms into teams with silly and suggestive names on their shirts, and coached their matches. He even managed to get a faculty team together. Stickball offered Phillips' pressured students a welcome escape from the rigidity of the school's traditional intercollegiate varsity team matches.

One day in his senior year, dressed in a top hat like some master of ceremonies at a circus, George W. rose in assembly and announced himself as the "High Commissioner of Stickball." This was followed by a twenty-minute speech during which he explained how he planned to organize the intramural stickball program for all the dormitories on campus. It may have been a spoof on the grave seriousness of the academy's competitive athletic meets against other schools, but his fellow students took him at his word. He outlined the rules, schedules and pledged to issue official membership cards to all stickball players. Years later, some students actually used these cards successfully and without encountering any questions, as fake IDs.

President George W. Bush may not have attended Phillips Academy, Andover by choice but he met the challenge presented him and made good friends there. Phillips taught him how to survive in an unfamiliar and difficult situation. George W. Bush understood how to make people feel better about themselves and found that he was particularly gifted as a cheerleader. ∞

BALLARDVALE BOY

⁊

Jay Leno, the host of NBC's *Tonight Show* has never forgotten his Andover roots. "Andover was a wonderful place to grow up. Just an ideal American town that never lost its innocence. People got excited over the littlest things…a magical town with everything a kid would want: a waterfall, creeks, a pond, a swimming hole, an old mill, a haunted house…I was a kid living in a little town. There was a river and there were frogs to catch and bicycles to ride."

Leno moved to Andover from New York in 1959, at the age of nine. His father, Angelo, a first-generation Italian, was the manager of an insurance company. Ballardvale, where the family lived on Clark Road, was then the quieter, less affluent section of Andover. Their home, built in the '50s, was demolished in 2001 by a developer in order to put up yet another half-million-dollar "trophy house." There was a line of evergreens along the driveway which were the Leno's Christmas trees, from the time Jay was nine until he turned eighteen. He and his father would dig up trees every season, then replant them after the decorations were removed.

Jay remembers Ballardvale as a place where teachers lived in the same neighborhood and sometimes, walked to school with their students. Summers, he and his friends swam in the Shawsheen River and rented kayaks from "an old Italian man." In the woods near their houses the boys discovered arrowheads and peered bravely through the broken windows of an abandoned house that they were convinced was haunted, since it still contained worn furniture and old clothing in bureau drawers.

Where Route 495 is now, Jay's father used to take him to ride his go-cart. Jay says he's liked cars and motorcycles and "tinkering with them since I was a little kid." Currently he has a web site called *Jay's Garage*. He first got wheels of his own, "an old Ford pick-up" at the age of fourteen, for which his parents bought him new upholstery.

During his years at Emerson College, one of his jobs was as a Rolls-Royce mechanic. Nancy Varnum, who went through public school with Jay, remembers that he once picked her up in Andover in a Rolls limo that he drove from Boston.

"By the time I was in high school, I had perfected a larger repertoire of pranks." Jay admits he was not a good student and was frequently sent to detention for cutting-up in class. "Come back when you're ready to learn!" teachers would say, sending him to the principal's office once again. Jay muses that he now gets paid for what he was formerly thrown out of class for doing. Life at Andover High eventually improved, and he now looks back on those years as most important in shaping his adult life. And Leno has been generous in giving back to the school. He recently donated $250,000 for the purchase of computers and software.

One English teacher took him aside to tell him that she'd heard him entertaining the class with funny stories and suggested that if he wrote some of those stories down on paper, she would consider it an assignment for credit. For the first time, Jay enjoyed doing his homework, then reading it out loud in front of the class the following day. He remains grateful to Sandra Hawkes for teaching him to believe in his own ability to write. Another teacher and one of the few who actually laughed at his jokes, asked Jay why he didn't consider going into show business. "When you grow up in a small town like Andover, show business is the furthest thing from being a career option," Leno later wrote.

Jay thinks that his modest mother, who emigrated from Scotland at the age of eleven, would probably consider his ten years of television success as a talk show host "showing off." Following his first appearance on the *Tonight Show* as Johnny Carson's guest, Jay sent his mother several photographs for the local weekly paper. She refused to submit them since she thought his hair too long and advised him to use his Andover High School yearbook picture instead.

When the first McDonald's opened in downtown Andover, Jay got an after school job which he kept through his high school years and where he acquired the nickname "French Fry Cut-Up." One classmate, Nancy Haggerty Varnum, recalls how Jay would present her with three or four bags of French fries when she had only ordered one, or two Big Macs instead of one…"always the funny guy!" Once, Leno beat out the competition and won a cash prize in a talent show sponsored by McDonalds, the first time he ever received money as a stand-up comedian.

James Leno was a member of the first class to graduate from the new Andover High School building in 1968. The prediction for his "Possible Future Career" in the yearbook is "Retired Millionair." Jay was also elected "Funniest Boy," and is pictured posing in a trash barrel.

Just as Jay Leno has never taken a sick day in his decade with NBC, he never stayed home sick from school, that is, not until one fateful day during his junior year. His mother, whom Jay says was "a terrible liar," feared someone from the school would phone. Her truant son reassured her that no one would call. That afternoon, Jay told his mother he had to go out to pick up something, but instead, he went cruising in the 1965 Buick Grandsport 401 V8 ("a genuine four-barrel, four-on-the-floor hot rod") that he'd bought with his McDonald's paychecks. His mother pleaded with him to stay home, terrified her son might be caught skipping school.

"Whatever you do, don't go near the high school!" But he did, and at the time many students and teachers were outside during lunch break. His buddies called out to him and challenged him to burn rubber so Jay raced his Buick around the parking lot and screeched up and down the school driveway. The assistant principal watched it all from his office window and telephoned Jay's house, asking his mother if her son was home. Mrs. Leno explained that he was sick and resting in his bed.

"Is that so? I hate to tell you, Mrs. Leno, but Jay was just here burning rubber in the school parking lot!" Jay received a three-day suspension and when he came through the door that night, his mother hit him over the head with a cooking pot.

Thirty years later, on October 15, 1998, Jay received a "Principal's Pardon" for "burning rubber" in the high school parking lot. "You see," Leno quipped on TV, "you *can* turn your life around!"

Jay's favorite teacher, David Robichaud, personally delivered the Official Pardon on a *Tonight Show* segment. "Try to stand up straight for the occasion," Robichaud reminded his former student as the proclamation was read, clearing Jay's bad record. "By the way, you still owe me a term paper," the history teacher said, exiting the stage. Later, the audience gets to see Mr. Robichaud race off in Jay's automobile, tires squealing.

Leno also invited Robichaud to join him as a presenter at the American Teacher Awards. Leno claims that the history and political current events he incorporates into his monologues come from Mr. Robichaud's teaching him to pay attention to the daily news in social studies. "For many, teaching is a stepping stone to somewhere else," says Leno, "But he was just proud to be a teacher."

When David Robichaud died in January, 2001, Leno phoned the high school principal to offer $10,000 to establish a social studies scholarship in Robichaud's name. "It was always a sense of pride for me that people would stop me on the street and tell me how proud Mr. Robichaud was of me. He never became President; he never circled the earth, but he affected my life in a way that those men never could have."

Jay Leno has learned how to share the very important gift of laughter. The famous comedian says that he learned solid values from his parents and from "growing up innocent in Andover." He credits high school teachers like Mr. Robichaud for teaching him "good citizenship…You remember what you were taught and how people behave and it makes you who you are."

Even though his parents are both gone now, there are occasional Leno sightings in Andover and he remains the Vale's favorite son. He recently donated funds for Ballardvale's playground equipment in his mother's memory. ∞

ENDNOTES: THE TWENTIETH CENTURY

☙

Page 159: Juliet H. Mofford. "AVIS: A History in Conservation," 1980, pp. 3-6

CHAPTER 56 – THE SUFFRAGE MOVEMENT IN ANDOVER
Page 166: Joan Patrakis. "Andover Suffragists Waged a Colorful Campaign."
Andover Historical Society Newsletter, Vol. 20, No. 2, 1995.
Eleanor Richardson. "Andover: A Century of Change," 1996. Andover Historical
Society, p. 49
Andover Townsman weekly columns "Shall Women Vote?" 1915.
"Their Voice Was Heard." Notes and labels for Andover Historical Society Exhibit,
Fall, 1988.
"Andover Men Wanted Women to have the Vote." Sunday Eagle Tribune,
August 20, 1995.

CHAPTER 57 – INDIAN ROGER'S REVENGE
Page 168: Eleanor Richardson. Op. Cit., pp. 50, 152, 187, 206
Juliet H. Mofford. "AVIS: A History in Conservation," 1980, p. 50
Andover Townsmans, December 17, 1897; February 14, 1902
Andover Town Meeting Records, March 6, 1899
Annual Report, Town of Andover, 1910
Andover: *What It Was; What It Is.* Andover Press, 1904, 1913.

CHAPTER 58 – COCONUTS
Page 169: Bessie P. Goldsmith. Townswoman's Andover, 1964; 1970, pp. 67-70
Charlotte Helen Abbott. Andover Townsman, June 4, 1920
Eleanor Richardson. Op. Cit., p. 141

CHAPTER 59 – THE "HORRIBLES"
Page 170: Eleanor Richardson. Ibid., p. 217
Andover Advertiser, July 9, 1853
Pages 170, 171: Andover Townsmans, July 2, 1937; July 8, 1982
Bernice Haggerty "Recreation in Andover in the Good Old Summertime"
Andover Historical Society Newsletter, Vol. 14, Summer, 1989.
Neil Fater. "Horribles Parade Wasn't Always For Kids." Andover Townsman,
July 1, 1999
Author's interview with Ruth Sharpe, 2000
Rebecca Griffin. "Andover Has Horrible History." Eagle Tribune, July 3, 2002

The Twentieth Century

CHAPTER 60 – THE ROBERT PEABODY MUSEUM OF ARCHAEOLOGY
Page 172: Frederick S. Allis, Jr., *Youth From Every Quarter: A Bicentennial History of Phillips Academy, Andover*, 1978, pp. 286, 353, 354, 614
Page 172-173: Author's interviews with staff and volunteers.
News from the Robert S. Peabody Museum of Archaeology, Phillips Academy, Andover. Fall, 1996; Fall/Winter, 1997; Fall, 1999
Lisa Boudreau. "At Phillips Academy's Peabody Museum of Archaeology: Setting a Mess of History Straight." Andover Townsman, July 25, 1991
Eagle Tribune, October 20, 1999

CHAPTER 61 – ANDOVER HISTORICAL SOCIETY: KEEPER OF ANDOVER'S PAST LOOKS TO THE FUTURE
Page 174: Eleanor Richardson. *Century of Change*, 1996, p. 34, 35, 41, 42, 96
Karen Koch-Weiser. "Edward Taylor." Andover Historical Society files.
March 19, 1991
C. C. Carpenter. *Andover Theological Seminary Necrology*. Boston: Beacon Press, p. 73-74
Page 175: Family files, "Blanchard." Andover Historical Society
Andover Historical Society By-Laws; grant applications by Barbara Thibault, Tom Edmonds and Elaine Clements
Page 176: "Organizations," and "Events" Andover Historical Society files and archives

CHAPTER 62 – LETTERS HOME FROM ANDOVER BOYS "OVER THERE"
Page 177: Joan Rollenhagen. "Exhibiting Andover's Total Participation in World War I." Andover Historical Society Newsletter, 1984. Vol. 9, No. 4.
"Over There…and Over Here." Andover Historical Society Exhibit, September 1984 - January 1985
Frederick A. Allis, Jr. Youth From Every Quarter: Bicentennial History of Phillips Academy, 1778, pp. 390-393.
Page 177 -180: Letters from local men serving overseas. Andover Townsman, 1916-1918
Page 178: Claude M. Fuess, Editor. *Town of Andover*, Andover Post #8, American Legion. Andover Press, 1921
Town Meeting Records, March, 1917

CHAPTER 63 – WILLIAM MADISON WOOD
Page 181: Edward G. Roddy. *Mills, Mansions, and Mergers: the Life of William Madison Wood*. North Andover: Merrimack Valley Textile Museum, 1982
Eleanor Richardson. Century of Change, 1996, p. 22-23
Page 182: Donald B. Cole. *Immigrant City: Lawrence, Massachusetts 1845-1921*. Chapel Hill: University of North Carolina, 1963

John B. McPherson. "William Madison Wood: A Career of Romance and Achievement." Bulletin of the National Association of Wool Manufacturers, April, 1926, pp. 245-257.

Page 181-183: Juliet H. Mofford. "Lawrence Strike of 1912." A high school role-playing curriculum for the Tsongas Center for Industrial History, Lowell National Historical Park & University of Massachusetts, Lowell, Mass., 2001

Sumner Keene. "A Business Genius Who Has Done What Others Said Was Impossible," *The American Magazine*, June, 1923

Page 183: Edward G. Roddy, Op. Cit., 1882, p. 93

James Batchelder and Barbara Thibault. West Parish Center Walking Tour, 1989; West Parish Chapel brochure, 2000, Andover Historical Society

CHAPTER 63 - WONDER VILLAGE

Page 184: ff. New York Times, May 1, 1919; February 3, 1926

D. M. Scott. "Shawsheen Village," Andover Townsman, February 9, 1923

__ __ _____. Shawsheen: The Model Community and The Home of the Office and Staff of the American Woolen Company. Promotional Brochure, 1924

Annual Report, Town of Andover, 1923

Eleanor Richardson. *Century of Change*, 1996, pp. 22, 23, 89-91, 180-183

Juliet H. Mofford. "AVIS: A History in Conservation," 1980, 69-70

CHAPTER 64 - CALVIN COOLIDGE CAME TO TOWN

Page 188: Juliet H. Mofford. "Presidents Who Passed Our Way." Script for Andover's 350th Anniversary Celebrations, (performed by the Rev. Calvin Mutti May, 1996 & February 2002)

Page 189: Andover Townsman, May 19, 1928

Author's Interview with Ruth Sharpe, 1996

Page 190: Frederick S. Allis, Jr., *Youth From Every Quarter*, 1978, p. 435-436; 445

CHAPTER 65 - BLACK LUCY'S GARDEN

Page 191: Adelaide K. & Ripley P. Bullen. "Black Lucy's Garden." Bulletin of the Massachusetts Archaeology Society. Vol. 4, #2, January 1945, pp. 17-28

Alfred Poor. Andover Advertiser, August 29, 1863

Page 192: South Parish Church Records. Andover Historical Society

Barbara Brown & Eugene Winter, Curators. Research and labels for Exhibition at Andover Historical Society, with the Peabody Museum of Archaeology, Phillips Academy, 2003-2004

CHAPTER 66 - HAROLD RAFTON: THE "CONSCIENCE OF ANDOVER"

Page 193-195: Author's Interviews with Harold Rafton, January, 1978; March 12, 1978

Page 193: Juliet H. Mofford. "AVIS: A History In Conservation," 1980, pp. 92-95 (Rafton's Letter) Andover Townsman, December 22, 1955
Page 194: Ibid., pp. 106-107; 117-119
Chris Young quoting Nat Smith in "AVIS Owes a Great Deal to the Raftons." Lawrence Eagle Tribune, December 12, 1977
Page 195: Ibid., June 8, 1967; November 14, 1973

CHAPTER 67 – THE MULTI-MILLION DOLLAR BUSINESS
THAT STARTED ON ROSE'S STOVE
Page 196: Eleanor Richardson. *Century of Change*, 1996, pp. 67-69
Christiana Robb. Boston Globe, October 18, 1989
Eagle Tribune, November 10, 1993
Page 197: "Frozen Yogurt Gets Its Licks In." Andover Townsman, July 18, 2002

CHAPTER 68 – ANDOVER'S MUSIC MAN
Page 198: Eleanor Richardson. Op. Cit. 1996, p. 29
Page 199: "Arts Award." Andover Townsman, September 26, 1983
Ibid., February 21, 1985; January 9, 1986
Mary Fitzgerald. Eagle Tribune, August 9, 1986
Obituary, Andover Townsman, August 14, 1986

CHAPTER 69 – OUTWARD BOUND OUT OF ANDOVER
Page 200: Eleanor Richardson. Op. Cit., 1996, p. 28
Barbara Thibault. Taped Interview with Joshua Miner. Andover Historical Society Oral History Collection.
Frederick S. Allis, Jr., *Youth From Every Quarter*, 1978, pp. 555-559, Page 197
Don Staruk. "Joshua Miner Inspires Us: Awakening an Excitement for Living." Ibid., September 24, 1992
_____ _____ "Outward Bound Names National Center for Joshua Miner." Andover Townsman, June 15, 1995
Judy Wakefield. "Miner's Early Outward Bound Days Remembered." Op. Cit., February 7, 2002

CHAPTER 70 – THE ANDOVER BOOKSTORE: "A SPECIAL PLACE"
Page 202: Eleanor Richardson. Op. Cit. pp. 150-151; 236
Karen Harris, Susan Lenoe, & Tom and Maribeth Edmonds. *History of the Andover Bookstore*. Andover Historical Society Video Production, August 13, 1997
See also PRINTERS INC., Chapter 45

CHAPTER 71 – THE HIGH COMMISSIONER OF STICKBALL
Pages 203-204: Phillips Academy Archives: Classes of 1942 & 1964

Pot Pourri: Phillips Academy Yearbooks
Page 204: Sam Allis. Boston Globe, March 28, 1999
Michael Kranish. Ibid., March 28, 1999
Time Magazine, July 2, 2001, p. 80

CHAPTER 72 - BALLARDVALE BOY
Page 205: Author's telephone interview, June 24, 2002
Author's Interviews: Andover High School classmates and Bernice Haggerty.
Page 206, 207: Jay Leno with Bill Zehme. *Leading With My Chin*. New York:
Harper Collins, 1996, pp. 27–28; 53–55; 57 ff.
Eleanor Richardson. *Century of Change*, 1998, p. 17
Eagle Tribune, February 1, 2001
Andover Townsman, February 8, 2001
Author's interview with Pauline Robichaud, 2002

ANDOVER HISTORY AT A GLANCE

❧

1645	Cochichewick Plantation settled; first meeting house built in what is now the old center of North Andover
1646	May 6, Town of Andover incorporated in Essex County; included what is now Andover, North Andover and a portion of the City of Lawrence
1675-06	Indian raids during King Phillips War nearly cause abandonment of Andover
1692	Forty-eight men, women, and children from Andover arrested during the Salem Witch Trials. Three are hanged and one dies in prison, awaiting execution.
1701	First school established.
1708	Massachusetts General Court orders division of Andover into two separate parishes.
1776	January, Mill established on Shawsheen River to produce gunpowder for the Continental Army
1778	Phillips Academy founded
1806-08	Essex Turnpike(now Route 28) cuts through South Parish
1808	Andover Theological Seminary founded
1807	Abraham Marland begins manufacture of cotton yarn at a spinning mill on the Shawsheen River, and by 1810, is producing woolen fabric
1815	Abel and Paschal Abbot open mill for manufacture of flannel and cashmere
1829	February 26, Abbot Female Seminary (later Abbot Academy) established
1834	Marland Manufacturing Company incorporated
1832	Samuel Francis Smith writes the song *America*
1836	Smith and Dove Flax Mill established at Frye Village: first successful manufacture of flax thread in U. S.
	Ballard Vale Manufacturing Company incorporated
	August 6, Andover and Wilmington Railroad: first train runs through town

1846	Free Christian Church founded by anti-slavery advocates
1845–47	Land along Merrimack River taken from Andover to establish new city of Lawrence.
1852	Harrriet Beecher Stowe moves to Andover
1855	April 7, Legal separation of Andover and North Andover into two towns Andover's population is 4,700. North Andover's population is 2,218.
1856	September 2, Dedication and opening of Punchard Free High School,
1860	Telegraph office opens in Andover
1870	June 13, Andover gets its first steam fire engine
1873	Memorial Hall Library built to honor the town's Civil War dead
	Women's Suffrage League formed
1894	Andover Village Improvement Society founded
1911	Andover Historical Society organized
1919–23	Development of Shawsheen Model Industrial Village for upper and middle-management employees of the American Woolen Company
1931	Addison Gallery of American Art opens on Phillips Academy campus.
1950s	Interstate highway system like Route 28, brings new high tech industries
1959	Route 93 intersects Andover
1960	Andover Conservation Commission formed
1965	Interstate 495 cuts through town
1970	Historical Commission formed to protect Andover's historic structures
1973	Abbot Academy is merged with Phillips Academy
2001	Annual Town Report estimates Andover's population at 31,6095 within thirty-two square miles

SOURCES

Abbot, Abiel *History of Andover from Its Settlement to 1829.* Andover, Mass.: Flagg & Gould, 1829.

Abbott, Charlotte Helen. Andover Families. Typescripts, Andover Historical Society Collections.

Allis, Frederick S. Jr., *Youth From Every Quarter: A Bicentennial History of Phillips Academy, Andover.* Hanover, NH, University Press of New England, 1979.

Allis, Sam. *Boston Globe,* March 28, 1999.

Andover: What It Was & What It Is.: 300th Anniversary Memorial Volume. Andover Townsman Press, 1947.

Andover Town Records, October 14, 1690-

Andover Advertiser, 1853-1866. (Sold to *Lawrence American* 1866, continued under joint title until 1907).

Andover Historical Society. Archives and manuscript collections, vertical files including Families, Streets & Structures, Organizations & Businesses) Quarterly Newsletters, 1976- 2002).

Andover Townsman, Bound Volumes 1887-October, 1936, then on microfilm to present.

Andover Village Improvement Society Records, 1894-1970.

Bailey, Sarah Loring. *Historical Sketches of Andover, Comprising the Present Towns of North Andover and Andover, Massachusetts.* Boston, Mass.: Houghton, Mifflin; Cambridge, Mass.: Riverside Press, 1880.

Beecher, Charles Beecher, *Spiritual Manifestations,* Boston, 1879, pp. 25-36.

Bennett, Mary Angela. *Elizabeth Stuart Phelps.* Philadelphia, PA: University of Pennsylvania Press, 1939.

Boyer, Paul & Stephen Nissenbaum, editors. *The Salem Witchcraft Papers: Verbatim Transcripts of the Legal Documents of the Salem Witchcraft Outbreak of 1692.* 3 volumes NY: Da Capo Press, 1977.

Bristol, Rev. Sherman. *The Pioneer Preacher: Incidents of Interest and Experiences in the Author's Life...* New York/Chicago: Fleming H. Revell, 1887.

Brooks, Van Wyck. *New England Indian Summer, 1865-1915.* NY: E. P. Dutton, 1940.

Buck, Alice, compiler. *Indian Ridge Scrapbook*, 1896-1907.

Bullen, Adelaide K. and Ripley P. *"Black Lucy's Garden."* Bulletin of the Massachusetts Archaeological Society. Vol. 4, No. 2, January, 1945, pp. 17-28.

Burr, George Lincoln, editor. *Narratives of the Witchcraft Cases 1648-1706.* New York: Charles Scribners, 1914. (Original Narratives of Early New England History) Barnes & Noble Reprints, 1946, 1972.

Business History of Andover: Anniversary Souvenir Number of the *Andover Townsman.* Andover, Mass.: Andover Press, May 20, 1896.

Campbell, Eleanor. *West of the Shawsheen.* Andover: West Parish Church, 1976.

Carter, Sarah Nelson. *For Pity's Sake.* Boston, Mass.: De Wolfe, Fiske & Co.; Andover, Mass.: Andover Press, 1897.

Dictionary of American Biography, Vol. X, Dumas Malone, Editor. New York: Charles Scribners 1936, pp. 418-419.

Donald, William C., *Address at Fiftieth Anniversary Observance in 1896.* Reprinted: *The History of Free Christian Church,* Andover, Mass., 1996, p.28.

Essex County Court Records, Quarterly Sessions, Salem, Mass.: Vol. I-X, 1665-1700.

Essex Co. Court Papers, Vol . I, p. 142, Jan. 2, 1692.

Fuess, Claude M., *Andover: Symbol of New England. Evolution of a Town.* Andover and North Andover Historical Societies, 1959.

_____ ,_____, *Andover, Massachusetts in the World War.* Andover Press & Andover Post #8, American Legion, 1921.

_____, _____, *An Old New England School*: A History of Phillips Academy. Boston, 1917.

Goldsmith, Bessie P., *The Townswoman's Andover.* Andover Historical Society, 1964; 1970.

Godbeer, Richard. *The Devil's Dominion: Magic & Religion in Early New England.* Cambridge, England: Cambridge University Press, 1991.

Greven, Philip J., Jr., *Four Generations: Population, Land, and Family in Colonial Andover, Massachusetts.* Ithaca, NY: Cornell University Press, 1970.

Hansen, Chadwick. *Witchcraft At Salem.* New York: George Braziller, 1969.

Hardy, Arthur Sherburne. *Life and Letters of Joseph Hardy Neesima.* Boston and New York: Houghton, Mifflin & Co., 1891.

SOURCES

Harris, Edward M.. *Andover in the American Revolution.: A New England Town In a Period of Crisis 1763-1790.* Marceline, Misssouri: Walsworth Publishing Company, 1976.

Hensley, Jeannine, editor. *The Works of Anne Bradstreet.* Cambridge, Mass.: Belknap Press, Harvard University, 1967.

Hill, Frances. *The Salem Witch Trials Reader.* Da Capo Press, Perseus Books Group, 2000.

Historical Manual of the South Church in Andover, Mass. Andover: Warren F. Draper, 1859.

Holmes, Oliver Wendell. *The School Boy.* Boston, 1878.

Jackson, Susan. *Reminiscences of Andover.* Andover, Mass.: Andover Press, 1914.

Kelly, Lori D. *Life and Works of Elizabeth Stuart Phelps, Victorian Feminist Writer.* Troy, NY: Whitston Publishing Co., 1983.

Kessler, Carol Farley. *Elizabeth Stuart Phelps.* Boston, Mass.: Twayne/G.K. Hall, 1982.

Kranish, Michael. *Boston Globe*, March 28, 1999.

Leno, Jay with Bill Zehme. *Leading With My Chin.* New York: Harper Collings, 1996.

____,____. Telephone Interview with Juliet Mofford, June 24, 2002.

Lenoe, Susan and Karen Harris, *History of the Andover Bookstore.* Video produced by Andover Historical Society, August 13, 1997.

Lynch, Shawn. "Our Sinne of Ignorance, Andover in 1692," and map. Andover and North Andover Historical Societies, 1995.

Mather, Cotton. *Execution of Hugh Stone, Magnalia Christi Americana*, II, 1698.

Mofford, Juliet Haines. *And Firm Thine Ancient Vow: The History of North Parish Church of North Andover 1645-1974.* North Andover, Mass.: Naimen Press, 1975

___, ____ ____. "The Anti-Slavery Movement & the Underground Railroad in Andover & Greater Lawrence, Mass.," Greater Lawrence Underground Railroad Committee, 2001.

___, ____ ____. "AVIS: A History in Conservation," Andover Village Improvement Society, 1980.

Nakatsukasa, Emi, "Joe Neesima Was First Japanese to Visit Andover," Andover Historical Society Newsletter, Winter 2001.

Nichols, Roy F. *Franklin Pierce: Young Hickory of the Granite Hills.* NY: Charles Scribner's, 1931.

Patrakis, Joan. Andover Historical Society Newsletters articles, 1982-2002.

Andover Massachusetts: Historical Selections from Four Centuries

Paradise, Scott M. *History of Printing in Andover, Mass., 1798-1931.* Andover Press, 1931.

Phelps, Elizabeth Stuart. *Chapters From a Life.* Boston: Houghton Mifflin, 1896.

___, ____ ____. "The Oath of Allegiance," *Atlantic Monthly,* April, 1894. Phillips Bulletin. Andover, Mass.: Phillips Academy, July 1917.

Poore, Alfred. "A Genealogical-Historical Visitation of Andover, Massachusetts in 1863." Essex Institute Historical Collections, Salem, Mass.,vols 48-55, 1912 1919.

Quintal, George, Jr. "Patriots of Color: A Peculiar Beauty" and "Merit: African-Americans and Native Americans at Battle Road and Bunker Hill." Boston National Historical Park and Minute Man National Historical Park, February, 2002.

"Railroad Catastrophe at Andover," *Lowell Daily Advertiser,* January 10, 1853.

Rafton, Harold R. Interviews with Juliet Mofford. Andover Village Improvement Society, 1978.

Raymond, Samuel. *Record of Andover During the Rebellion.* Andover: Warren F. Draper, 1875.

Richardson, Eleanor M., "Andover: A Century of Change 1896-1996." Andover Historical Society, 1995.

Robbins, Sarah Stuart. *Old Andover Days: Memories of a Puritan Childhood.* Boston: Pilgrim Press, 1908.

Robichaud, Pauline M., Interview and Video Clips on Jay Leno and Andover High School teacher, David Robichaud. August, 2002.

Roddy, Edward G. *Mills, Mansions, and Mergers: The Life of William Madison Wood.* North Andover, Mass.: Merrimack Valley Textile Museum, 1982

Rowe, Henry K. *History of Andover Theological Seminary.* Newton, Mass., 1923.

"Sad Railroad Accident/Son of General Pierce Killed," *New York Times,* January 7, 1853, p. l.

Scott, D. M., "Shawsheen Village" *Andover Townsman,* February 9, 1923.

Sharpe, Ruth, research & narration. *Ballardvale in Its Heyday.* Video produced by Andover Historical Society, 1987.

Shawsheen: The Model Community and The Home of the Office and Staff of the American Woolen Company. New York: American Woolen Company promotional brochure, 1924.

Siebert, Wilbur H., *The Underground Railroad in Massachusetts,* 1898. Reprint: Worcester, Mass.: American Antiquarian Society, 1936.

South Parish Church Records, Andover Historical Society Collections., 1708-1932.

SOURCES

Smith, Mary Byers. "The Founding of the Free Christian Church of Andover." Essex Institute Historical Collections, Vol. LXXXII, Oct., 1946, pp.1-15.

_____, ____ ____. "Founding of Memorial Hall Library, Andover, Mass.," Essex Institute Historical Collections, Vol. 79, 1943, pp. 246-255.

Staruk, Don. "Josh Miner Interview," *Andover Townsman*, June 15, 1995.

Stowe, Charles Edward. *Life of Harriet Beecher Stowe*, compiled from her letters and journals. Boston: Houghton-Mifflin, 1890.

Taylor, John L.. *Memoir of His Honor Samuel Phillips, LLD*. Boston: Congregational Board of Publishers, 1856.

Thompson, J. Earl, Jr. "Abolitionism and Theological Education at Andover." *New England Quarterly*, 47, 1974, pp. 238-261.

Time Magazine, July 2, 2001, p. 80.

Wright, George Frederick. "Some Remarkable Gravel Ridges in the Merrimack Valley." Proceedings of the Boston Society in Natural History, 1876, Vol. XIX, pp. 47-63.

.

INDEX

INDEX

INDEX

INDEX

INDEX

INDEX